A HISTORY OF
RAF DREM
AT WAR

A HISTORY OF
RAF DREM
AT WAR

MALCOLM FIFE

FONTHILL

In memory of my friend Andrew Weddell
4 January 1941–9 July 2013

Fonthill Media Language Policy

Fonthill Media publishes in the international English language market. One language edition is published worldwide. As there are minor differences in spelling and presentation, especially with regard to American English and British English, a policy is necessary to define which form of English to use. The Fonthill Policy is to use the form of English native to the author. Malcolm Fife was born and educated in Edinburgh, and still lives there; therefore British English has been adopted in this publication.

Fonthill Media Limited
Fonthill Media LLC
www.fonthillmedia.com
office@fonthillmedia.com

First published in the United Kingdom and the United States of America 2016

British Library Cataloguing in Publication Data:
A catalogue record for this book is available from the British Library

Typeset in 10pt on 13pt Sabon
Printed and bound by CPI Group (UK) Ltd, Croydon, CR0 4YY

Contents

Spitfires of 602 Squadron over the Bass Rock. From a painting by Alexandre Jay.

Acknowledgements

Particular thanks to Ross Dimsey for editing and assistance with the text
Andrew Dennis—Assistant Curator, RAF Museum
Nick Forder—The First World War Airfield
Hania Frackiewicz—Polish translation (307 Squadron)
Alan Hayman—609 Squadron Association
Colin Hendry—RAF Drem Museum (now closed)
Arthur Jones DFC—226 Squadron's deployment to Drem
Philip Judkins—Radar and Electronic Warfare
Bob O'Hara—Research in the National Archives
Wilhelm Ratuszynski—Polish Squadrons Remembered website

Preface

The tranquil landscape of East Lothian today, with its golden fields of wheat and picturesque villages, gives little clue to the turbulent events experienced in earlier times. Invading armies would march up the coast from Berwick-upon-Tweed and along the low-lying coastal plain of East Lothian. The threat was not only land-based. In the Dark Ages, Vikings raided the coast. The Romans transported troops and supplies along the North Sea coast, and later the Auld Enemy (the English) supported their incursions into Scotland with a fleet of ships sailing into the Firth of Forth. When the Union of Scotland and England took place in 1707, the threat from south of the border melted away. It was replaced by fears of French invasions, first under Napoleon I and later Napoleon III. Fortifications were built along the coast, but the threat was never realised.

When the First World War broke out, it had been only eleven years since the Wright Brothers had been airborne for just a few hundred yards. At first, most British military commanders were sceptical of aircraft as a weapon and those that accepted flying machines saw them only as a means for carrying out reconnaissance in support of ground forces. Meanwhile, the Germans had been experimenting for more than a decade with airships. Many, built by the Zeppelin Company, were over 500 feet long—longer than a Boeing 747. They could carry heavy loads, so their potential threat to Britain as long-range bombers was not long in being recognised.

The first Zeppelin raids in early 1915 caused great alarm. What was to prevent these aerial monsters roaming the night skies over Britain at will? It was even rumoured that a Zeppelin was operating from a clandestine base near Grasmere in the English Lake District and the question was raised as to whether the British Government should be evacuated temporarily to North Berwick, Scotland, if there was a sustained aerial bombardment of the capital. However, even Scotland was not exempt from the threat of an aerial attack. On 2 April 1916, two German Navy Zeppelins (L14 and L22) bombed Edinburgh.

In August 1914, the Admiralty ordered Royal Flying Corps coastal patrols to be flown from the Moray Firth to Dungeness, the northern and southern extremities of the east coast. Over the next two years, a chain of landing grounds was established along the coast.

1

The First World War Airfield

In September 1915, the Director of Naval Air Services gave approval for a large air station to be constructed at East Fortune—already serving as a sub-station for the Royal Naval Air Station at Dundee—with an additional satellite airfield for this facility to be built at West Fenton. It appears that the landing ground was to consist of more than the usual grass airstrip, as a 2-foot narrow-gauge light railway, or tramway, was laid to carry the construction materials to the site. The line ran from Gullane station eastwards for approximately 200 yards, reaching a point close to Muirfield Farm Cottages. It then turned south, crossed the Peffer Burn by means of a trestle bridge and then crossed a road near Craigend Cottage before entering the site of the airfield.

North British railways delivered materials to Gullane station, where the loading bank to the south of the passenger platform had been especially extended in May 1915. Initially, the wagons of cement, lime, and timber were then hauled part of the way by horse on the tramway, before being unhitched and allowed to roll downhill towards West Fenton Airfield, powered by nothing more than gravity. At a sharp bend in the track, the wagons would sometimes derail and scatter their contents across the surrounding countryside, much to the delight of the local children. In 1918, a small saddle tank engine was introduced. Although the railway fell out of use when West Fenton airfield closed in 1919, another short tramway was built during the Second World War for transporting ammunition within Drem airfield.

West Fenton landing ground was probably used by the fighter aircraft of 77 Squadron—headquartered at Turnhouse and providing protection for south-east Scotland—only on an occasional basis from 1916 onwards. There were also numerous small airfields and landing grounds, used from time to time by detachments of BE2 and BE12 aircraft. These included Cairncross, near Reston, Eccles Toft, near Greenlaw, Haggerston, in Northumberland, Old Heaton, near Cornhill, and Tynehead, in Midlothian. In East Lothian the main base for 77 Squadron was at Penston, near Tranent, which became the location of RAF Macmerry during the Second World War. Other landing grounds included South Belton (near Dunbar), Skateraw (near Innerwick), Townhead Farm (near Gifford), and West Fenton (close to Dirleton). Taking its name from the nearby hamlet, West Fenton was to become Drem airfield.

When East Fortune airfield began operations in 1916, it was base to Avro 504s, BE2Cs, and a small number of Sopwith Scouts. The nearby airfield at West Fenton was probably used from time to time for practice landings and take-offs. Sopwith 1½ Strutters, Camels, and Pups arrived in 1917 and were used to train pilots. On completion of their course, newly qualified pilots would fly these types from modified warships. Large airships were also based at East Fortune only a couple of miles away, flying anti-submarine and convoy protection duties.

In 1917, the Royal Flying Corps reformed its organisation for the instruction of new pilots. Training Depot Stations (TDS) were established with the objective of making economies in personnel and transport and of minimising the use of agricultural land for airfields. Nos 9, 19, and 35 Training Squadrons were initially merged to form 2 TDS at Lake Down Airfield on 15 August 1917, and then transferred to West Fenton (Gullane) on 15 April 1918. At this time, the future of the home defence squadrons came into question, as the risk of Zeppelin attacks was felt to have greatly diminished. No. 77 Squadron moved its headquarters from Turnhouse to the smaller airfield of Penston at the beginning of 1918.

At West Fenton, a large construction programme to redevelop the airfield for use as No. 2 TDS began. The station commenced operation in April 1918, the same month that the Royal Naval Air Service and Royal Flying Corps were merged to form the Royal Air Force. It was renamed RAF Gullane, after the nearby passenger railway station. In 1932, the passenger station closed at Gullane and the nearest station was now Drem. Hence the change of name when the airfield reopened in 1939.

Although flying training commenced at the airfield in April 1918, many of the new buildings were still being built in the summer, with their completion scheduled for 15 August of that year. The structures included seven hangars or 'aeroplane sheds', as they were then called, each 170 feet × 100 feet. One was set aside for aircraft repairs. Other buildings included three unit commander's offices, an officers' mess, and four officers' quarters for staff with a further three for pupils. There was also a reception station and a women's hostel. Written in 1918, an official description of RAF Gullane described the airfield as follows:

> Maximum dimensions, 1,100 yards × 900 yards, area 186 acres of which 33 acres are occupied by technical buildings. Height above sea level, 60 feet. Soil–heavy loam. Surface–fair, improvements being made. The ground slopes to the south-west. The general surroundings are good, open and fairly flat, with fairly large fields and a few small woods.[1]

The designated function of No. 2 TDS was to train pilots to fly single-seat fighter aircraft. Its strength, on paper, was thirty-six Royal Aircraft Factory SE5s and thirty-six Avro 504A/J/Ks. Other types were also used by the unit—Bristol F2Bs, Bristol Scouts, Sopwith Camels, and Sopwith Pups, the latter on strength in July 1918.

New recruits usually first flew the Avro 504, before graduating to Sopwith Pups and SE5s. On completion of their training, some pilots were posted to No. 27 Training Service Depot at RAF Crail on the opposite side of the Firth of Forth, where they received instruction on fighter reconnaissance aircraft. RAF Gullane also retained one of its original functions as a landing ground for 77's fighters.

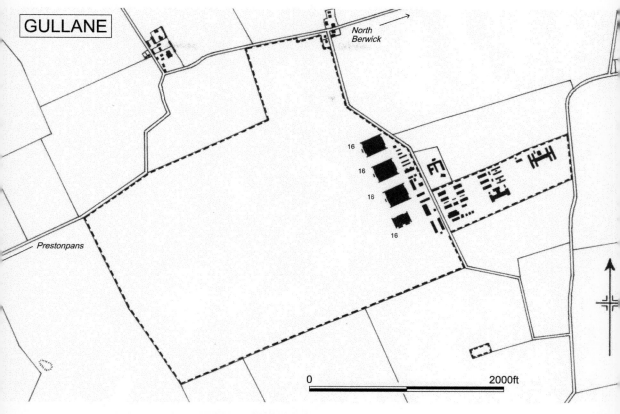

A plan of RAF Gullane in 1918. (*Mick Davis*)

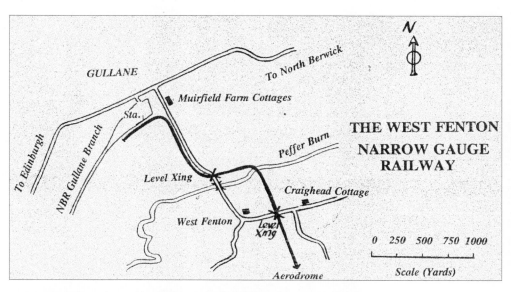

Plan of the West Fenton narrow-gauge railway. (*Andrew Hajducki*)

Above and below: RFC boy trainees in the station workshops in January 1918. (*IWM*)

Boy trainees of the RAF watch a Maurice Farman Shorthorn aircraft they have helped prepare for flight take off from RFC West Fenton (Gullane) in January 1918. (*IWM*)

Another aerial view of 2 Aircraft Training Depot, RAF Gullane in November 1918. Fifteen aircraft, including Avro 504's, are lined up in front of the hangars, some of which are still under construction. (*IWM*)

An aerial view of 2 Aircraft Training Depot RAF Gullane in November 1918. The accommodation blocks are visible in the foreground at West Fenton. (*IWM HU91006*)

The personnel on strength of No. 2 Training Depot on 1 August 1918:

Officers	51
Officers under instruction	120
NCOs under instruction	60
WOs and NCOs above the rank of Corporal	47
Corporals	25
Rank and File	320
Forewomen	7
Women	155
Women (household)	54
Total	839

In an age when most transport was by rail, RAF Gullane appears to have been particularly well furnished with motor vehicles. The following are recorded as being on its charge: one touring car, ten light tenders, ten heavy tenders, eight motor cycles, eight sidecars, and five trailers.

Among the RAF personnel to serve at Gullane was Air Mechanic William Smith. As a boy, he had witnessed the crash of the German Schutte-Lanz airship SL11 in

Hertfordshire and later saw a formation of Gotha bombers over the Thames on their way to bomb London. This was sufficient motivation to join the RFC at the age of sixteen. He was trained as an Air Mechanic at RFC School of Technical Training at Halton, near Wendover, and, in early 1918, on completion of his training, he was posted to No. 2 TDS at RAF Gullane. Smith recalled 'that the flying field there was V-shaped with a dip in the middle'. The mechanics slept in a large barracks and worked undercover, mainly in canvas Bessonneau hangars. These were portable timber-framed structures, first introduced in 1916. In winter, when the canvas doors froze, Bessonneau hangars were cursed by all, but they played a vital role in protecting the flimsy aircraft, supplementing the seven permanent brick-built hangars mentioned earlier.

William Smith was assigned to service the Monosoupape rotary engines that powered the Avro 504s. These engines were quite reliable, and the mechanics seldom had a backlog of repairs requiring them to 'burn the midnight oil', as Smith put it. One of his duties was to start engines, a hazardous task involving swinging the propeller by hand. The mechanics worked a seven-day week, but were given a day off from time to time, sometimes to fly as passengers in the training aircraft. When the work was done for the day the personnel were generally left to amuse themselves. On Sundays, all ranks attended a church parade at the airfield, a feature of life at the airfield during both world wars.

The cadets at RAF Gullane were mostly new pilots undergoing initial training, so there were numerous accidents. Fortunately, due to the low flying speeds of the biplanes, the pilots often escaped with nothing more than a few cuts and bruises. They would then be flying again later in the day. Several planes crashed into the waters of the nearby Firth of Forth, but open cockpits enabled the pilots to usually escape the sinking machine without too much difficulty.

However, the flyers' luck sometimes gave out and there were several fatalities in the eighteen months of No. 2 TDS's existence. Such an incident occurred when Smith was eating in the Mess. There was a loud noise, followed by the sudden exodus by all in the building, as they rushed to see what had happened. A student pilot, flying low over the airfield, had misjudged his height and flown straight into the side of an unused concrete building. He was killed instantly. The pilot had been due to go on leave and had been showing off to some of his friends on the ground. Smith was detailed to attend the funeral as a member of the firing party. It was the only occasion that he attended a funeral, although he recalled that the local cemetery received regular visits following flying accidents at RAF Gullane.

The following casualties are known to have occurred to No. 2 TDS:

Donald Cheers, 2nd Lt, 3rd Bn, East Surrey Regiment attached to RAF—killed while flying Avro 504 J B4206, 17 April 1918, aged seventeen.

William Dando, Flight Cadet, 4th Bn, King's Own (Royal Lancaster Regiment)—killed while flying, 22 October 1918.

Hugh Glanville, Capt., 1st Bn BWI Regiment—died of injuries on 24 May 1918 sustained while flying Avro 504 D44, 23 May 1918, aged thirty-three. Buried in Dirleton Parish Cemetery. His passenger was unhurt.

Boy trainees of the RFC at West Fenton (Gullane) being trained in January 1918 to swing a propeller to start an aircraft engine. Some are barely tall enough to reach the blades. (*IWM*)

A pilot and gunner prepare to take-off for air gunnery practice in 1918. (*IWM*)

William Hunter, 2nd Lt RAF—killed while flying Sopwith Camel D6680, 3 July 1918, aged twenty-one. Aircraft landed in the sea after aerial firing practice and the pilot drowned.

George MacAllister, 2nd Lt RAF—killed while flying Sopwith Camel C8329, 12 August 1918 aged twenty. Born in Canada.

Rolfe McKiel, 2nd Lt RAF—killed while flying Avro 504 D5851, 6 September 1918, aged twenty-one. Born in Canada. 2nd Lt H. A. Murton was also flying in the aircraft but escaped unhurt.

Donald Parr, Flight Cadet—killed while flying Avro 504 D4464, 13 August 1918, aged twenty-one. Buried Comley Bank Cemetery, Edinburgh.

Lewis Wilkinson, 2nd Lieutenant RAF—killed while flying Sopwith Camel D6670, 18 June 1918, aged eighteen. The aircraft crashed out of control from 2,000 feet on to the North Berwick Railway Line.

William Wright, 2nd Lt 5th Bn, The Kings Royal Rifle Corps attached to RAF—killed while flying RAF SE5a D3497 on 1 October 1918, aged twenty-nine. Starboard wings of aircraft folded back at 1,000 feet while diving steeply.

The fate of the pilots is unknown in the following reported incidents:

Sopwith Camel C6750—engine failure and stalled during forced landing at Gullane on 3 September 1918.

Sopwith Camel D9535—engine failure on take-off and spun in at West Fenton on 24 February 1919.

Numerous Canadian airmen are interred in graveyards near training bases, but far fewer British, as natives of mainland Britain were shipped home for burial. Those pilots whose bodies were not returned to their families were buried at Comely Bank Cemetery in Edinburgh, where their last resting place is today marked by a simple white headstone. Next to them are several other RFC aircrew killed at Turnhouse airfield and elsewhere. Capt. Glanville was the only No. 2 TDS fatality to be buried near the airfield at Dirleton, because he was resident overseas when he enlisted.

When the USA entered the war in 1917, it sent both soldiers and airmen to assist the Allies fighting on the Western Front. This included 41st US Aero Squadron, which had been formed at Kelly Field, Texas, in July 1917, and was posted to Britain in the spring of the following year. The Squadron spent some time at RAF Montrose before arriving at No. 2 TDS, RAF Gullane.

Sgt Wilfred Mack, a flight rigger, was among the Americans and fortunately recorded his experiences for posterity. His diaries give an interesting insight into life at the airfield in a way that the few surviving official records do not:

Our airdrome at Gullane, Scotland, was situated far out in the hills with no town within miles. The only railroad track was about two miles or more away. From our barracks we could see the Edinburgh Express train as it passed by on its way to Edinburgh, which was about twice daily. From the distance it appeared to be a miniature train with the light or dark smoke puffing from its chimney.

From this airdrome we could plainly see the British Royal Naval Air Station [East Fortune] which houses quite a few dirigibles or blimps [airships] and other naval craft, used in patrolling the surrounding area as well as the North Sea area, weather permitting.

Our food at Gullane was much better than at Montrose. When they served oatmeal for breakfast, they served jam with it and not milk. Then as the troops were eating, the Officer of the Day [British Orderly Officer] on his rounds would enter the mess hall and the mess sergeant would yell out, 'Orderly Officer, will one man stand up at the end of each table'. This was to hear the complaints, if any. I wouldn't want to be in the shoes of the Tommy who would stand up. He could be in the kitchen for a month perhaps, just for complaining. Therefore no one would stand up.

War or no war, these same British Tommies always knocked off for their tea and cakes twice daily, morning and afternoon. This was their custom.[2]

The 41st Aero Squadron arrived at Gullane from Montrose divided into two flights. The squadron was given complete charge of the flights and the maintenance facilities, but the British had overall control of the training program. After the first week, the total number of flying hours and the total number of aircraft repaired from the 41st exceeded that of the British flight, which was serviced entirely by British mechanics. Following an inspection by Col. Mitchell, Inspector General for the American Expeditionary Forces in Britain, the 41st Squadron received a mark of 85 per cent, the highest grade received by any squadron in Britain. Lt Warren C. Woodward, who was in command of the unit and of all other American troops in Scotland, left in July to renew his flying training. A couple of months later he was killed in a mid-air collision while on a practice flight over France.

As Sgt Wilfred Mack recorded:

We were fortunate to have a very fine British officer of the RFC in charge of the Student Officer Training Programme. He was Captain Corchoran [possibly a misspelling] who at one time served as a combat pilot on the Western Front. He was wounded and as a result was of no further use for combat duty [many of the instructors at the training airfields were in the same condition]. This is when he was assigned to this aerodrome. His injuries do not seem to have impeded his flying abilities as I always got a thrill watching him fly, especially when he came in for a landing. He would side-slip his plane towards the earth and with the wingtip only a few feet off the ground, he would kick over his rudder and ailerons, bringing the plane to a smooth landing in a short space of ground. Captain Corchoran usually made the early morning air test flight before allowing any student pilot to take off. He usually used the Avro 504 for this purpose as being slower than the others, it gave him more time to observe all the conditions necessary to safe flying in those days. This was when he made most of his side-slipping tactics. This type of flying was considered dangerous, but the British did a lot of it and seemed to enjoy it.[3]

The mechanics for the 41st Aero Squadron were housed in Bessonneau hangars, made from heavy canvas that was in turn supported by heavy wood uprights and had a

An American officer, in training as an observer, receives instruction on clearing a stoppage on a machine gun. (*IWM HU91024*)

RFC Observers testing their aim on a machine gun. (*IWM HU9100*)

cathedral-type roof support. The hangars were not very large, but could be dismantled and moved whenever necessary.

> We usually stored six or seven planes in each hangar which gave us ample room to do our work without any congestion. Our repairs were limited to small crashes of all types. In very severe crashes the planes were sent to the main reclamation depot for overhaul.

Wilfred Mack witnessed at least one fatal accident while on station at Gullane. The undercarriage of a Sopwith Camel struck high-tension cables while landing and the aircraft then hit a steam engine that was still hot from its day's labours.

> [The Camel burst into flames on contact and] in a few seconds nothing remained except a charred form of a man and a few pieces of wood and wires. We couldn't get near enough to do anything as it happened so fast. There was no such fire-fighting equipment in those days as we see being used in similar crashes today. As we tried to recover the remains, they simply disintegrated but we recovered whatever was possible.[4]

Sometime later a friend of this pilot crashed into the hills near the aerodrome.

The mechanics that salvaged crashed aircraft would sometimes 'liberate' the more valuable artefacts, particularly the propellers that were French-polished for potential buyers.

Initially, the American airmen were welcomed by the British, but as time went on there were a number of incidents that created tension between the two nationalities. One occurred on 4 July 1918, when the American personnel were given the day off to celebrate Independence Day. In the morning they began parading around the barracks area drumming on pots and rubbish bins, accompanied by a bugler playing what he could of 'Yankee Doodle'. The British were at first bemused. Then an American hoisted the Stars and Stripes flag up the parade ground flagpole. Now the British were

A line-up of Avro 504Ks at RAF Gullane in 1918 (*Museum of Flight, National Museums of Scotland*)

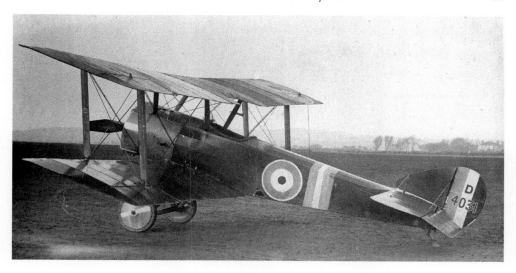

This Sopwith Pup is one of the later variants equipped with a larger rotary engine. It was used for pilot training at the No. 2 Training Depot Station at RAF Gullane in 1918. Pilots would graduate to the single-seat fighter after completing their basic training on the two-seat Avro 504K trainer. (*East Lothian Museum Service/SCRAN*)

RAF war graves at Comely Bank Cemetery in Edinburgh. They include several of airmen killed at RAF Gullane in 1918. (*Malcolm Fife*)

Gravestone of 2-Lt G. W. MacAllister RAF, who died on 12 August 1918 in a flying accident at RAF Gullane. It is located with other Commonwealth War Graves in Comely Bank Cemetery, Edinburgh. (*Malcolm Fife*)

annoyed, and matters took a turn for the worse. The commanding officer of the 41st Aero Squadron informed all his personnel that it was unlawful to fly any foreign flag on British soil unless it was flown under the Union Jack. The Americans defused the situation by agreeing to remove their flag and forget the affair.

Wilfred Mack was under the impression that had the squadron stayed at Gullane for many more months, matters would have gotten out of hand. On 14 August 1918, he and his colleagues departed for France where, at Collombey-les-Belles, they received their aircraft, the Spad XIII. While training they had used the Sopwith Camel, so the pilots were less than happy. The Spad was faster, but in the hands of a good pilot the Camel was the more agile of the two. The officers did a deal with 138 Aero Squadron to exchange 41st's Spads for their Camels. Only one operational flight was flown before the Armistice was signed. The squadron was demobilised in April of the following year, but Wilfred Mack elected to remain in Germany with the Army of Occupation and did not return home until 1923. His CO, Lt Henry Clay, never returned, dying of influenza in Europe.

With the end of hostilities there was a rapid contraction of the newly created RAF. Nos 151 and 152 squadrons arrived at Gullane on 21 February 1919 and were disbanded there on 10 September and 30 June respectively. The last service unit at Gullane, 2 TDS, soldiered on until 21 November 1919, when it was dissolved. The airfield closed a short time later.

2

Between Wars

The contraction of Britain's military air power in the years immediately following the cessation of hostilities was as rapid as its expansion during the four years of conflict. Demobilisation began almost immediately. On 11 November 1918, the newly formed RAF had some 204 squadrons on strength. This had shrunk to just twenty-nine by 1 March 1920, seven of which existed only as cadres. Many squadrons were scattered across the globe to police the British Empire; only eight were in Britain itself. There was no need to retain many of the newly built airfields, and all the landing grounds in East Lothian had been abandoned by the early 1920s. The inhabitants of Scotland would occasionally cast their eyes skyward to see a silver-winged biplane supporting military insignia flying towards Donibristle or Leuchars on the Firth of Forth. These were the only two functioning RAF airfields in the whole of Scotland at this time, providing training and support for aircraft operating from Royal Navy aircraft carriers.

In the autumn of 1923, the Disposal Board of the cash-strapped government sold 17 acres of land and along with all the buildings that once constituted Gullane/West Fenton airfield to the local farmer, Dr. Chalmers-Watson. He and his wife began to establish at Fenton Barnes farm what was to become the first large-scale dairy enterprise in the east of Scotland. Two of the four First World War hangars were adapted for the livestock, one as a barn for the dairy herd and the other as a storage shed for stock feed. The other two stored wheat and barley grown on the farm. The new accommodation enabled the harvested crops to be threshed indoors, usually by travelling steam mill. Dr. Chalmers-Watson was also a well-known teacher of medicine at Edinburgh University and had developed a vaccine for inoculating cattle against tubercular disease. His herd of dairy cows was the first in the country to be fully certified as tubercular tested.

According to an article that appeared in a 1924 edition of the local newspaper, *The Haddington Courier*:

> A beautiful herd of 80 pedigree Ayrshire heifers are already grazing in the meadows and the piggeries, run on the latest lines in feeding and production and including Irish, Scotch and Cumberland breeds are well stocked. Six blocks of buildings which had been the officers sleeping quarters were adapted to house them.

The four large hangars of the aerodrome, efficiently drained and wired throughout for electric power and with running doors at top and bottom, provide ideal accommodation for harvesting operations, dairy stock and for the elaborate processes which Grade A milk has to undergo from the cow to the sealed can and also sterilising of the dairy utensils.

The men's and women's original quarters are being refitted for the living accommodation of the dairy staff and other livestock attendants with a club and recreation room. Mrs. Chalmers-Watson proposes to employ only educated women to ensure the highest standard of hygienic service.[1]

Throughout the 1920s, Fenton Barnes farm continued to expand and prosper and former airfield building were renovated to house egg-laying hens, guinea pigs, and Angora rabbits. In 1928, it was selected as a demonstration farm for the visiting delegates of the World Dairying Congress in Edinburgh.

Despite having been reclaimed for farming, it was still possible for the site to revert back to its function as a military landing ground. In the last few days of September 1933, 602 (City of Glasgow) and 603 (City of Edinburgh) Auxiliary Air Force squadrons used it briefly as a refuelling depot for their biplane bombers, at the time engaged in a coastal defence exercise involving mock attacks on capital ships of the Royal Navy. No further RAF aircraft were sighted at Drem until 1939.

In 1935 Wg Cdr Victor Goddard flew north to Edinburgh from RAF Andover, Hampshire, for a weekend visit. During his brief stay he decided to visit Drem to look at the remains of the First World War airfield. According to his account, 'four hangars were in disrepair, barbed wire divided the [air]field into numerous pastures and cattle grazed everywhere'. After his weekend stay, Goddard took off from Turnhouse airfield to return to England. Low cloud and rain had developed over the Lothians—far from ideal flying conditions at a time when the pilot sat in an open cockpit and had to navigate without today's electronic devices. Flying through cloud, with driving rain bombarding his flying goggles, Goddard tried to climb above the turbulent weather. On reaching a height of 8,000 feet the conditions improved, but the machine began spinning earthwards at a rapid rate. As he lost altitude, Goddard noticed that the sky was becoming darker and the clouds turning a strange yellow-brown. The Hawker Hart continued towards the ground with the pilot fighting to regain control. At this stage death seemed certain. Suddenly Goddard burst through the bottom of the cloud, finding himself over 'rotating water', which he recognised as the Firth of Forth.

At a height of only a few feet, he regained control and shortly after levelling out, found himself flying inland only a few feet above the ground. He narrowly missed a seawall and a young girl pushing a pram. Even at this low altitude the visibility was very limited, but as he regained his bearings, one of the first landmarks he recognised was the road to Edinburgh. Shortly after, he sighted the outline of Drem airfield, which he had visited the previous day. The biplane was again shaken by turbulence, but then emerged into clear sky, bathed in golden sunlight. It was as if he had entered a different world.

Drem airfield was now below him, but it bore little resemblance to the abandoned site he had seen the day before. The derelict hangars appeared to have been rebuilt and there were now four aircraft parked on the forecourt, where yesterday cows had grazed. Goddard recognised three of the machines as Avro 504N trainers, the fourth was a monoplane of an unknown type. Strangely for 1935, all the aircraft were painted yellow and the mechanics that tended them were clad in blue overalls, rather than the usual brown. The wing commander flew across the airfield, narrowly missing the hangars, but the personnel on the ground seemed oblivious to the Hart's sudden appearance. No sooner had he left the airfield, than he was again engulfed in cloud and battered by turbulence. Eventually, by climbing to a height of 21,000 feet, the cloak of mist and rain was left behind. Goddard eventually managed to pilot his machine safely back to his home base in southern England.

Goddard was met with ridicule and scepticism when he related his eerie experience to his fellow officers, so he decided to keep silent in case it affected his career. In 1939, the RAF began to paint some of their training aircraft yellow and the mechanics had their brown overalls replaced by blue ones. A new training monoplane, the Miles Magister, was introduced. It was identical to the aircraft he had seen in his flight over Drem. Around the same time the airfield was reopened to train pilots for the RAF. Goddard remained silent about his strange, possibly supernatural experience until he wrote about it in 1966. Four years after Wg Cdr Goddard's vision, it had became a reality. Drem airfield was refurbished and returned to use.

The catalyst for the rapid expansion of British air power was the discovery that Germany had been building up a large air force in total secrecy. At the beginning of 1935, there were some sixty-five operational squadrons in the RAF. This number doubled within just three years. To meet the demand for new pilots, training schools were established across the length and breadth of Britain. Civilian flying schools taught some the basics and those that made the grade were posted to advanced flying schools at RAF airfields.

In 1939, three flying training schools (FTS) were established in Scotland—at RAF Drem, Kinloss, and Lossiemouth, all sites of First World War airfields. The latter two were a few miles apart, close to the shores of the Moray Firth. No. 13 FTS was formed on 17 March at Drem under the command of No. 21 Group. While the No. 14 FTS and No. 15 FTS at Kinloss and Lossiemouth were housed in brand-new buildings on recently constructed airfields, No. 13 had to make the best of the existing structures at Drem. The landing ground was a large grass field and the huts were refurbished as accommodation for the servicemen. The surviving hangars were left derelict, to be eventually demolished and replaced by nine transportable Bellman hangars. The most common steel hangar on RAF airfields, these were obsolete by 1940 due to their relatively small size.

On 15 March 1939, the opening-up party for No. 13 FTS included CFI Sqn Ldr T. H. Carr, Sqn Ldr J. Grandy, Sqn Ldr B. Chadwell, Flt Lt H. Wardle, and fifteen aircraftsmen. Soon riggers and airframe fitters with a vast range of experience descended from bases in Britain and overseas. The mechanics 'know every nut, bolt and split pin on Cheetah, Kestrel, Pegasus and Merlin engines'. The projected strength of No. 13 FTS was ninety-nine officers and 508 airmen to be assisted by seventy civilian employees. It was intended that the unit would be able to train sixty-two officer and thirty-four airman pilots in the skills of advanced flying. For the first week or so after opening 'chaos reigned supreme', but after just one month, RAF Drem was ready to accept the first pupils for the No. 1 Course. The fifty trainee pilots came from several Elementary and Reserve Flying Training Schools in England, including Filton, Gatwick, Sywell, and White Waltham.

It was originally intended to equip No. 13 FTS with twenty-six Airspeed Oxford twin-engined trainers, with a further twelve instrument-rated machines for advanced flying. In addition, eighteen Miles Master two-seat high-speed monoplane trainers and eight instrument-rated versions were to be delivered. The Master had just entered production in 1939 and none were immediately available for Drem, so Hawker Audax and Hart biplanes were supplied instead. Unfortunately, official records for No. 13 FTS do not contain much detail and shed little light on its day-to-day activities. Flying appears to have taken place on most days due to favourable weather conditions, as 1939 was blessed with a brilliant summer. Audax, Hart, and Oxford aircraft were 'lined up wingtip to wingtip and stretched the whole width of the field, north to south, over half a mile'. The residents of the nearby villages of Drem and Gullane would have had their peace frequently disturbed by aircraft flying low overhead in continual circuits, practicing landings and take-offs. When night came there would sometimes be little respite, as night flying formed a significant part of the trainee pilot's syllabus.

RAF Drem was commanded by Sqn Ldr Charles Keary, who was 'a strict disciplinarian of the old school who seldom flew. He was also very pedantic'. With an intensive flying programme, airmen and mechanics were kept very busy and were sometimes required to work on Sundays, which led to some complaints to their superiors. On 8 August 1939, a further fifty trainee pupils arrived for training on No. 2 Course. These included nine acting pilot officers, five airmen pupils and ten Royal Navy volunteer reserve officers from No. 7 Elementary and Reserve Flying School Desford, Leicestershire. Others came from Elementary Flying Schools in Scotland, including ten pilot officers from Scone airfield near Perth and three airmen pupils from Prestwick.

On 1 September 1939, just two days before Britain declared war on Germany, 13 FTS received instructions to mobilise. The unit was placed on a war footing, all ranks were recalled from leave and the airfield defence scheme was put into operation. At that time 546 personnel were based at Drem:

Group Captain	1
Squadron Leaders	6
Flight Lieutenants	12
Flight Lieutenants or Flying Officers	12
Flying Officers or Pilot Officers	2
Other Officers	4
TOTAL OFFICERS	37
Warrant Officers	3
Flight Sergeants	51
Corporals	56
Aircraftsmen	330
Civilian Staff	69
TOTAL OTHERS	509
GRAND TOTAL	546

The fine summer weather continued into September, allowing flying training almost every day in the month. On some days, as many as eighty-six hours were flown by the Initial Training Section and forty-seven hours by the Advanced Training Squadron. On 4 September, Air Chief Marshal Sir Arthur Longmore, C-in-C Training Command, visited and on 11 September, a change was made from 'peace' to 'war' training. The following month, aircraft belonging to the Advanced Training Squadron flew north to Evanton armament training camp on the shores of the Cromarty Firth for bombing and gunnery practice.

The weather began to break down, and on some nights flying training could not take place. In the autumn, the first Avro Anson trainers began to arrive to replace the Oxfords. There was no sign of the single-engine Masters, of which only seven had been delivered to the RAF by the outbreak of war.

On 14 September, at approximately 4 p.m., No. 13 FTS suffered its first air fatality. Hawker Audax K7479 crashed into a hill in the grounds of Whittinghame House near Gifford. The pilot APO K. Chiazzari, aged nineteen, from South Africa, and his passenger APO F. A. Bishop, aged twenty-three, both sustained fatal injuries. They were pupils on No. 1 Course. Four days later they were buried in the Dirleton Cemetery, not far from the edge of Drem airfield—'Full service honours were afforded'. They were the first of many airmen to be interred there.

There had been a number of serious non-fatal accidents before the loss of the Audax, but the official records make little mention of the many heavy landings and minor accidents. On 2 April 1939, Airspeed Oxford N4576 was flying north on a delivery flight to Drem when it made a forced landing at East Boldon, County Durham. It overturned in the boggy ground and was written off. On 8 September, another Oxford (N6383) was written off when it stalled and hit the ground during an undershot approach to the forced-landing practice ground at Barberfield, near Haddington. The following month an Oxford flew into the ground at night, while overshooting a landing at Drem, damaging the machine beyond repair.

Two weeks later, on 25 October, Oxford N4592 suddenly dived into the ground at Lammerlaw, the highest point of the Lammermuir Hills. Both trainee pilots, Cpl Basil Evans and Cpl Charles Thorpe, were killed. Like the casualties of the earlier Audax crash, they were buried in Dirleton Cemetery.

Although Britain declared war on Germany on 3 September 1939, for a month or so after there was little sign of immediate threat to Central Scotland. Life continued much as before at RAF Drem until 13 October, when a detachment of 602 (City of Glasgow) Spitfires touched down, heralding a change of role. Just three days later they were in action against a force of German bombers attacking Royal Navy ships. A detachment of Gloster Gladiator biplanes arrived the same day to re-enforce the defences around the Firth of Forth. The tempo of activity suddenly became very hectic as Fighter Command fine-tuned the country's defences by redeploying many of its squadrons to new locations. No sooner had the 607's fighters returned south to RAF Acklington than, on 17 October, 609's Spitfires arrived from the same airfield. On 18 October, Spitfires of 41 Squadron passed through Drem on their way north to Wick, returning south a week later. The airfield's role as a training airfield was drawing to a close.

On the 27 October, instructions were received from Headquarters Training Command that 13 FTS was to be dispersed. No time was lost in executing this order. The following day, twenty pupil pilots on No. 2 Course, with a flight commander and four instructors, migrated north to No. 15 Flying Training School at Lossiemouth. Ten Avro Ansons and six Hawker Harts of the Advanced Training Squadron went with them. No. 1 Course had been completed on 21 October and its graduates had already been posted elsewhere. Nine Ansons and four Hawker Harts of the Initial Training Squadron departed on the 30 October to their new home at RAF Montrose, where 8 FTS was based. Ten remaining Ansons and three Hawker Hart trainers also flew north to 14 Flying Training School at Kinloss, close to Moray Firth. Kinloss and Lossiemouth were to enjoy perfect flying conditions for the remainder of the year, while most of the rest of the country was in the grip of a bitter winter. It was remarked that 'Drem was the coldest place on earth'.

At the end of October, RAF Drem was officially transferred to Fighter Command. However, Grp Capt. Charles Keary remained in command and a number of other officers stayed on, including Sqn Ldr Harrison, the station chaplain. The following fighter squadrons were resident when Drem opened for business as a fighter airfield, all equipped with the Spitfire Mark I—72 Squadron, 602 Squadron and 609 Squadron. The airfield now came under the command of 13 Group, which had its administration headquarters in the city of Newcastle-upon-Tyne and was responsible for all fighter airfields in Northern England and Scotland. Nos 11, 12, and 22 Groups commanded the air defences in the rest of Britain south of the Humber Estuary.

In November 1939 there were still just three fighter airfields in Scotland (RAF Drem, Grangemouth, and Turnhouse), all in Central Scotland. Turnhouse was the Sector Airfield for the area, from which operations at the other two were controlled. At the outbreak of hostilities, it was one of only two Fighter Command bases to have paved runways. The RAF still operated large numbers of biplanes, including over 300 Gloster Gladiator fighters that, with their low landing and take-off speeds, were ideally suited to such conditions. Previously, the very wet winter of 1936–37 led C-in-C Fighter Command to ask for concrete runways to be laid in place of the usual grass at certain fighter stations. Government finance officials were not keen on spending money on innovations such as this, so the Air Ministry produced many excuses against the construction of runways with hardened surfaces in place of grass, including the arguments that practice bombing of airfields would no longer be possible, there would be no natural braking effect for landing aircraft and paved runways were impossible to camouflage. Sir Hugh Dowding stated in 1938 that Fighter Command must have concrete runways if their aircraft were to be able to operate by day and night during a wet winter:

> This eternal tinkering with the drainage of aerodromes will not be necessary. In wet weather only the runways will be used and the rest of the aerodrome will not become a swamp and can be used again without repair as soon as the weather improves.[2]

As far as Drem was concerned, these were to become very poignant words. In 1939, like almost all other airfields, it had grass runways. Most of the major RAF airfields had their grass runways replaced by concrete or tarmac during the course of the war. No such innovation occurred at Drem. It ended the war as it begun and its grass landing ground proved a great asset to the enemy, causing many RAF machines to be written off.

In distant centuries there had been confrontation on the Anglo-Scottish border. Now there was close co-operation from military units based either side of it to meet a new external threat. South of the border, 13 Group had two important airfields at Catterick and Church Fenton, both in Yorkshire. Further north, in Northumberland, was the Sector Station at RAF Acklington, located about 8 miles south of the market town of Alnwick. It was opened in 1938 for 7 Armament Training School, but like Drem had been used as a landing ground by 77 Squadron fighter aircraft in the First World War. As soon as hostilities commenced in the autumn of 1939, the training units flew off to be replaced by fighter squadrons. Acklington was to become the most important fighter base in north-east England, being responsible for the defence of Newcastle and its industrial hinterland. The airfield's history in the early years of the conflict is closely bound up with that of Drem, as squadrons based at Acklington were often posted to Drem and vice versa.

One other installation of critical importance for the air defence of south-east Scotland and Northumberland was the radar station at Drone Hill, Berwickshire. Britain invented radar and put it into practical use long before the Germans. It was probably as important as the Supermarine Spitfire in giving the RAF the edge over the Luftwaffe. By giving advanced warning of attacks, the limited numbers of RAF fighters were able to remain on the ground until they were required and once airborne, to be effectively deployed.

In 1933, when Hitler came to power, air defence exercises indicated that less than half of any attacking enemy bombers would be intercepted by RAF fighters. These disturbing figures gave added impetus to development of an early warning system. In the 1920s, the development of a death ray utilising radio waves to destroy enemy flying machines had been seriously considered. The initial experiments were an abysmal failure, but it was discovered that when radio energy is directed at a distant flying object, some of the energy is reflected back to the transmitter. Further trials were carried out, leading to the invention of radar. In 1936, plans were made for a chain of radar stations to defend the Thames Estuary. It was then decided to extend the radar coverage along the east coast of Britain as far north as the Firth of Forth. When war came there were nineteen radar stations in the chain, giving them the name 'Chain Home Stations'. Early radar only worked over the sea and as a consequence all the stations were located near the coast. Enemy aircraft approaching the coast flying at altitudes of over 5,000 feet could be detected from between 100 and 200 miles away.

Drone Hill station was built at the edge of Coldingham Moor, not far from the rocky coast of St Abbs Head. The early radar apparatus was a cumbersome affair and bore little resemblance to modern equipment. Chain Home Stations usually consisted of three steel transmitting towers, some 360 feet tall. There were also four shorter (240 foot) receiving towers. Despite their lower height, they were more conspicuous than the transmitting towers as they were constructed out of wood with extensive lattice work, resembling miniature Eiffel Towers. Such installations could hardly be concealed from the enemy and it was expected that, due to their vital role, they would come under heavy attack. There was also a fear that German parachutists might attack them. Each station, including Drone Hill, was to be defended by anti-aircraft guns, supported by Lewis machine guns, to deal with low-flying aircraft, and manned by around forty soldiers. A further sixty men, led by two lieutenants and one captain, were responsible for ground defence.

Numerous fortifications, including a large number of pillboxes, were built round Drone Hill. The fears of an aerial assault on Britain's radar stations were fortunately never realised. Bombs fell on a small number of sites in Southern England, but Drone Hill survived the war unscathed, despite the fact that German aircraft often crossed the Berwickshire coast close by. Later in the war a second radar station (Chain Home Low) was built at Cockburnspath, not far from Drone Hill. Its function was to track the movements of low-flying aircraft that could not be picked up by the main radar station.

The radar station at Drone Hill, Berwickshire. Although this photograph was taken in 1954, it would have appeared much the same in 1939. (*RCAHMS/SCRAN*)

3

The Auxiliary Spitfire Squadrons

The Spitfire is one of the icons of the twentieth century. In popular tradition it has been credited with winning the Battle of Britain and thus saving Britain from invasion by Hitler's legions. Although it was an outstanding aircraft and highly regarded by its pilots, its role in history has been somewhat overblown—Hawker Hurricanes actually shot down more enemy aircraft in the Battle of Britain. The newly invented radar also played a vital role in greatly increasing the effectiveness of the limited number of RAF fighters.

At the beginning of the Second World War, the first versions of the Spitfire were based at Drem. Sixteen versions later, it was still flying from the airfield when the Germans surrendered.

Rather surprisingly, the air defence of Central Scotland in 1939 was the responsibility of the Auxiliary Air Force Squadrons, manned by weekend pilots, many of whom were lawyers, doctors, and other professionals. No. 602 (City of Glasgow) Squadron was based at Abbotsinch, now Glasgow Airport and 603 (City of Edinburgh) Squadron flew from Turnhouse, now Edinburgh Airport.

602 (City of Glasgow) Squadron

This was the first auxiliary squadron created by Lord Trenchard, the early Chief of the Air Staff. He had the idea of a territory-based civilian force, a *corps d'elite* of the air. It was decided in the early 1920s that a number of these squadrons would be established. They were to be based in the centres of population, where not only would there be a local pool of aircrew but, of equal importance, engineering expertise essential for the maintenance of the aircraft. Glasgow was one of the leading centres for engineering at that time, and provided 602 Squadron with a ready pool of mechanics and fitters.

At the beginning of 1939, both this squadron and the neighbouring 603 (City of Edinburgh) Squadron were equipped with obsolete biplanes, the Gloster Gauntlet and Gladiator. It is rather surprising that these part-time units began to receive the new Spitfire I in the latter part of that year, as the first Spitfires had only entered service with front-line squadrons in August 1938. By the outbreak of war, Fighter

Spitfires of 602 Squadron in front of a hangar in late 1939. (*602 Squadron Museum*)

Command fielded nine full squadrons, of which two were auxiliary squadrons. Two other auxiliary squadrons, including the City of Edinburgh, were partly equipped with the aircraft.

No. 602's personnel received their call-up papers ten days before Prime Minister Chamberlain declared war on Germany. On 7 October 1939, the Spitfires departed for Grangemouth Airfield, opened a few months earlier as the main civil airport for Central Scotland. Their stay there was short-lived, as Sqn Ldr Farquhar thought that the training airfield at Drem would provide shorter interception times. The CO, Grp Capt. Charles Keary, was not so enthusiastic. Furious, Farquhar flew back to Grangemouth and phoned his superior, AVM Saul. A week later 602 got the go-ahead to move, flying training was transferred to Northern Scotland, and, on Friday 13 October, thirteen pilots in thirteen Spitfires arrived at Drem.

On that day, Fg Off. A. Johnston's Spitfire ran down a slope at speed, hit a muddy patch at the bottom and dug its nose in. This would become an all-too-frequent occurrence throughout the war. The following morning Spitfires scrambled from Drem for the first time, when four unsuccessfully investigated a suspicious radar plot.

On 16 October, a formation of twelve Ju 88s of KG30 flew up the Firth of Forth towards the Royal Naval base of Rosyth. The Drone Hill radar had suffered valve failures and was inoperative, so the Ju 88s were not detected. Two He 111s of KG26 were flying over the Lammermuirs, providing details on the weather and targets for the bombers. No. 603's Spitfires from RAF Turnhouse were sent after one He 111 flying in the vicinity of Galashiels—to no avail. Flt Lt George Pinkerton and Fg Off. A. McKellar of 602 Squadron briefly engaged the other Heinkel, in the vicinity of Dunbar, before it made good its escape. At 2.22 p.m., Blue Section of the squadron was on patrol and Yellow Section was scrambled to investigate an unconfirmed report of enemy planes heading towards the Forth Rail Bridge. In a contemporary account in the magazine *The War Illustrated* entitled 'We Saw the First Air Raid at Rosyth', A. Neilson, a former member of the RAF, described it as follows:

On Monday, 16 October at 2.30 p.m., my wife and I chanced to be travelling along a coast road on the Firth of Forth, at a point exactly opposite two cruisers, the *Edinburgh* and the *Southampton*. Suddenly there was a loud cracking noise, which seemed to be within the car and which I immediately diagnosed as a broken ball-race. Again! But this time the cracking noise was a few hundred yards away and easily recognizable as machine-gun fire. I stopped the car and jumped out just in time to see a great volume of water shoot up within a few yards of one of the cruisers. The attacker had gone but presently the cruisers started losing their shells to a height of about 6,000 feet. Up among the white puffs of smoke my wife spotted something. 'Look there he is!' As she spoke the machine banked and came down in a fast dive from the west. Down, down he came, until directly over the Forth Bridge he released two large bombs whose course we were able to follow until they plunged into the river within a few yards of one of the cruisers. Several times this happened and of the bombs which were dropped I should say more than one was as near as 30 yards from one or other of the cruisers. Certainly a lucky day for them. Right behind us in a wood an anti-aircraft battery blazed away and as we were not more than 400 yards from the cruisers the noise was terrific and all about us we could hear quite distinctly the orders given on the ships' loudspeakers.

As we were on rising ground and looking down on the scene we had a perfect view of the whole affair. My wife was a bit afraid to begin with but I insisted we were tremendously fortunate to get such a view and that we might never have such an opportunity again. I continued to reassure her, however, and pointed out that there was not a chance in a million of a bomb dropping near us as the marksmanship was far too good for that. The danger of shrapnel dropping on us was slight as we were too close to the guns. One large piece did, however, land within 50 yards of my car. What I dared not think about was my secret fear of what would have happened to us if one of the bombs had made a lucky hit where the raider was aiming ... it was a most thrilling experience which I could not have missed for a great deal.[1]

The target of the raiders was the battleship HMS *Hood*, which was being shadowed by German maritime reconnaissance. When the Ju 88 arrived over Rosyth, its crew saw to their frustration that their main target was out of reach, as it had already docked. Hitler had given the order that bombs were not to be dropped on British soil lest civilians be harmed, as he still had hopes of negotiating a peace deal with the British government. They turned their attention to the other warships anchored close to the Forth Rail Bridge. In fact, the battleship they had under observation was HMS *Repulse* and not HMS *Hood*.

The Germans believed that the Firth of Forth was defended by a few elderly Gladiator biplanes and that there were no Spitfires in Scotland. This was despite the fact that high-flying He 111 reconnaissance aircraft had been regularly over-flying and photographing Drem airfield and other potential targets in the Lothians in late September and early October 1939.

Ju 88A-1 4D+AK was shot down by Fg Off. G. Pinkerton and crashed into the sea off Fifeness. On board was *Hauptmann* (Captain) Helmut Pohle, the chief test pilot for the newly introduced Ju 88 and the commander of the bomber formation. He later recalled:

In the Forth lay HMS *Southampton* and HMS *Edinburgh* at anchor and these we dived-bombed. I was flying one of the first Ju 88s to go into attack but during the dive the top part of the canopy came off. Although I was now flying with my crew in the half-open plane, I nevertheless remained in the area to observe the results of the other aircraft. However, I was surprised by a Spitfire which I could not get away from. Also, we could not defend ourselves with the rear top gun as this had gone with the canopy. After other attacks, during which two of my crew were killed, one of the engines failed. Flying on with one engine I managed another 20 kilometres [12 miles] when some distance off the Scottish coast and flying in an easterly direction, I saw a trawler through the slowly lifting mist. There was no sign of any crew, but I thought it might be Norwegian—then a neutral country.

I was just able to clear the trawler before ditching the Junkers, although the sea was running at strength 4. The crew of the trawler did not rescue me; instead I was picked up by a Navy destroyer, as well as my badly injured fourth crew member. However I collapsed on deck with concussion and facial injuries. My crewman died from his injuries the next day. A few days later I regained consciousness. A white bed and a nurse. I thought I was in Norway and for some reason I asked if I could make a phone call to Italy. However, I was in the Royal Navy Hospital near Edinburgh. About ten days later I was transferred to a military hospital in Edinburgh Castle. After that, and shortly before Christmas, I was taken to the Tower of London and finally off to No. 1 POW Camp at Grizedale Hall.

A second Ju 88A-1 4D+DH was shot down by 603's Spitfires based at Turnhouse. It crashed into the Firth of Forth, some 4 miles to the north of Port Seaton. Three of its crew members were rescued by the fishing yawl *Dayspring*. The fourth had been killed in the air battle and his body had sunk with the aircraft. The machine was later salvaged by the Air Ministry, almost intact. A third Ju 88 was damaged, but managed to return to its base at Westerland on one engine. For a long time afterwards it was believed that three or even four of the enemy bombers had been shot down over Scotland, but there is no evidence for this. Many years after the end of the war, it was discovered that one of the damaged Junkers Ju 88s failed to make it back to its base on Sylt, and had crashed, killing all on board, miles off course in the Netherlands (then a neutral country).

At the time of the attack there was considerable confusion. 602 Squadron diaries state that they had shot down a He 111 and not a Ju 88 and the Royal Navy almost succeeded in shooting down a Spitfire piloted by Sandy Johnstone. He had been at RAF Leuchars when the Ju 88s had commenced their attack. Flying at great speed towards the Forth Bridge to join his colleagues, he found himself under attack from the aircraft carrier HMS *Furious*, whose anti-aircraft guns were firing at his aircraft with everything they had. Fortunately he survived the experience unscathed.

Reinforcements in the form of sixteen Gloster Gladiators of 607 Squadron were dispatched from RAF Acklington. Orders were received by telephone at 12.45 p.m., and all aircraft had arrived at Drem by 2 p.m. The first patrol was flown over the Firth of Forth by six aircraft of A-Flight at 2.30 p.m. and a second was mounted by five Gladiators of B-Flight at 3.20 p.m. The main party of ground crew arrived in the evening by road, only to be ordered to RAF Acklington the following day. The Gladiators arrived back at base at 8 a.m. AOC A. Saul arrived by air from RAF Usworth to get a first-hand account of the raid. There was a celebration the same night in Edinburgh's Caledonian Hotel. Not long after, numerous telegrams were received, the most notable one from ACM Sir Hugh Dowding, containing the now famous words 'Well done … First blood to the Auxiliaries'. The following day, German aircraft raided the northerly naval base of Scapa Flow. Again they were thwarted as the British fleet had moved three days previously to Loch Ewe in north-west Scotland to be less exposed to German attack. The raids on Rosyth and Scapa Flow were part of the overall strategy to destroy the British Home Fleet and North Sea convoy system by 150 bombers of KG26 based on the Island of Sylt.

Drem's fighter strength was boosted on 17 October when 609's Spitfire Is arrived. No. 72 Squadron also sent a detachment of aircraft. On 21 October, twenty-two airmen arrived from Abbotsinch, 602's home airfield. They could not be accommodated on base, so they were put up in the Marine Hotel in Gullane. The squadron strength was now twenty-three officers and 169 NCOs and airmen. For the remainder of October, 602's Spitfire Is flew patrols over south-east Scotland.

The Spitfire I had a maximum speed of 346 mph, with a recommended ceiling of 30,500 feet. Its range was 415 miles, but by reducing cruising speed to 175 mph its range could be extended to 600 miles. But on the ground, the Spitfire was like a fish out of water, particularly when operating from grass airfields like Drem. Donald Jack, a 602 Squadron member, recalled:

> … even just getting out onto the airfield you would have an airman on each wing tip because the Spitfire was very blind on the ground—it had a huge nose that stuck up in the air, so you had really to move your nose backwards and forwards so that you could see where you were going.[2]

Another of the squadron members recalled:

> The Spitfire was a lovely aeroplane to fly but it had terrible problems for the beginner. If you were not frightfully careful you would go onto your nose, particularly if there was any mud. Because of the huge engine forward of the wheels the centre of gravity was really too far forward. The slightest interruption, if your wheels stuck in the ground, the plane could go onto its nose and break its prop. That's where 602 Squadron had most of its accidents.[3]

Taking off at night was even more fraught with difficulties. Donald Jack described it in the following terms:

> At night we were just flying off with a flare path of paraffin lamps. It was pretty fraught because you'd probably been taxying [*sic.*] on the ground for quite a few minutes and the engine got very hot and when you opened up to full throttle the glare from the exhaust stubs was blinding. So it was very difficult just to keep your line on the flare path to see

if you were going in the right direction. Then when you eventually took off you had to forget about the flare path, get your head inside the cockpit and on to your instruments. Now that was fine, but it was difficult seeing the instruments sometimes because you were still dazzled by the flare off of the exhaust. But not only that, the instruments—the rate of climb instrument and your artificial horizon—when you first lifted off, appeared to read that you were diving and that you were losing height. This would go on for maybe eight or ten seconds so you just had to remember that you were not losing height and then the instruments would settle down. But it was very fraught, landing was not much fun either.[4]

At the beginning of the war, the RAF night-fighter force was virtually non-existent. No. 602 Squadron had been deemed 'night operational' and until the end of 1939 was the only unit at Drem given this responsibility. Many pilots were not very happy with this, as flying at night was difficult enough, let alone while trying to locate enemy planes. Specialised night-fighter units, which appeared the following year, always had two crew members—a pilot and a navigator.

For the remainder of October and much of November, 602 carried out routine flights and 'just kept on doing these wretched convoy patrols and night patrols too, which were murder in a Spitfire'. Providing air cover for merchant shipping operating in the vicinity of the Firth of Forth was a role that Drem-based fighter units were to play for most of the war. The convoy patrols were not very popular with the RAF aircrew, but then some of the enemy pilots were not that enthusiastic about attacking Allied ships either. One captured German stated it was estimated that most bomber crews would only survive six attacks on North Sea convoys. They had named the area around the Firth of Forth, defended by Drem's Spitfires, 'Suicide Corner'.

On 28 October, a He 111 was observed flying at high altitude over Drem, apparently on a reconnaissance mission to monitor the movement of British shipping. At 10.45 a.m., Yellow Section of 602 Squadron was ordered to take off and pursue the enemy. The intended operational area for the He 111 was the Firth of Clyde, but due to low cloud it made its way back to the east coast of Scotland, where the weather was better. Anti-aircraft batteries opened up over the Firth of Forth and inflicted some damage. During this, 602's Yellow Section Spitfires intercepted a twin-engined aircraft flying near May Island. It was only after they had opened fire on it, wounding the pilot in the jaw, did they realise their mistake—it was actually an RAF Avro Anson.

Meanwhile, the He 111 was flying in the vicinity of RAF Turnhouse, where both Red Sections of 602 and 603 Squadrons were patrolling. The exploding anti-aircraft shells alerted them to the presence of an unwelcome visitor. The Heinkel tried to escape by diving into thin cloud, but it provided little protection. A total of six Spitfires from both squadrons launched the first attack at 10,000 feet, riddling the He 111 from stem to stern with machine-gun fire. Despite being under continuous attack, pilot Kurt Lehmkuhl, who had been hit several times in the back, headed towards the Lammermuir Hills—a remarkable piece of flying. With both engines dead and too low to parachute, Lehmkuhl glided the aircraft towards the inhospitable terrain. The landing speed was too high on approach, but Lehmkuhl skilfully slowed the aircraft, allowing it to touch the ground just as it had reached the stall and had zero forward speed. The Heinkel came to rest on a hillside between High Latch and Kidlaw, to the east of Humbie Village. It had smashed through a dry stone wall, tearing off its starboard tailplane, breaking its back, and smashing its glass canopy. A contemporary description of the incident was published in the magazine *The War Illustrated* on 25 November 1939. Mr John K. Irvine of Long Newton Farm was on the spot within a few minutes:

I am the grieve [manager] at Longnewton Farm, close beside the Lammerlaw Hill. I was filling up sacks of barley at about quarter past ten when I heard a noise like the hurling of a barrow. That's what I thought it was at first but it went on and on and came nearer and then I knew it was the noise of guns. Then we saw a big black machine with two engines coming over the trees from the north-west. There were four British machines with it. They were circling all round and rattling bullets into the German as hard as they could do it. I thought we ought to take cover—there were women workers here. But curiosity brought us out again—while we were running in and while we were running out—so that we saw the German go over the houses, so low that it almost touched the chimneys. Then they all went out of sight up over the hill and a few minutes later I saw our fighters going back—all four of them. They seemed to be finished with their job. So we ran up the hill to see what had happened.

Two of the crew were dead. I expect they would be the gunners [they were the wireless operator and flight engineer, who doubled as air gunners] and they must have been shot before they came my length because I never saw them firing at our planes. The machine had scrapped its tail over a dyke and come down on the moor on an even keel. One of the crew wasn't hurt at all. He was pulling out his mate. By the time we got up he had him drawn out and lying on the ground. We tried to talk to the unwounded man but he didn't know what we were saying. But he spoke a little English. The wounded man wanted a drink but the doctor said he ought not to have one. He had two bullet wounds in the back. The police took the unwounded man away. Before he went he shook hands with his mate. We got a gate off one of the fences and carried the wounded man down to the road and waited there, till the ambulance came for him.[5]

Another witness reported:

… a policeman appeared shortly afterwards and the pilot speaking good English said, 'We surrender as prisoners of war. Please see to my gunners in the back of the aircraft'. But both gunners were dead. The German pilot and his companion were taken as prisoners to Edinburgh.

The shooting down of this aircraft received much publicity at the time. Officially, He 111 H-2 1H+JA, from KG26 based at Westerland was awarded as a joint kill to 602 and 603 Squadrons, with no credit given to the anti-aircraft gunners. Interestingly, the 3rd (Scottish) Anti-Aircraft Division report for this day states:

The wreckage of Heinkel He 111 1H+JA of KG 26, which was shot down on the Lammermuir Hills, near Humbie, by Spitfires of 602 and 603 Squadron. (*Museum of Flight, National Museums of Scotland/SCRAN*)

... no AA gun stations opened fire, so it must be assumed that the damage inflicted on the machine originated from the considerable number of naval vessels lying at anchor near Rosyth.[6]

There was little other enemy activity in the autumn of 1939 other than these reconnaissance and anti-shipping flights over the North Sea. The Heinkel was the first downed German aircraft to crash on the British mainland. However, the first aircraft to be brought down on British soil was Ju 88A-1 4D+EK, which exploded on the Island of Hoy in the Orkneys after being hit by anti-aircraft fire on Tuesday 17 October, a day after the raid on the Royal Navy ships in the Firth of Forth.

On 26 November, there was a collision on landing involving two of 3 Yellow Section Spitfires, one of which was L.1009. Fortunately, there were no injuries:

There were an alarming number of bent Spitfires as the field at Drem alternated between a bog and an ice rink. It was far from being the ideal fighter base, too small for high performance machines to operate with a generous safety margin, it had a slight hill right in the middle. And of course, the weather produced such extraordinary ground conditions that on one occasion a Spitfire skidded sideways on landing on ice and then promptly dug its nose into an unfrozen patch of mud at the bottom of the more sheltered slope. Some of the pilots didn't even get into their machines that winter. A number went down with flu, while Harry Moody slipped climbing onto the wing of his Spitfire. Somersaulting spectacularly on the ice, he broke his collar bone.[7]

In December 1939, an aircraft broke its propeller after overshooting on a night landing. Undercarriage legs were frequently damaged as the Spitfires bounced on the soft ground and ground crews became well-versed in rapidly repairing such damage; they were able to replace the airscrew, jack the wings, change the oleo leg, fit the wheel, check the hydraulics, clean the wing, and dope the scratches in less than four hours. In one of the coldest winters experienced for many decades, the mechanics worked twenty-four hours a day to keep the Spitfires airworthy. Their Merlin engines had to be started and run every few minutes to stop the oil freezing in the feed pipes. During that entire winter there was not a single time when pilots could not start their engines for a scramble.

Enemy aircraft put in a fleeting appearance almost every day and 602 Squadron were scrambled to intercept, placing a great strain on the squadron. Climbing was not one of the Spitfire's strongest points, so interceptions were frequently made over the North Sea at extreme range. Often the raider would disappear in the clouds before the fighter could catch it.

According to the rulebook, three aircraft had to investigate any unidentified radar plot. The Spitfires were required to fly in tight 'vic' (vee) formation, with the leader in the centre and wingmen on either side. This required constant adjustments to speed and position, which told on both the pilots and their machines. The servicing facilities simply could not cope with the frequent maintenance checks. In the end, the pilots decided to disregard this—and many other regulations in the Fighter Command rulebook—and decided to fly in pairs instead. This experience led to the abandonment of many widely held ideas about air combat and the new tactics evolved here would be of great value in the forthcoming Battle of Britain.

At 11 a.m. on Tuesday 12 December 1939, residents of North Berwick watched Blue Section, 602 Squadron engage a He 111 overhead. No. 602 was joined in the fray a short time later by Spitfires of 72 Squadron from RAF Leuchars and 603 Squadron based at RAF Turnhouse. None of the pilots made a positive claim concerning the Heinkel's destruction, but an Icelandic ship reported picking up a distress call at 1.35 p.m. from an enemy aircraft, which had crashed 40 miles out to sea. That night, the Germans confirmed that one of their aircraft was missing.

One cloudy winter's day off the Fife coast, a section of 602's Spitfires caught a glimpse of a twin-engined aircraft diving through the mist and managed to fire several bursts of machine-gun fire. Later in the day RAF Dyce telephoned, complaining that one of their Avro Ansons had landed with its fuselage full of holes. Four days before Christmas, there was a more serious mistaken identity incident; a formation of Hampden bombers, returning from a raid on Germany, were attacked and two of them shot down by 602's Spitfires with fatal consequences. Full details of this can be found in Chapter 11. These incidents led to the squadron being accused of being trigger-happy by some other RAF pilots, which did not endear 602's pilots to the station commander, whom the pilots went to great lengths to avoid after this incident.

The following day, 602 made amends for this. At 10.29 a.m., east of May Island, Flt Lt J. Urie, Fg Off. C. Maclean, and Fg Off. Strong succeeded in destroying a Heinkel He 115 floatplane, one of two laying mines in the sea. At the beginning of August 1940, another He 115 was involved in an attack on a convoy off the east coast. It misjudged its attack and flew so low that it hit a lifeboat davit and crashed on to the deck of the merchantman SS *Highlander*. The ship later arrived at Leith Docks, Edinburgh, with the aircraft still entangled in its superstructure. Enemy aircraft were frequently deployed in mine-laying operations off the coast of Britain during the first few months of war. The magnetic mines dropped by these aircraft claimed many Allied ships and were much feared by sailors.

The year ended badly for 602 Squadron. On 30 December 1939, Sgt Bailey was killed in Spitfire K9977, when it crashed near Haddington after a wing detached while recovering from a loop. The bitter winter weather continued throughout January 1940, but the Luftwaffe continued to mount attacks on shipping whenever conditions allowed. On 9 January, eight attacks were made on convoys between Aberdeen and Cromer, including one in the vicinity of St Abb's Head. No. 602 Squadron and 111 Squadron from RAF Turnhouse and 64 Squadron from RAF Leuchars were sent to intercept the German bombers, but no contact was made due to the poor weather.

On 13 January 1940, 602's luck changed. Marcus Robinson led Red Section against an enemy aircraft reported north of St Andrews. The Spitfires successfully attacked the reconnaissance He 111 H-2 F6+LH, knocking out one of its engines. No. 111 Squadron's Hurricanes then arrived on the scene to join the battle, and soon after the enemy aircraft crash-landed in the sea, 15 miles off Carnoustie. The three NCOs

Spitfire (Mk I) of 609 Squadron in the winter of 1939–40. (*RAF Museum*)

on board were later listed as missing, but the pilot, *Unteroffizier (Sgt)* G. Kahle, was fished out the water. He later sent his congratulations to 602 Squadron on their good shooting. Shortly before the Heinkel crashed, one of its gunners had managed to put a bullet through the windscreen of Fg Off. McLean's Spitfire, narrowly missing him. After actions such as this, the Spitfires would fly low across the airfield so that the ground crews could see that they needed rearming and be ready when they landed, in case the enemy's next target was the airfield.

However, flying accidents continued to inflict far more damage on 602's Spitfires than the Germans. For example, in early February, after a gunnery exercise, John McAdam succeeded in putting a Spitfire on its back at RAF Acklington. Then back at Drem he tipped another Spitfire onto its nose and the following day attempted to land a third with its wheels up. A crash was averted by a quick-thinking member of the squadron, who fired a Very Light across the landing path. Not to be left out of the ever-mounting number of accidents involving aircraft, 602's 1½-ton motor lorry succeeded in skidding into *Hannibal*, a Handley Page HP 42E four-engined biplane airliner—once the pride of Imperial Airways—which had just landed with 609 Squadron's equipment and personnel. Some damage was done to the wing-leading edge, but the pilot, Capt. Peacock, was said to have been 'remarkably philosophical' about the accident. *Hannibal* was one of several former Imperial Airways machines used to deliver airmen to Drem in the early years of the war. Unfortunately, within a short time of being commandeered, several of them were lost in accidents or destroyed by bad weather.

The inclement weather also claimed another victim in the person of Charles Keary, the station commander. Keary had a strong dislike of the members of the auxiliary squadrons, regarding them as a long-haired, ill-disciplined bunch who paid little attention to regulations. No. 602 Squadron personnel had to turn out for the Station Commander's Parade and Inspection on 23 January 1940. Efforts had been made to clear just enough snow from the tarmac to accommodate the personnel of the three squadrons plus the headquarters staff, but a recent fall of rain turned the surrounding area into a skating rink. Charles Keary, in his immaculate uniform, stepped out of his highly polished staff car, lost his footing on the icy surface and landed flat on his back, much to the delight of many of those on the parade ground.

A break from the routine patrols was provided when Green Section was instructed to escort Sir John Salmond's aircraft through the Sector to RAF Leuchars. At the beginning of February, B-Flight's Spitfires departed to RAF Acklington for several days practice of their gunnery skills.

On 9 February, Red Section engaged He 111 H-3 1H+EN 6825, from their old adversary KG26, flying south about 20 miles out to sea. Sqn Ldr A. Farquhar fired just 625 .303 rounds (a four-second burst) at it, but this was enough to wound a crew member and cause thick black smoke to pour from an engine. The crippled aircraft made a forced landing in a field at Rhodes Farm, immediately to the east of North Berwick. The three crew members clambered out and were taken prisoner by the local police. The gunner had a bullet wound to his lung. He was taken to the hospital at RAF Drem, where he died a short time later. Many locals and pilots from Drem visited the downed enemy aircraft, which had landed intact.

A Handley Page HP.42 in the snow during the severe winter in January 1940. The former Imperial Airways airliner was impressed into RAF service for ferrying war supplies. This aircraft suffered damage to its aileron while at Drem, caused by strong winds. Scaffolding can be seen under the port wing in an attempt to repair the aircraft. (*Museum of Flight, National Museums of Scotland/SCRAN*)

The Heinkel was dismantled by 63 Maintenance Unit. The intention was to rebuild it at Drem using parts from a He 111, salvaged from the Lammermuirs in 1939, but it could not be moved on the narrow roads near the airfield so it was taken to RAF Turnhouse. After some months it was moved south and rebuilt. In September 1941, bearing RAF serial number AW177, it was transferred to the Air Fighting Development Unit at RAF Duxford, established to study the relative performance of Allied and Axis aircraft. Two months later, the Air Ministry formed No. 1426 Enemy Aircraft Flight with the Heinkel as its first machine. It led the opening demonstration tour of RAF airfields, which commenced on 11 February 1942. The following year it featured in *Combat America*, a training film for American air gunners narrated by Maj. Clark Gable the Hollywood star. In November 1943, on a tour of US Army Air Force bases in Britain, the Heinkel came to grief while landing at Polebrook, Northamptonshire. The pilot executed a steep left turn to avoid an oncoming Ju 88. The Heinkel stalled, spun in, and exploded, killing seven of the eleven crew on board.

Back at Drem, 602 Squadron continued to patrol the sea lanes around south-east Scotland. When a Dornier was reported shadowing the *Argent*, the Spitfires were dispatched only to chase their own radar plots. This could happen when there was a delay between plots being co-ordinated in the operations room and being radioed to the fighters, by which time they could be muddled with the plots of the fighters themselves. A few days later, on 18 February, the squadron's Spitfires acted as targets for the airfield's anti-aircraft guns. Gun cameras enabled the results of the exercises to be assessed later. Occasionally, 602's aircraft provided targets for naval vessels in

This Heinkel He 111 of KG26 was damaged by a 602 Squadron Spitfire flown by Squadron Leader Farquhar. It crash landed at Rhodes Farm, North Berwick, on 9 February 1940. (*Museum of Flight, National Museums of Scotland/SCRAN*)

the Firth of Forth. The squadron insisted that one of their personnel be on board the ships, as the sailors had a reputation of shooting live rounds at any aircraft, Allied or enemy, that flew too close.

Early in the war there were no specialised missing aircraft search units, so the Spitfires sometimes performed this role. On 21 February it was reported that a Hurricane had crashed into the sea near May Island. The Spitfires were scrambled, but no trace of wreckage was seen. A risky landing awaited them back at Drem due to a sudden thaw. No Hurricane was missing—it was a false alarm.

On 14 January 1940, Spitfire L1007 and its pilot, Plt Off. George Proudman of 65 Squadron, RAF Northolt, was attached to 602 Squadron. This was the only Spitfire equipped with 20-mm Hispano cannon in the RAF at the time. When this new type first entered service there was a problem with the cannon jamming, but this fault was rectified in later versions. Proudman was a regular pilot and an excellent shot. He once demonstrated his marksmanship by shooting a pheasant stone dead with a service revolver from a moving car at a range of 30 feet. To some of his fellow pilots, he was regarded as a 'cowboy of the air'. When he flew, he smoked a pipe and was impervious to the cold, wearing only a shirt front and little else under his flying jacket. On 8 February he was given permission to fire his Spitfire's cannon into the sea off North Berwick. A few days later, on 22 February, he had the opportunity to test them against the enemy.

Flying with Red Section, the cannon-equipped machine was vectored onto an unidentified aircraft approaching the coast near St Abb's Head. It was identified as He 111 P-2 T5+0H, belonging to 1(F)/Ob.d.l. Sqn Ldr Douglas Farquhar was the first to attack in Spitfire K9962, in case L1007's cannon did not operate correctly. Farquhar's aircraft was also equipped with a recent innovation in the form of a camera gun. The film of the air attack ran for just six seconds, but it was Fighter Command's first pictures of aerial combat. After the first four seconds, the images showed a puff of white smoke from the Heinkel's left engine. Less than a second later, the engine exploded. This was then followed by an attack by Proudman, who managed to fire sixty-four rounds from his cannons before they jammed. The pilot of the stricken Heinkel headed towards the coast and managed to make a successful landing on remote moorland at Dowlaw, north of Coldingham. In the distance were the huge masts of Drone Hill Radar Station, where some of the personnel had probably witnessed the demise of the hostile plane. What followed next would have astonished them even more.

The Spitfire flown by Douglas Farquhar approached to land beside the downed aircraft. Farquhar wanted to prevent the Germans from destroying their aircraft, as he wanted to assess the effectiveness of the attack by the cannon-firing Spitfire. Unfortunately, his Spitfire bounced down a steep hill into soft ground, the nose dug in, and it tipped on its back. Farquhar found himself hanging upside down only inches from the ground. Meanwhile the four German airmen, one wounded in the legs, had managed to extract themselves from the wreckage and were in the process of setting fire to it. However, Feldwebel (Sgt) Sprigath went to the Spitfire to extricate Farquhar. The squadron leader then found himself a prisoner of the Germans, with three of them pointing Lugers at him, but after some discussion he persuaded them to put away their weapons.

A detachment of elderly Local Defence Volunteers (later called 'The Home Guard') trudged across several miles of moorland from the nearest road to eventually arrive on the scene. Douglas Farquhar's troubles were not over yet. The leader of the volunteers was convinced that he was a member of the enemy aircrew. It was only when he produced his income tax form and showed his captors the crashed Spitfire that they realised their error. The fire did not take hold and destroyed only the forward fuselage of the Heinkel. On examination, no trace of hits by cannon fire could found.

No. 63 Maintenance Unit, which had salvaged the other two He 111s shot down over Scotland in the early months of the war, began work on this wreck on 26 February 1940. The unit was to return to this area at the end of the war to carry out one of its most demanding recovery operations. A Sea Otter had hit the cliffs at St Abb's Head and fallen into the sea below. Some of the pieces were lifted by boat from the sea, while a tractor was used to drag other pieces lodged on the 300-foot precipice to the top of the cliff.

On 28 February 1940, the deeds of 602's pilots were acknowledged when the king and high-ranking members of the RAF visited Drem. By the end of the month, the bitter winter weather had relinquished its grip. The clocks were changed to summer time, a move that pleased the pilots as dawn patrol would commence an hour later.

Chart of 72 Nazi Raids on Britain in Six Months

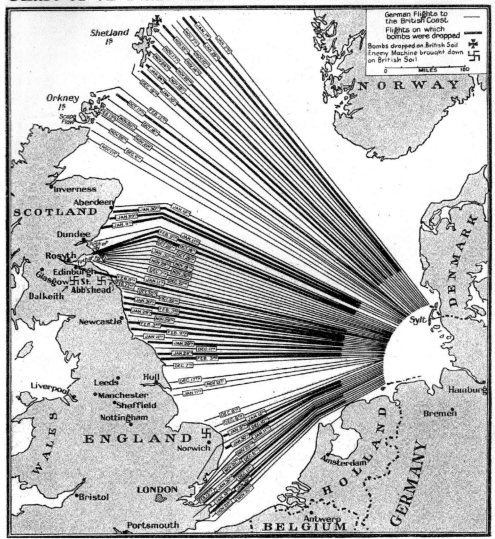

A contemporary chart of German air raids directed towards the British Isles, from September 1939 to 22 February 1940. There had been twenty-five bombing raids (mostly on shipping) and forty-seven reconnaissance flights, but few German aircraft crossed the coast line and those that did dropped no bombs inland. Most raids were directed on Scotland or the north of England. (*War Illustrated Vol.1*)

As the days began to lengthen, there was no let-up in enemy activity. Late on the night of 2 March, three Spitfires were scrambled in response to a report of an enemy attack on a convoy south of St Abb's Head. The pilots saw a number of bright flashes, but no sign of enemy aircraft. They returned, refuelled, and were ordered to investigate a report of an enemy aircraft flying over Perth. Again, no German aircraft was encountered. The Spitfires were ordered back to St Abb's Head to check on the convoy. The weather was now deteriorating and it took some time to locate the ships. By now the Spitfires had been airborne for over an hour and a half. One of them was running short of fuel, so its pilot, Plt Off. G. Proudman, had to make a wheels-up landing in a field near Dunbar. Fortunately, it was just beginning to get light at the time and the pilot escaped with minor injuries. No. 602's motor transport section also suffered an accident a few days later, when one of its drivers accidentally set fire to a refuelling bowser.

There continued to be frequent false alarms and scrambles, putting considerable strain on the ground crews to keep the fighters airworthy. B-Flight alone flew more than 300 hours during March 1940. On 25 March there was another scramble in the middle of the night to go to the assistance of a convoy off Montrose. Unfortunately, when the Spitfires returned to base to be refuelled the ships were attacked with one of them reported sinking. Two days later, dawn and dusk patrols were flown over convoys entering and leaving the Firth of Forth. There was no enemy activity, but the gunners on a Royal Naval ship near May Island, who were engaged in target practice, managed to direct some of their fire close to a Spitfire being flown by Plt Off. Sandy Johnstone.

The troublesome cannon-equipped Spitfire L1007 was returned to its makers at Southampton by Plt Off. Proudman. A replacement was collected from RAF Catterick, but it was not much of an improvement as it leaked large quantities of oil. A couple of weeks after its arrival it nearly came to grief by taking the top off the windsock with its wing while taking off in formation. The windsock suffered more damage than the aircraft, which managed to land safely. During March 602 Squadron suffered several other mishaps. An accident-prone flight sergeant taxied Spitfire L1004 into L1019 on 19 March, after which he was promptly posted to another unit; though neither aircraft was badly damaged. Around the same time there was increasing concern that the Germans would step up operations against targets in the south-east of Scotland, including Drem. Several steps were taken to disperse its Spitfires at nightfall to make them less vulnerable to attack. On 20 March six Spitfires of 602 were flown to RAF Turnhouse to stay the night. Fg Off. Alastair Milne Grant crashed on landing into the setting sun, but fortunately was unhurt.

Some relief for the overworked pilots arrived at the beginning of April in the form of 29 Squadron's Bristol Blenheims, the first specialised night-fighter unit to be deployed to Drem. The Blenheims had a crew of two, making night flying considerably less stressful. The special equipment and mechanics arrived on board *Scylla*, a former Imperial Airways Short L17 four-engined biplane airliner, of which only two were built. The winter weather at Drem had given way to gales of up to 50 knots. While the ground crew were picketing down the machine for its overnight stay, a violent gust caught her broadside and *Scylla* rolled slowly onto her back, accompanied by the sound of tearing metal and snapping rigging wires. Two aircrew were trapped inside. Sandy Johnstone of 602 Squadron witnessed the event:

> What happened next was like the Charge of the Light Brigade as everyone nearby grabbed empty tins, bowls, jam jars, teapots, anything which would hold liquid—in which to catch the petrol as it flowed from Scylla's recently fuelled tanks. Everybody was intent on augmenting their meagre petrol ration and I even saw some of the maintenance chaps rolling out a fifty gallon oil drum which I thought showed commendable enterprise! The two occupants trapped inside were eventually released from their lofty prison but not until the last drop of petrol had stopped flowing.[8]

In April 1940 the Germans invaded Denmark and Norway. Britain promised military aid to both countries, and there was a rumour that 602 Squadron could be dispatched to Scandinavia. This did not occur, but A-Flight was instructed to move north to RAF Montrose and B-Flight to RAF Dyce where they would be closer to the fighting than at Drem. No Imperial Airways airliners were provided to transport the personnel or their equipment; ground crews were told to find their own way to their new postings. If some of 602's pilots thought that Drem was far from ideal when they had first arrived from Glasgow, they were in for an even greater shock when they landed at RAF Dyce. It was another grass airfield—even muddier than Drem—and it frequently rained and snowed. In addition, in early 1940, the radar coverage did not extend this far north; Dundee was the northern limit.

On 18 April, Spitfires chased what they thought was a Ju 88, but spotted the RAF roundels just before opening fire. It was a long-nosed version of the Bristol Blenheim. At RAF Dyce, 602 Squadron marked out a strip the size and shape of an aircraft carrier deck to prove they could, if necessary, fly from such a type of ship without catapult or arrester gear.

With the fall of Norway there was an increase in enemy activity over northern Scotland, especially against the Royal Navy base at Scapa Flow. The Germans now had the advantage of operating from captured airfields, which reduced the flying time to their targets.

On 19 May, as a Spitfire's guns were being lined up against the sighting markings on a hangar door at Dyce, the armourer accidentally pressed the trigger, sending a hail of bullets from all eight machine guns straight through the building. One of these punched its way through several walls before landing on the desk of Ghandar Dowar, the owner of the airfield in pre-war days. He immediately wrote a letter to the station commander, complaining that 602 Squadron had tried to kill him.

On 28 May, both A- and B-Flights of 602 Squadron were very happy to return to Drem. The last aircraft touched down close to midnight, thus completing the first night unit move. 'It was great to be back at Drem, for it has a happy atmosphere about it'. Charles Keary's (the station commander) face fell when he was informed of their return. The following day the battle-scarred 605 Warwickshire Hurricane Squadron arrived to rest and reform. In the previous six days, while resisting the German

Shorts S.17, G-ACJJ, *Scylla* after being blown over by gales. The former Imperial Airways airliner had been *en route* to Wick, but was damaged beyond repair when it called in to refuel at Drem. (*RAF Museum*)

Another view of the wreck of Short S.17 in a gale on 1 April 1940. (*Museum of Flight, National Museums of Scotland/SCRAN*)

invasion of France, they had lost nine aircraft and four pilots. No. 605's pilots passed on what they had learned to 602 Squadron, who up until then had not encountered any enemy fighter aircraft. No. 602's Spitfires were immediately fitted with rear view mirrors, mounted just above the canopy in streamlined casings designed by Sgt Simpson. He had worked at Stevenson's, the coachbuilders, before the war. The aircraft's worst blind spot was now virtually eliminated.

On 3 June the squadron was ordered to RAF Northolt, London, to provide fighter cover for the evacuation from Dunkirk. Equipment was loaded onto two Bombay transports, but the following day Churchill announced that the withdrawal had been completed; the transport aircraft were unloaded and departed empty.

During the first two weeks of June, East Lothian sizzled in a heat wave. The warm conditions favoured the formation of the coastal fog known as 'haar'. On 10 June Red Section's Spitfires had difficulty landing due to the haar, one making several abortive attempts, then damaging a landing flap and wingtip on touching down. The ground crew had it airworthy again within four hours. The haar returned towards the end of the month, when a German reconnaissance plane was heard overflying the field, but visibility was so bad that the Spitfires could not take off.

There was considerable enemy activity over south-east Scotland at the end of June 1940. On 25 June, at 11.30 p.m., approximately fifteen KG26 Heinkels were detected approaching the area from their new base at Stavanger, Norway. At 12.35 a.m. five Heinkels were seen crossing the coast at North Berwick. They flew inland, dropping bombs on the Broxburn and Livingston area. At 1.25 a.m. Sqn Ldr George Pinkerton and Sandy Johnstone were ordered up on patrol; half an hour later, they saw anti-aircraft fire in the direction of Edinburgh and heard 603's call sign 'viken'. Suddenly, a He 111 was illuminated by three searchlights and Sandy Johnstone took chase. On his first pass he flew so close to the bomber that he almost collided with it, but fortunately the searchlight operators were able to keep the enemy trapped in their beams, allowing the Spitfire to carry out another attack. The bomber's engine caught fire, splattering the attacking Spifire's windscreen with oil. As the crippled aircraft descended slowly towards the sea, its landing lights suddenly illuminated the pitch-black night. It hit the water off Barns Ness, south of Dunbar. As it sunk below the waves it presented an eerie sight as its lights were still glowing. Sandy Johnstone then fired a double-red Very light to mark the spot. Three of the four crew were subsequently rescued by the local lifeboat. The pilot, who was only eighteen, did not make the best impression with his captors, spitting on a nurse attending to his superficial injuries. Much of the air battle had taken place over Drem and was witnessed by the personnel there.

The following day Johnstone was called into the station commander's office to face two irate Army officers from Edinburgh. They demanded an explanation as to why two red Very lights had been fired over Dunbar—unknown to the RAF, this was the signal that an invasion was imminent. Many soldiers stationed between Fife and the Borders had a sleepless night because of the false alarm. The station commander, Richard Atcherley, who had recently replaced the unloved Charles Keary, apologised to the Army officers for the misunderstanding. He was a most approachable person as well as a brilliant pilot, so it was not long before any ill-feeling was dispelled. The same evening (26 June) Sandy Johnstone was on patrol when, at 11.30 p.m., he saw bombs being dropped on Leith. Flying towards Edinburgh he caught a fleeting glimpse of a He 111. It managed to escape by diving into the darkness. Earlier in the day, Spitfire I N3190 was abandoned by Fg Off. J. Haig over the Pentland Hills—he survived without injury.

At 7.35 p.m. on Monday 1 July, two enemy reconnaissance aircraft were detected approaching North Berwick. Blue Section 602 Squadron intercepted one, a Junkers Ju 88 of 1 (F)/121, at 6,000 feet. At 8.05 p.m. it jettisoned its bombs on the foreshore at Belhaven, Dunbar, and then flew in and out of cloud in an attempt to escape the pursuing Spitfires—2,400 rounds were fired at it by Paul Watt's Spitfire before it disappeared. Watt claimed one of its engines was emitting smoke. RAF Intelligence refused to credit him with damaging the Junkers, but later relented. It was not until after the war that the fate of the aircraft became known. One engine had been knocked out, the compass shot away, and the instruments seriously damaged, but the pilot had nursed his crippled machine across the North Sea before crashing in Northern France.

On 3 July a Dornier 17 managed to fly under the radar cover to machine gun Drem airfield and escaped unscathed. The radar station at Drone Hill was unable to detect low-flying aircraft, but this was later rectified when a Chain Home Low station was established at Cockburnspath. Later the same day, while 602's Blue Section was flying north to patrol over Arbroath, a Dornier 17 was sighted flying in and out of cloud at 14,000 feet. Sandy Johnstone met his opponent head on and managed to fire a short burst. The enemy gunner returned fire, but also missed before the Dornier disappeared.

There were rumours that the Germans were about to step up their attacks, particularly on coastal convoys. No one was allowed to leave Drem for several days, but it wasn't until 7 July that a pair of Ju 88s of KG30 were intercepted by Hector McLean and Findlay Boyd, 25 miles east of May Island. Both pilots witnessed one of the enemy crash into the sea. At evening of the following day, Green Section was scrambled to intercept an enemy aircraft that had been reported flying towards Fife. When the Spitfires reached 20,000 feet, a Heinkel was sighted flying in an easterly direction and they gave chase. After disappearing in thick cumulus the Heinkel re-emerged and was engaged by Sandy Johnstone and Paul Webb. Its right engine in flames, and with its gunners returning fire, the aircraft dived steeply towards the protection of the nearest bank of cloud. This time it did disappear. A few bombs had been dropped on Crail, Fife, without doing much damage.

On 9 July 602's Spitfires were in action again. Two fighters of Red Section intercepted a couple of Ju 88s, 2 miles off Fifeness. The German flyers were engaged in mine-laying and were taken by surprise. At 5.50 p.m. Dunlop Urie hit one aircraft, which dived into the sea some 20 miles east of May Island. Donald Jack, flying the second Spitfire, riddled the other Junkers with machine-gun fire, but it made good its escape and, despite being badly damaged, managed to return to its base at Westerland, never to take to the air again. No. 602 Squadron had now brought 13 Group's total number of kills to over fifty.

The Battle of Britain is widely regarded to have begun on 10 July 1940. While Scotland had seen the brunt of enemy air operations in the first months of the war, this was about to change drastically. Enemy units that had previously mounted these operations were now transferred to France to attack targets in the south of England. The brief glory days of Drem were coming to an end, and the press who had publicized the exploits of its pilots in the early days of war, would now focus its attention elsewhere.

On 12 July four pilots of 602 Squadron were sent to collect new Spitfires from RAF Carlisle. Flt Lt Sandy Johnstone was appointed to command the unit in place of Sqn Ldr Pinkerton. On 18 July it was recorded 'still raining heavily, aerodrome and tarmac looking like the Lake District'. Supermarine's Chief Test Pilot, Geoffrey Quill, arrived at Drem flying a Spitfire with a variable pitch airscrew instead of the standard two-speed model. Sqn Ldr Sandy Johnstone was given the opportunity to fly the new machine, which he remarked gave a very smooth ride compared with their current aircraft.

On 18 July the Germans mounted twenty-four raids against the east coast, targeting convoys, Crail and Montrose Airfields, and Leith Docks. On 22 July a Ju 88 streaked low across Drem airfield in the direction of Edinburgh, taking everyone by surprise. It dropped some bombs on Leith cemetery, by a strange quirk of fate exposing the bodies of several German airmen killed in the raid on Royal Navy ships in the Firth of Forth the previous October. As 602's log book recorded:

> It is believed that the only parts of Scotland 'Forever Germany' have been evacuated by their own bombs as the permanent residence of Forth raid casualties is now a mere conjecture.[9]

At 12.40 a.m., on 24 July, searchlights at East Linton illuminated a He 111 at around 4,000 feet. Sgt Andrew MacDowall, on patrol at the time, made a head-on attack and saw his tracers hit. The Heinkel immediately jettisoned two parachute mines and dived towards the sea. It was later confirmed as having been shot down. This was the last 'kill' for 602 Squadron during its stay at Drem. Around the same time Sqn Ldr Sandy Johnstone, flying Spitfire Q, with its newly fitted variable-pitched airscrew, latched onto another He 111, some distance off the Fife Coast. It also dropped its ordnance, but escaped by rapidly descending almost to sea level. Sqn Ldr Sandy Johnstone remarked in his diary:

> General Stumpff's boys must like Scotland, for they are frequent visitors to our shores these days. The General's Squadrons are operating from Norway, part of Luftflotte Five—Stumpff's Funf, we call them—but although a few of them venture inland during the hours of darkness, they seldom come further than landfall in their daylight operations. They do not seem to be showing the same aggressive spirit that they used to.[10]

At the end of July the Germans were mounting operations against shipping off south-east Scotland, almost on a nightly basis. While flying over St Abb's Head, the squadron leader witnessed the convoy escort *Royal Archer* strike a mine and sink rapidly, its bows blown away. The haar returned in August; after a night patrol, Plt

Off. Moody and Flt Lt Boyd had difficulty in returning in the dense fog. Boyd diverted to RAF Leuchars, but Moody, short of fuel, attempted to land at Drem. With visibility at about 50 yards, he made several attempts, overshot, and ended up in the boundary hedge. He was unhurt, but the Spitfire never flew again. On 5 August 602 Squadron's Spitfires were vectored to a raid near Arbroath where they intercepted a He 111 some miles off the Fife Coast. When the German pilot realised he was under attack he performed a stall turn and escaped into the cloud tops.

A few days later 602 Squadron received instructions that it was to move south to RAF West Hampnett to relieve 145 Squadron, which in turn was to move to Drem. Two Handley Page Harrows transported the mechanics to their new base, which was in the forefront of the Battle of Britain. After a weather delay, at 12 p.m. on 13 August, 602's Spitfires lined up on Drem's runway for the last time. As they opened their throttles and bumped over the grass field, the station commander drove his Humber staff car alongside them. Padre Sutherland was in the back seat, hanging out the window and playing the lament 'Lochaber No More' on his bagpipes. Sgt McDowall, however, had to land almost immediately with engine trouble.

No. 602 Squadron would never return to Drem. It continued to fly Spitfires until 1951—one of the last units to do so—by which time Drem had been closed for several years. Sqn Ldr Sandy Johnstone was promoted to Air Vice-Marshal, retiring in 1968. Fortunately, he kept diaries of his stay at Drem, despite this being frowned upon by officialdom. These later formed the basis of several books on his flying career. Without this record the history of the airfield would be all the poorer, as the official squadron records for the first few months of the war are very brief.

A Spitfire of 602 Squadron in a dispersal next to the perimeter track in 1940. (*Aldon Ferguson*)

609 (West Riding) Squadron

This was the second Spitfire squadron to arrive at Drem and operated alongside 602 (City of Glasgow) Squadron for much of the war. The West Riding is one of the three historic subdivisions of Yorkshire.

Based at RAF Catterick, Yorkshire, on 27 August 1939, it was equipped with just two Spitfire Is and one Fairey Battle, with more aircraft to be delivered. The unit moved north via RAF Acklington in Northumberland. With the declaration of war on 3 September 1939, the Spitfires were put on an operational defensive state similar to most other fighter squadrons:

> One section at Readiness—airborne in 5 minutes.
> One section at Available—airborne in 15 minutes.
> One section at Released—airborne in 30 minutes.
> One section stood-off for training, weather permitting.

At this stage, 609 Squadron had only twelve pilots. On 16 October, it played a small role against the first major German raid of the war, an attack by Ju 88s on Royal Navy ships in the Firth of Forth. Its planes were sent over Alnwick and Berwick-upon-Tweed in an unsuccessful attempt to intercept four of the enemy bombers, reportedly flying south. Although officially a non-mobile squadron, 609 were ordered to deploy to Drem at dawn the following day for 'immediate duty'. Civilian transport was requisitioned, including two White Horse Whisky trucks. Due to the shortage of transport aircraft, the flight servicing crews and more essential stores were transported in Whitley bombers.

After only five days, 609 Squadron had to move again—this time to RAF Kinloss to provide fighter cover for the hitherto unprotected north-east coast. Essential personnel were transported in three former Imperial Airways Ensigns. These were large, four-engined monoplane airliners, which, reputedly being underpowered, required longer take-off runs than the former Imperial Airways machines that used Drem. They were to make several subsequent visits. According to Kenneth McDowall, a plane spotter and eyewitness to many of the events at Drem:

> I saw a Handley Page HP42 which easily coped with Drem but the Armstrong Whitworth Ensign took the whole strip and every revolution to get off. Nevertheless it managed the traditional beat-up of the hangers [*sic.*] before heading away.[11]

The deployment to RAF Kinloss was short-lived and 609 returned to Drem just two days later. It was rumoured that the squadron would soon move back to RAF Catterick, but nothing came of this. In the meantime, the pilots had already managed to cross swords with the station commander, Charles Keary, and his staff, who resented squadrons that 'blew in' and impaired their comfort and code of discipline. No. 609's pilots had no sooner dispersed their aircraft and entered the mess than they were reprimanded by Keary for walking on the grass.

From October until the end of the year there were numerous uneventful scrambles. On one occasion, Green Section's Spitfires chased a group of enemy aircraft and were about to open fire when it was realised that they were Red Section's aircraft on a practice flight. Squadron Leader Geoffrey Ambler took every opportunity to teach his pilots how to perform the numerous types of fighter attacks. A North American Harvard was borrowed (probably from 602, which had one on strength) to instruct the pilots who were not fully operational.

As winter set in the billets became very cold. Airman Waterson recalled that water spilt during an evening 'brew up' soon froze to the floor, and that half of 609's personnel went down with the flu. The runways had to be cleared by hand to remain serviceable. In late November a batch of regular RAF pilots arrived. The auxiliary squadrons still consisted of volunteers from a specific town or region, but they began to lose their distinct regional identity as personnel were posted to them from other units and training establishments. Among the group of new pilots was an American, Fg Off. Hank Russell, a former commercial airline pilot. He was described as 'as an unscareable tough guy'. He chain smoked while he flew and dressed in clothing more suited to the Arctic, as he felt the cold severely. It was said he looked like an Eskimo in the cockpit. He was the first squadron pilot to use his parachute, on an occasion when his undercarriage refused to lower properly.

North American Harvards were brought in to train new pilots, who had flown only biplanes, from a Service Flying Training School.

On 5 December 1939, 609 departed again for RAF Kinloss, a move intended to be for just one week, but extended for five. Equipment was prepared during the night and some of the ammunition and flight equipment left before dawn on a lorry. The civil aircraft detailed for use by the squadron failed to arrive until after noon, so the fourteen Spitfires were unable to leave until 2.15 p.m. The one de Havilland DH86 that did arrive left at 2.30 p.m. with eight men. Arrangements were made to send the remainder of the men and equipment to RAF Kinloss by rail, but great difficulty was experienced in obtaining transport to the railway station. Eventually 602 Squadron supplied a lorry. No. 609's administration remained at Drem.

While at RAF Kinloss, 609's Spitfires carried out patrols with 64 Squadron over the Home Fleet, which had been moved from its main anchorage at Scapa Flow to Loch Ewe, north-west Scotland, in response to German attacks. No. 609 returned to Drem on 12 January 1940, after the Home Fleet had departed the Loch. On 25 January there was another instance of an undercarriage leg sticking, this time with Fg Off. A. Edge's aircraft. He eventually got the undercarriage leg down and landed safely. On the same day Fg Off. Hank Russell damaged his airscrew and flaps by running into a small snowdrift on landing.

On 29 January 1940, three Spitfires were practicing 'circuits and bumps' when they were instructed to investigate a report of an enemy aircraft attacking a trawler at the mouth of the River Tay. Fg Off. Presse-Joynt and Plt Off. Desmond Ayre eventually caught sight of a He 111, and attacked it. The Heinkel managed two passes at the trawler before disappearing into cloud, apparently undamaged. The third Spitfire I, L1082, was the oldest in the squadron and could not keep up with the other two in the

A Spitfire of No. 609 (West Riding) Squadron being armed and refuelled. The Spitfire 1A had four machine guns in each wing. The .303 bullets were loaded through the access panels above and below the gun mounting positions. These panels can be seen hanging down in the photograph. (*Museum of Flight, National Museums of Scotland/SCRAN*)

Spitfire 1A undergoing an engine test with cowling removed in the snow in the winter of 1940.

chase. Several months later the same He 111 was shot down over northern Scotland, near Wick. Its pilot survived and told his captives that, after his earlier encounter with 609's Spitfires, his machine was riddled with bullet holes.

During February 1940, frequent convoy patrols were flown over the Firth of Forth. It was on such a mission that 609 Squadron destroyed its first enemy aircraft. On 27 February, Red Section was on convoy patrol off St Abb's Head when a He 111 H-31H+AK of KG26 was sighted flying at only 500 feet above the sea towards the ships. Fg Off. Persse-Joynt pursued it, but the Heinkel climbed rapidly into cloud. Flying at a lower altitude, the two other Spitfire pilots saw it reappear and attacked. The enemy aircraft hit the sea, its engines on fire. The crew of four were later rescued by a trawler and taken to Dundee. They had not given up without a fight, as seen by Plt Off. G. Ayre's Spitfire, which had been hit by about fourteen bullets that damaged his elevator trim-tab control and punctured the oil and glycol tanks.

Around the same time, a further two Spitfires were damaged in an accident. The engine of L1065 was being run up, with two airmen sitting on its tail, when the chocks slipped on the frozen ground. The aircraft then moved forward, damaging the main plane of another aircraft (N3025) with its airscrew. The fitter running up L1065 was looking at the instruments and did not realize the aircraft was moving until too late.

There was intensive patrol activity through the first three weeks of March, without contact being made. An instruction was issued that 'day' pilots should become operational by night as well, meaning an end to days off. The Spitfire was quite unsuitable for night flying in a blackout and several accidents soon occurred. As always, the pilots had their excuses. Flt Off. Dundas in L1084 after a perfect three-point landing—on two wheels and the airscrew—stated that '[he] was landing uphill'. An ambulance and fire tender were ordered to search for an aircraft reported by police to have crashed in flames at North Berwick. It was merely Sgt Bennett in L1058 losing a parachute flare: 'It just dropped out ... it might have been the fault of those bloody armourers'. Plt Off. Bisdee appeared to land L1082 about 20 feet in the air, before the aircraft fell the remaining distance with a distinct crunch: 'Two oleo legs, port main plane and tail unit written off'.

No. 609 Squadron suffered further losses to its fleet when Drem's Spitfires were dispersed each night to Turnhouse. The RAF had just raided the German naval base at Kiel and retaliation was expected. Coincidentally, a stray Hampden bomber involved in that raid, lost and short of fuel, landed at Drem during the night. On 20 March, one of 602's Spitfires ended up on its nose at RAF Turnhouse while putting the evacuation plan into effect. Both this squadron and 609 decided to send some of their aircraft to RAF Grangemouth instead. Here, conditions were no better and a total of nine Spitfires became bogged. 'A similar farce' took place the following night with two damaged aircraft being left behind at RAF Grangemouth. All the pilots were suffering severe fatigue and no night flying could be done. On 2 April, two Spitfires collided and were badly damaged when a pilot failed to see an aircraft ahead when taxiing to take-off position. He was subsequently charged with negligently damaging aircraft.

April was an extremely quiet month for operational flying so every opportunity was taken to get in the maximum amount of practice flying, particularly mock attacks on flights and sections of Blenheim fighters, but weather conditions were against night-flying practice.

No. 29 Squadron's Blenheims departed Drem on 10 May, leaving 609's Spitfires as the only aircraft on the airfield. When the City of Glasgow Squadron departed in April, Plt Off. G. Proudman and his second cannon-firing Spitfire was attached to 609. On 15 May he was responsible for 'the most memorable prang in 609's whole history'. He was demonstrating the landing technique formerly employed in the Sopwith Camel, which required the switching on and off of the ignition, but the Spitfire's Merlin engine did not like being treated like the Bentley Rotary that powered the First World War plane and, at a vital moment, stopped altogether. George Proudman's aircraft descended rapidly on top of one of 609's Spitfires. Both aircraft caught fire and shells and bullets exploded all over the place. Remarkably, Proudman walked away from the inferno totally unscathed. His luck ran out a short time later when, at the end of May, he flew south to rejoin his squadron and was wounded by cross-fire from Dornier Do 17s.

At 6 p.m. on 18 May, 609 was ordered to move to RAF Tangmere on the south coast of England, but this changed almost immediately to RAF Northolt, near London. The CO was playing golf on Muirfield at the time, but 'it seems unlike Drake, he did not deem it essential to complete his game'.[12] The first rail party left at 10 p.m. the same day, followed by the fifteen Spitfires the next day. While at Drem, the West Riding Squadron had claimed only one enemy aircraft, but, in a comment clearly directed at 602 Squadron, 'it could at least boast, unlike many squadrons, that in over eight months it had shot down no aircraft of its own side'. Drem was to become 'one of the 609's most happily remembered stations of the war'.

603 (City of Edinburgh) Squadron

No. 603 Squadron first came south to Drem from RAF Dyce (near Aberdeen) and RAF Montrose (between Aberdeen and Dundee) on 14 April 1940 to replace 602 Squadron, which had departed in the opposite direction. Armstrong Whitworth Ensigns ferried 603's ground crews. When war was declared, this unit was based at RAF Turnhouse, Edinburgh, from where they had flown with 602's Spitfires, based at Drem, against the Ju 88s raid on Royal Navy ships in the Firth of Forth. In early 1940, Turnhouse was having its surfaces extensively resurfaced and returfed so that 603 Squadron could not operate from there.

Former pilots recalled that Drem was an airfield with a severe slope, the cause of many crashes. As with RAF Grangemouth, the long grass was also an ever present problem. Drem was described in the following terms: 'There were some basic wooden huts, a wooden mess and a number of hangars. Once again the airmen were billeted off base'. While based there, 603's pilots flew frequent training flights when not on readiness duties, generally using a Harvard I. The first day brought their first mishap. Berry was on descent in poor weather when an inexperienced controller gave him incorrect bearings; suddenly, his Spitfire I broke through the cloud and he found he was hurtling towards the heather-clad slopes of the Lammermuir Hills. He pulled back on the control column so hard that he bent the wings. After successfully landing back at base his aircraft was fitted with a new set.

Two days later, on 17 April, Plt Off. B. Douglas crash-landed on a nearby ploughed field while attempting to land in heavy rain. The undercarriage of his Spitfire K9956 sunk into the soil, causing the aircraft to flip over, with its wheels pointing skywards. Fortunately, the pilot managed to crawl from the inverted cockpit uninjured. For the next few days, 603's Spitfires flew patrols and practised night flying. As noted earlier, the Spifire I was far from ideal for night flying—the long nose made it difficult to see a runway flare path, and the exhaust flames destroyed the pilot's night vision. Plt Off. Stapleton was attempting to land his Spitfire L1025 at night on 26 April when he damaged his undercarriage. The aircraft remained airborne and Stapleton was instructed to climb and bale out. In doing so, he landed heavily, injuring his knee, but he kept quiet about this in case the medical officer forbade him from flying. The injury would still trouble him some fifty years after the incident.

On 5 May, 603 Squadron returned to RAF Turnhouse. Like 602 (City of Glasgow) Squadron, it would soon be sent to the south of England to participate in the Battle of Britain. Unlike many of the other fighter squadrons, both units had some combat experience, but it was only against German bombers and not their fighters:

> It was tragic that once the Squadron moved south to 11 Group, despite the many hours that the pilots had spent working in the air, death came swiftly for the experienced and inexperienced alike.

After spending many months in the forefront of fighting over the south coast, where they were credited with destroying numerous German aircraft, 603's Spitfire IIAs returned to Drem on 17 December 1940 from RAF Rochford, Southend, refuelling *en route* at RAF Catterick, in Yorkshire. Arrangements had been made in advance for lunch to be prepared for them on arrival at Drem, but when they touched down the pilots discovered that 602 (City of Glasgow) Squadron had already eaten, consuming their food as well as its own.

More seriously, when three of 603's Spitfires landed in formation two of them briefly collided. The machine flown by Sgt Sheep Gilroy bounced into the air, flipped over, and burst into flames. Another pilot in the formation did an emergency stop, climbed out of his Spitfire and ran to drag his colleague from the stricken aircraft. A fire tender arrived promptly and the fire was extinguished. Sgt Gilroy suffered serious injuries, but was able to return to flying two months later.

Over the next few days, the new pilots carried out numerous practice flights, which were also not incident free. On 21 December, Sergeant Pilots Jack Stokoe and John Strawson both crashed on landing, severely damaging their undercarriages. The following day, Sqn Ldr George Denholm hit an 'unlighted obstruction' on landing after a night-flying exercise. Due to the difficulty of operating Spitfires at night, 603 Squadron seriously considered using Gloster Gladiator biplanes for this role. Although nothing came of this idea at Drem, it was adopted for a brief time at RAF Acklington.

On Christmas Day, three Spitfires (P7749, P7528, and P7359) were scrambled. They caught sight of a Ju 88 over the sea at 1,000 feet, 12 miles north-east of St Abb's Head. This was one of a very few German aircraft seen over Britain on 25 December, as the Germans had suspended all offensive operations in accordance with an unofficial Christmas truce. Plt Off. B. Carbury attacked the Ju 88 twice, knocking out the right engine. Trailing black smoke, the Junkers lowered its undercarriage during the air battle, a sign that it was in distress. It was decided to award it as 'damaged' to Carbury. Between 7 December 1939 and 25 December 1940, Carbury claimed fifteen enemy aircraft destroyed, two shared destroyed, three probable, and four damaged. A short time later he was posted to 58 OTU at RAF Grangemouth.

Fighter Command had been primarily concerned with defence, but by the beginning of 1940 it began to go on the offensive. No. 603 experienced the first accidents of the year on 12 January, when both Sgt Jack Stokoe and Sgt John Strawson crashed their aircraft on landing, although neither was injured. A contributory cause of was again the sloping runway. Two days later, the slope claimed yet another victim when Sgt A. Darling was injured. Tragically, Sgt Liddell was killed at Aberdeen while ferrying an aircraft from RAF Kinloss.

A few days later on 24 January, five Spitfires of B-Flight (P7750, P7359, P7564, P7528, and P7597) took off to patrol RAF Turnhouse at cloud base, when they received vectors to an enemy aircraft. When 10 miles east of May Island they saw a Ju 88 climbing into cloud and the Spitfires performed a steep climbing turn, but only Sgt Strawson was able to fire—a one-second burst at 400 yards without any visible result. The enemy aircraft was then lost in the cloud.

Flying training continued for the remainder of the month, as did landing accidents. Sgt Cook crashed on 27 January. On 30 January Sgt Compton was injured in a similar incident. The routine of practice flying, accompanied with operational patrols, continued through February, but was punctuated by a tragedy on 16 February. Sgt J. Boulter, a veteran of the Battle of Britain, had just touched down with one of his colleagues and was taxiing towards the hangars, when he was struck side-on by another Spitfire taking off. Reduced visibility due to the infamous slope was said to be a contributing factor. Sgt Boulter suffered horrific injuries. His legs were almost severed at the knees, and, despite being rushed to the nearby East Fortune Hospital, he died the next day. His body was buried in Dirleton Cemetery, which overlooks the site of the airfield.

Bad weather prevented flying between 18 and 23 February, but some further training was carried out a few days later. No. 603 Squadron returned to RAF Turnhouse on 28 February 1941. 'A' Flight returned to Drem on 1 May to undertake a week of night-flying under the command of Fg Off. Scott-Malden, to be followed by the rest of 603 on 9 May. By 11 May, some aircraft had arrived, but three days later the move was cancelled and 603 was informed it was to proceed to RAF Hornchurch instead. At around 9 a.m. on 16 May 1941, thirteen pilots took off for Hornchurch from RAF Turnhouse and RAF Drem respectively, refuelling at RAF Church Fenton *en route*.

After spending the latter years of the conflict in North Africa, 603 squadron returned to Britain at the beginning of 1945. A short time after hostilities ended in Europe, their aircraft touched down again at Drem. Further details in Chapter 17.

611 (West Lancashire) Squadron

Arriving in November 1941, 611 Squadron was the last of the auxiliary squadrons to serve at Drem during the war. In 1939, like the City of Edinburgh and Glasgow Squadrons, the Lancashire unit was equipped with the Spitfire I. With war threatening, 611 was soon incorporated into the regular RAF along with the other auxiliary squadrons. It left Speke airport, on the outskirts of Liverpool, in the summer of 1939 and would not return to its home base throughout the years of conflict.

No. 611 spent most of 1941 based at RAF Hornchurch and RAF Southend, from where it carried out offensive operations over France and the English Channel. Towards the end of the year, it was ordered to change places with 64 Squadron, then based at Drem. Rather unusually, the squadrons left their aircraft behind. On 12 November, two Handley Page Harrows flew forty men north to their new base. The remainder travelled to Scotland on board a special train which arrived the next day in pouring rain. The pilots also travelled by rail and arrived a few days later. No. 64 Squadron had left fifteen Spitfire IIAs and three Spitfire IIBs for them.

Many of 611's members were less than impressed with their new posting:

> As compared with Hornchurch, Drem has a very long way to go. The men have four wooden huts in which to sleep (35 men to each) and heated by 2 coal stoves. Senior NCOs and Officers both have the old type messes. Dispersal point is situated along the south-west side of the flying field. There are 5 wooden huts, 2 for pilots, 1 each for A- and B-Flight's ground crews and 1 for signal and armament personnel. Squadron HQ is on the opposite side of the flying field and is very reminiscent of the wooden HQ which the Squadron had in pre-war days at Speke. It must be realized that Hornchurch has been completely modernized and everything is most up to date whilst here no modernization has been carried out yet.[13]

On 17 November, 611 Squadron flew their first operational flights from Drem and several convoy patrols were carried out during the remainder of the month. Training was hindered by indifferent weather, but sector reconnaissance, aerobatics, homings, formation flying, army co-operation, and dusk landings were all undertaken. Plt Off. Jones 'had the misfortune to prang on landing from his first flight in a Spitfire' on 21 November, having arrived just the day before. On 12 December, six aircraft of B-Flight were detached to Montrose, a flying training airfield that, like Drem in the autumn of 1939, did not exactly welcome intrusion by operational squadrons. The accommodation was uncomfortable, but fortunately the detachment's stay was short-lived, with the Spitfires returning on 16 December.

No. 611 Squadron continued its training programme—including air-to-air firing—during December: 'The pilots do not appear to be capable of raising sufficient hatred of a drogue to do very much damage, the average score being 0.1% hits'. The routine was broken on 19 December, when several Spitfires were sent to look for survivors from two downed Ju 88s in the sea near St Abb's Head. While on a non-operational flight from RAF Turnhouse, Wg Cdr Meagher had attacked one of the planes and it had then collided with its companion—no survivors were found. On 22 December:

> The Squadron did its first squadron formation since the arrival as a change from the endless air-to-air firing. It is obvious we will have to practice this type of formation very much more if we are to maintain our reputation when we go south again.[14]

Many pilots went on leave over Christmas, although on Christmas Eve they had to assist 340 Polish Squadron (also based at Drem), which could muster only four aircraft. No. 611 supplied another four aircraft and pilots. This was an annoyance as it held back the training programme. Like other auxiliary units, the squadron retained its regional identity in name only, and at the end of 1941 had 'become very "cosmopolitan". We now had 5 New Zealanders, 3 Australians, 2 Canadians, 1 American, 1 Dutch and 14 English pilots'. The year finished on a bad note for Drem. Although none of 611's aircraft were involved, the squadron diary for 30 December relates:

> Two Defiants from East Fortune and one Master were in difficulties over this base for a long time—one Defiant crashed at Drem station and the pilot was killed, another bailed out near Haddington and the Master landed OK. A bad business—the weather was very tricky.[15]

1942 began with a hard frost, followed a few days later by snow. The adverse weather lasted for much of January:

> The weather during the month has been exceedingly poor—on 4 days flying was impossible and on 17 days less than 10 hours could be obtained—total flown-ops 50 hours, non-ops 233 hours, the lowest monthly total for a year.[16]

There was some good news for the Squadron on 1 February 1942 when its first two Spitfire Vbs were delivered. Further aircraft arrived the following week. By the middle of the month, the weather had began to improve and on 14 February, a He 111 was observed flying over Drem at a height of around 30,000 feet. Six aircraft of 611 Squadron were scrambled and were in pursuit of the unwelcome visitor when it disappeared into cloud. The following day there was another scramble. One of the Spitfires collided with a Miles Master, but fortunately neither of the pilots was hurt.

The weather closed in again with heavy falls of snow. At 8 p.m., on 22 February, every available airman was called out to help clear drifts from No. 1 landing strip. They worked all night to ensure the strip was operational the next day. By 26 February, most of the snow had disappeared and training flights could be resumed. FS Munro's Spitfire BL354 collided with Fg Off. Van den Honert's (BL445) while practicing formation flying. Munro made a forced landing near Longnidddry, suffering a cracked rib and other minor injuries, while Van den Honert put his aircraft down near RAF MacMerry.

During the first week of March the airfield was covered in snow to a depth of 6 inches, but there were drifts of up to 8 feet on the perimeter, closing all roads in the vicinity. By 8 March temperatures began rising and a thaw set in. The remainder of the month was spent flying convoy patrols and carrying out mock attacks on the airfield to provide practice for the anti-aircraft gunners. At the end of March, the squadron received the shock news that a flight commander and fourteen pilots were to be sent overseas. This would render the unit temporarily non-operational until replacements could be drafted. The last operational flight for April was flown in the first week of the month. There followed a continuous wave of postings.

Such actions caused much discontent among the several fighter squadrons sent to Drem to rest and regroup. The experienced pilots often found themselves being posted to new units as soon as they had trained the recently arrived recruits. On 7 April, FS S. Neill, in his first flight in a Spitfire, succeeded in ripping off the right undercarriage leg of BL255. He was promptly relegated to 4 Delivery Flight at RAF Turnhouse. His short stay with 611 Squadron was not an isolated instance. Many of the recently arrived personnel stayed only briefly before receiving another posting. An entry for 14 April 1942 in the squadron records sums up the frustration with the situation:

An everyday scene which is occurring in the squadron orderly room at the present time is not without its humorous side. Enter three new pilots with a very special salute—Sergeant Straddle reporting for duty—'I am posted to this squadron'. Orderly Room Corporal—'Ah yes, here is your warrant and your train leaves Drem Station in 30 minutes, you are posted to No ... Squadron at ...' At the moment the Squadron does not bother to accept any new pilot or permit him to unpack anything but a toothbrush for three days, as a new posting follows immediately. Of the six fully operational pilots sent to form the basis of our new squadron, there remains but one, the rest having been returned to their old units by Group. A squadron dance is being arranged in an effort to cheer up the airmen who are almost as bewildered as the Orderly Room staff, the CO and the Adjutant. It has been suggested that a back door be fitted to the orderly room to form a one-way traffic route.[17]

Despite the upheavals, a substantial amount of flying was done in April, 'but it will take a good deal of hard work to bring the Squadron up to the standard required for Channel Sweeps etc'. Flying hour totals for the month:

Operational	Daytime 44 hours	Night-time 1 hour
Non-operational	Daytime 424 hours	Night-time 45 hours

On 19 April, Spitfire BL367 suffered a glycol leak and force-landed in a field near Dunino, Fife. The squadron's Miles Magister P2501, flown by Plt Off. M. Graham, was sent to pick up the pilot. On taking off from the field where the Spitfire had come down, the Magister hit a tree and crashed. The aircraft was written off, but fortunately both pilots escaped with only minor injuries. Sgt John Misseldine also had a narrow escape when flying Spitfire BL614 with two other aircraft, carrying out

simulated attacks on anti-aircraft gun sites near the coastline of the Firth of Forth. The station commander, Wg Cdr Peter Townsend, was piloting one of the other Spitfires. The formation of three aircraft were flying along the coast of the Firth of Forth in the early morning, at a height of only 50 feet, when Misseldine's Spitfire briefly came into contact with the water. He managed to retain control and nurse the aircraft back to Drem, where he found that about 6 inches of the propeller tips were missing. It was fortunate that the propeller was wood, because a metal one would have dragged the Spitfire into the sea. A few days later, Misseldine was in trouble again for carrying out aerobatics in a Tiger Moth directly over the airfield. He was giving Army personnel flights when he lost his bearings. Although threatened with numerous charges for flying aerobatics without authorisation and endangering both his aircraft and property on the ground, he was let off with a warning from Townsend.

On 31 May, 611 Squadron received news that it was to move to RAF Kenley on the southern outskirts of London. This month was the best for flying since October 1941. Flying hour totals for the month:

Operational	Daytime 27.05 hours	Night-time 0 hour
Non-operational	Daytime 597 hours	Night-time 19.04 hours

On 1 June, 611 scrambled with 165 Squadron, which had that day been posted to Drem to reinforce the Sector in expectation of enemy activity. This was 611's last day at Drem. On 2 June:

> We all rose this morning rather late after a hectic farewell party—our aircraft have been handed over to 242 Squadron. A slight argument as to who should maintain today's state resulted in a 'commando' by the Squadron against 242 at 1.00 hours in which the enemy were dispersed and beaten (not to mention soaked) while our casualties were very slight—chiefly financial.[18]

At 7.45 p.m., 611's rail party left Drem after 'six tiring but not unpleasant months'. After marching to the station, the party boarded a special five-coach train, which was to take them to Kenley. The next morning, when the train was close to London, the squadron log book records:

> It was a pleasant change to see the crowds in the streets and houses waving as the train went by and I think that all of us felt that once more we were doing a really full time job for the country.[19]

The Regular Spitfire Squadrons

The first regular Spitfires to deploy to Drem were the A- and B-Flights of 72 Squadron, which arrived from RAF Leconfield on 28 October 1939. No less than three former Imperial Airways airliners—two Ensigns and a HP42 Hannibal—were enlisted to move the personnel. Headquarters remained at the previous base. Nos 602 and 609 Squadrons had flown into Drem a week or so earlier with their Spitfires (Mk I), but 72 Squadron was the only regular fighter squadron between RAF Catterick, in Yorkshire, and Wick, in the north of Scotland.

During November, daily patrols were flown over North Berwick and the mouth of the Firth of Forth. On the afternoon of 23 November, Yellow Section was ordered to patrol Crail at the cloud base to investigate an unidentified aircraft, but it was a 'friendly'. There was a further alarm close to midnight when 72's Spitfires were ordered to patrol over Drem at 5,000 feet, but the searchlights could not pick up an enemy aircraft. At around 9 a.m. the following day, a similar patrol saw no enemy aircraft due to heavy cloud. On 28 November, 72's Spitfires were ordered to investigate an unidentified aircraft flying towards the coast, but it proved to be an RAF Hudson returning from a North Sea patrol. There were several other alarms in the latter part of the month, but not a single enemy aircraft was seen.

Over the next few weeks there were several more false alarms involving the Hudsons based near St Andrews at RAF Leuchars. On 5 December, one of the Spitfire pilots had a lucky escape. His section had been ordered to climb through cloud and then split up and patrol individually. No enemy were seen and the aircraft were instructed to return. While descending he was given faulty information from the air traffic controller, and on breaking through the cloud base he found himself flying amongst hills. He clipped the top of one, but managed to land his damaged aircraft safely at Drem.

Two days later, 72 Squadron scrambled to intercept two unidentified aircraft over Turnhouse airfield. They proved to be a Gladiator and a Spitfire. Shortly after, the five aircraft of B-Flight were ordered to patrol the area around Montrose. A radio report had been received of seven enemy machines flying south along the coast, and for once this was not a false alarm. The fighter pilots caught sight of seven He 111H-3s from 1/KG26 flying in two formations of four and three aircraft just north of Arbroath. As

An impressive formation of Spitfires flies over RAF Drem. (*IWM*)

the Spitfires closed in, the bombers dived to fly just above the waves in a very tight formation, which they then maintained throughout the engagement. Three Spitfires of Green Section attacked the leading group and two fighters of Blue Section began shooting at the rear group. Three Spitfires of 603 Squadron (then based at RAF Montrose) also joined the attack, but they had to break off as they were operating at the limit of their range. As they did, one of the Heinkels dropped its undercarriage, an indication that it was in distress. Individual attacks were then carried out, with all pilots except Fg Off. Elsdon engaging the rear section. Elsdon continued attacking the leading formation with deflection shots until he ran out of ammunition.

While chasing the rear formation, Fg Off. Desmond Sheen, an Australian, twice wounded in the leg, had a lucky escape when a bullet penetrated his canopy, smashed his earphone, and then exited the same side of the aircraft. Undaunted, he commenced another attack, but found the fumes from his damaged petrol tank were so bad that he had to break off the engagement just 30 feet above the sea. Sheen landed his crippled machine at RAF Leuchars, where he later learned that the air battle had finished only 15 feet above the water. From Leuchars he was taken by ambulance to a hospital in Edinburgh in which he spent a month before rejoining his unit. Sheen returned later in the war to Drem as the station commander, having destroyed a total of six enemy aircraft during his time with 72 Squadron.

The other Spitfires made it back to Drem, although one of them had been hit by a Heinkel rear gunner. Shortly before they landed, other Spitfires were ordered up to patrol over May Island. By the time they arrived there 'the enemy had decided that discretion was the better part of valour and had turned out east and headed for home'. During the air battle, none of the Heinkels were seen to crash, but it later became known that two of them had come down in the sea east of the Bell Rock Lighthouse. In each case, the aircraft sank and the four crewmen perished. This was 72 Squadron's single contact with the enemy while stationed at Drem.

Another of 72's pilots was Flt Lt James 'Nick' Nicolson. His CO, Flight Lieutenant F. Smith, wrote of him:

> We were required to do long periods on duty, day and night as there was a great shortage of operational pilots.No.72 Squadron was the only regular squadron between Catterick and Wick and the two Auxiliary Squadrons—Nos 602 and Nos 603—were in the process of re-equipping with Spitfires and were't fully operational. Nick had flu and should have been in bed but insisted on doing his full period, huddled in a full leather Irvin Suit by the stove in the flight hut. He refused to go off duty but luckily no order came to scramble.[1]

Nicolson was posted from Drem to join the newly formed 249 Squadron and on 16 August 1940 he participated in an air battle near Southampton. Despite being seriously injured in a dogfight with a Bf 110, and with his Hurricane in flames, he managed to press home his attack on another enemy machine, destroying it completely. Only then did he parachute to safety. For his actions he was awarded the Victoria Cross, the only fighter pilot to receive this honour in the Second World War.

For the remainder of December 1939, numerous patrols were flown over the coast, but most were uneventful. At 2 p.m. on 18 December, Red Section's Spitfires were ordered to attack six enemy aircraft 13 miles east of Crail. The enemy fled east towards Germany, possibly because the cloud base was at only 200 feet. The weather remained poor the following day and Yellow Section were forced to land at RAF Leuchars because of fog. A 72 squadron pilot recollected:

> The winter of 1939/40 was particularly cold and Drem, I am quite sure was the coldest spot on earth. The aircraft, always in the open, were frequently covered by a film of ice, which to remove, using lead weighted wire bristled brooms, kept both pilots and untiring ground crews constantly busy, especially in the early morning. Everyone alert, pilots in the dispersal trying to keep warm by an antiquated iron stove and playing 'Uckers' [a form of Ludo].[2]

New Year 1940 began with a number of dawn patrols. On 2 January, 111's Hurricanes (Mk I) were deployed to Drem. On 5 January, 72 Squadron was ordered to return to RAF Church Fenton as soon as possible, but were prevented by persistent fog across south-east Scotland and northern England. By 8 January, the weather had improved except at Church Fenton airfield, where visibility was around 90 feet. Two days later, 13 Group issued instructions that 72 Squadron was to maintain standing patrols over the coast until it was relocated. The weather then improved over much of the country, allowing patrols to be flown, but RAF Church Fenton was still fog-bound. Eventually it was decided that the move could be postponed no longer, and on 12 January some of the ground crews left by road. The air party, consisting of fourteen Spitfires, one Miles Magister, and two Handley Page HP 42 airliners, departed in the early afternoon for RAF Leconfield, to fly on to RAF Church Fenton once conditions improved.

It was some time before the next regular Spitfire Squadron arrived at Drem. No. 64 Squadron were based at RAF Hornchurch in Essex at the beginning of May 1941. An entry in its log book records the dismay at being posted to Scotland:

> The Squadron was available in the early morning and we were still busily congratulating themselves on being back 'at home' when the bombshell burst, we were to exchange with 603 Squadron at TUR-R-R-RNHOOSE on the morrow! With time for no more than a fleeting thought of Haggis, Hogmanay and other phenomena liable to fox the puir (we were careful to cultivate this accent) wee Sassenach, we busied ourselves with movement orders, maps and recalls from leave.[3]

The air transport party was ferried in two Harrows, 'which found the landing and take-off runs at Hornchurch none too long'. By 9 p.m. on 16 May they had arrived at RAF Turnhouse: 'Considerable progress was made with shaking in. What a gentlemanly war is waged in these parts—sections or at the very worst, flights at readiness!' After only two days at Turnhouse, A-Flight flew to Drem for nominal readiness duties (ready to scramble at short notice). It was decided to move B-Flight to Drem permanently. On 18 May, two 64 Squadron Spitfires (Mk Ia) were scrambled to patrol over St Abb's Head. A few days later, the entire squadron decamped from RAF Turnhouse and travelled the short distance to Drem. The closing days of May were spent providing air protection for convoys and the occasional scramble. Routine patrols were flown utilising two aircraft. On one late night patrol, the pilots had their first experience of the Drem lighting system, which they declared resembled 'a Christmas tree'. Training flights were also carried out to familiarise pilots with the airfield, sometimes using a Miles Magister aircraft: 'Plt Off. Beake [...] was detailed to shoot up the local ground defences and was pained at the scant interest his activities aroused at one post'. Apparently, one of the soldiers was more interested in his sandwiches than the Spitfire buzzing his gun post.

Despite the onset of summer, the weather curtailed flying on some days, and 64's log book makes several references to the poor conditions:

> 26 May—a very wet day with clouds on the deck. Even the hardier Scots birds found walking preferable. Late in the evening the rain stopped and one had fleeting glimpses of the blue sky, but visibility near the ground was still far too bad for flying. A big fire, an easy chair, a book and pint of beer was each officer's choice of whiling away the evening.[4]

Conditions had not improved much by the 28 May, with 'rain in the morning, usual cold east wind, not noticed by the natives but very trying for the English'. Two sections of Spitfires were ordered up on patrol, but there was no sign of the Germans. There was some improvement in the weather by the 30 May: 'A fine sunny day—usual non-stop east wind, which takes most of the gilt off the gingerbread'. On the last day of the month 'the peaceful monotony' was disturbed by an order to scramble, but this was soon cancelled. The same evening, an aircraft had difficulty in finding the airfield due to mist.

At the beginning of June 1941, the squadron strength stood at twenty pilots, including the squadron leader. Poor weather continued through the first days of the month: 'Still cool and cloudy. Even the natives have now given up hope of seeing the sun'. By 8 June the sun had come out, but the piercing east wind had not abated. This lead to more comments about the weather in the squadron log book: 'Cold again—Oh to be in Scotland? Now that June is there'.[5] At this time it was decided to move the squadron's orderly room to the woods on the western edge of the airfield, where a long wooden hut was erected:

It is rumoured that it is to be built of bamboo poles and grass. The site chosen certainly lends itself to the vivid imagination worthy of Fenimore Cooper [the nineteenth century writer of *The Last of the Mohicans* and other stories of the American Frontier].[6]

By the middle of June, summer finally arrived, allowing more flying to take place:

A wizard morning and the weather maintained its high standard ... yet another grand day, in fact a scorcher. Pilots seem to favour flying in shirt sleeves, at least one in a polo shirt.[7]

As well as training, the Spitfires flew patrols. On 15 June:

The squadron did early readiness, but were not called upon to operate. Jerry doesn't appear over keen to visit Scotland, although there's a very warm welcome awaiting him and a strong feeling that he will not return to his beloved Deutschland![8]

The Germans obliged by putting in an appearance a few days later. Just before midnight on 27 June, Red Section Spitfires flown by Sergeants Slade and Thomas were vectored onto a He 115 seaplane, 6 miles east of May Island:

... which they shot up in fine style and when finally they lost it in cloud, the starboard engine was afire and the rudder and fin very tattered and torn. A really good interception from a very accurate plot.[9]

The combat report recorded 'unconfirmed', but it was thought the enemy aircraft had been destroyed. A few days earlier, a Whitley arrived to act as a target for attack practice by the Spitfire pilots. Flt Lt Ashton from 64 Squadron went up in the Whitley, while his colleagues carried out interceptions on it. He did not enjoy the experience, stating 'I've never been so (...) scared in my life—I don't like it!' On 22 June, the adjutant went on a evening flight in the Whitley and was greatly impressed by the pilot's evasive tactics as he met each attacker head on. The Whitley returned home the following day, with its crew agreeing that their trip to Drem had been a busman's holiday. Numerous training flights were flown and there were the inevitable accidents. The most serious involved a collision between Spitfire P7747 and Spitfire R7204, which was landing. Although both aircraft were seriously damaged, the pilots escaped without injury.

The entry for 64 Squadron's log book for 1 July reads:

> Yet another month dawns and we are vastly changed squadron. Five of our pilots have been posted south to reinforce the southern sector and we have four new arrivals. Today, there is little flying. A spot of gun 'co-op' in the afternoon which didn't impress the gun crews at all. They much preferred to sunbathe and regarded the Spitfires as one does a fly on such a day—as an unwelcome intruder.[10]

Little operational flying was undertaken during July. Plt Off. Watson was roused from bed at 1.20 a.m. one morning to chase a group of enemy aircraft, but was unable to engage, despite pursuing them for half an hour. The pilots on twenty-minute's readiness now began sleeping at the dispersals to be closer to their aircraft. On 17 July, it took only one minute and forty seconds for aircraft to become airborne during a scramble.

Fighter squadrons based at Drem for any length of time found its best pilots spirited off to other parts of the country. So many experienced pilots had been posted to other units that only one flight was operational. The following complaint is not unique to 64 Squadron and the same sentiments are found in several other fighter squadrons' records: 'Everyone is fed up at the way the Squadron is being pulled apart and in addition training twelve new people has done little to pacify frayed tempers'. A dog-fight practice between Plt Off. Campbell and Sgt Inkster ended abruptly when the latter's aircraft began emitting an ominous trail of black smoke. The Spitfire managed to land safely. Later in the evening of 9 July, A-Flight's formation flying was watched by their squadron leader and the unit doctor standing on top of North Berwick Law. Two days later, drogue-towing gear arrived to facilitate air-to-air firing practice, the introduction of which was not without incident. After one exercise, the Spitfire towing the drogue was unable to release it and had to land with it trailing behind.

Recently trained pilots were posted to the squadron, some of whom had never flown a Spitfire before:

> The new pilots were taken on an oxygen climb to 34,000 feet. One aircraft was seen to be pouring smoke and made a hurried descent, landing very well with smoke and flames pouring from its intake. The fire wagon had a glorious time covering everything with foam. The pilot climbed out very unconcerned from a smoking cockpit.[11]

Three days later, on 22 July, two Spitfires collided while dog fighting. Both managed to land safely with some minor damage. The next day, Plt Off. Chadwick, resplendent in a new uniform, had to belly-land on the airfield after his engine seized at 700 feet over the coast. With the flying hours accumulated on training flights, several Spitfires reached the 240-hour inspection mark and had to be flown back to the manufacturer's factory. It was noted that 'not many Spitfires can live long enough to achieve this'. August started with more prangs. The wing of Sgt Morgan's Spitfire struck a landing light post, causing the aircraft to slew round, and collapsing one of the undercarriage legs. Just five days later, Plt Off. Taylor clipped the top of a hedge while taking off, damaging an aileron. Later that day, Sgt Morgan was again in trouble when his aircraft hit a hedge on take-off. He managed to get airborne, but his undercarriage had been damaged, forcing him to crash-land—Sgt Morgan was uninjured.

On 6 August, 64 Squadron moved back to RAF Turnhouse. The Reverend Sutherland gave them the traditional Drem send off, playing his bagpipes while the Spitfires taxied out towards the runway: 'It was a long take off but the Reverend's lungs stood up to it well'. No. 64 Squadron's absence was short-lived. The next day, B-flight was back at Drem on readiness duties. On 9 August, Sgt Morgan was involved in yet another accident. While coming into land he forgot to lower his undercarriage:

> ... and so another Spitfire was reduced to produce. The large number of prangs in the last few weeks unnerved the CO and Flt Lt Ashton so much that release in the evening allowed them to seek oblivion in Edinburgh.[12]

No. 123 Squadron exchanged bases with 64, and their Spitfires (Mk I) arrived at Drem from RAF Turnhouse on 5 August 1941. No. 123, formed on 10 May 1941, became operational on defensive duties on 8 June. A small number of operational flights were flown during its stay at Drem, together with the occasional sortie to provide anti-aircraft gunners with a live-practice target. Sgt Ferguson crashed his Spitfire (Mk I) N3288 while taking off on a non-operational flight. He raised his undercarriage before the aircraft had become airborne. On 16 August, Sgt De Salo Hall damaged his Spitfire (Mk I) X4253, while making a landing at dusk.

September commenced with a similar accident. Sgt Aylott broke off part of an undercarriage leg of his Spitfire R6914 while landing in fading light. He attributed the accident to 'grit in his eye'. Matters took a turn for the worse on 5 September when two of 123's Spitfires collided while flying over Edinburgh on a practice formation flight. Plt Off. A. Searle, a Rhodesian, died when his parachute failed to open. He was subsequently interred in Dirleton Cemetery. His Spitfire X4560 crashed into the grounds of the Royal Botanic Garden. Plt Off. Simpson, in X4910, parachuted and was unhurt. No. 123 Squadron lost another of its pilots when Flt Lt Webb, on temporary attachment to 602 Squadron at RAF Kenley near London, failed to return from a mission. On 21 September 1941, 123 departed Drem, shortly after being re-equipped with the Spitfire Mk IIA. A special train transported the ground crews to their new home at RAF Castletown, near Thurso, in the north of Scotland.

Although 64 Squadron's aircraft had been on detachment at Drem from RAF Turnhouse on several occasions, on 3 October 1941, the squadron returned to Drem for its final deployment there. The weather deteriorated shortly after its arrival and not much flying was done for the next few days, but once the weather improved, gunnery practice kept the squadron busy. The squadron leader successfully tried out a cannon-firing Spitfire on a drogue. There was trouble with the cone-type drogues, which kept breaking away from the towing aircraft, so low-drag ones were used instead. Practice squadron formations were flown and 'looked good but quite impracticable'. No. 122 Squadron Spitfires (Mk II) from Yorkshire provided interception practice for 64 Squadron towards the end of the month and B-Flight Spitfires paid a return visit when seven of their aircraft flew to RAF Catterick for further exercises of a similar nature: 'we stayed for tea, returning to land at Drem at about 18.00 hours'. On 15 October, Sgt Doherty led a practice formation of A-Flight's Spitfires, with some acting as 'bombers', while others flew as their escort fighters. Waverley Station, Edinburgh, was the intended target. Both 'bombers' and escort fighters were intercepted by B-Flight, but not before the target had been 'severely damaged'. At the end of the month, four aircraft flew to RAF West Freugh, near Stranraer, for four days detachment. Here, fighter affiliation exercises were flown, this time against real bombers with the results being recorded on camera guns.

During the autumn months, 64 Squadron was also responsible for having aircraft ready to scramble at Drem. There was a small number of alerts, but all were false alarms. There was a fatal accident on 1 November 1941 when Sgt Kaye crashed after descending through a rainstorm. Training continued during the first part of this month with the weather fluctuating between very good and vile. On 8 November:

> … highlight of the day was a flight formation of nine aircraft led by F/Lt. Prevot … [then two days later] … there was little flying as the weather was vile and there were near gale force winds.[13]

However, this did not prevent the Germans putting in an appearance. A Ju 88 flew across Drem airfield at less than 100 feet, before disappearing in cloud. A convoy patrol was carried out a few days later. No. 64's stay in Scotland came to an end on 16 November, when it began moving back to RAF Hornchurch. The squadron's Spitfires (Mk IIa) were left behind for 611 Squadron, its replacement at Drem. In turn, 64 Squadron took over 611's Spitfires (Mk Vb) when they returned back south.

During the winter of 1941–1942, there were no regular Spitfire Squadrons at Drem. The next regular units to be based there arrived on 1 April. It was a detachment of B-Flight of 81 Squadron, equipped with the Spitfire Mk Va, from RAF Turnhouse. The following day, the pilots were called on to perform an operational mission:

> On this day, an event of some interest took place. From 17.15 to 17.40 hours, A Flight took off from Drem with seven pilots, joining B-Flight pilots already there. Some Norwegian ships, the majority of which were sunk or turned back, had escaped from Swedish waters. At 17.55 hours, Blue Section were sent to convoy one of them, a large tanker of some 12,000 tons. They were relieved by Red Section who landed at 20.30 hours. Yellow Section were scrambled but landed again in ten minutes.[14]

The Norwegian ships had been stranded in Sweden when Germany invaded. Eventually, some of the captains decided to flee to join the Allies rather than remain impounded in a neutral country. A-Flight returned to RAF Turnhouse on 3 April, but two sections came back to Drem in the afternoon. The following day, they were joined by the remaining section of A-Flight. Both Flights then spent part of the day escorting a Norwegian ship.

Over the next week, there was a daily shuttling of 81's Spitfires between Drem and Turnhouse. On 6 April, A-Flight sent two sections of aircraft across to Drem at 8.40 a.m. and 8.50 a.m. Both sections were assigned 'readiness in the air' from 10.50 a.m. to 12.20 p.m., returning to RAF Turnhouse at 1 p.m. Aircraft of B-Flight then landed at Turnhouse from 6.30 p.m. to 6.45 p.m. The detachment at Drem had ceased by 12 April, although some of 81's Spitfires remained at RAF Turnhouse. Others were posted to RAF Ayr and RAF Ouston.

No. 165 Squadron, flying the Spitfire Mk Va, was formed at RAF Ayr during April 1942, being declared operational on 1 May 1942. At the end of that month, it too detached some of its aircraft to Drem, along with seven pilots under Sqn Ldr Winskill. Ground crew followed by train. On 31 May, two of its Spitfires were scrambled to join a further two aircraft already *en route* to intercept an incoming raid. The first two pilots lost each other in cloud and were ordered back to Drem. The latter two failed to establish any contact and the raid faded uneventfully from the radar screen. The following day, there was a further abortive attempt to intercept enemy aircraft some 25 miles east of the airfield. The short stay by the detachment of 165 Squadron came to an end on 2 June, when they flew back to RAF Ayr.

Just before 165 departed, 242 Squadron, recently formed at RAF Turnhouse, arrived at Drem. No. 611 Squadron was due to move south the next day, 2 June, and its CO refused to continue its own readiness state so that the whole responsibility fell on the detachment of 165 Squadron from RAF Ayr. No. 242 Squadron made every effort to be available as soon as possible, which lead to a tense atmosphere between it and the departing 611. On their first full day at Drem, inspections were carried out on the Spitfire Mk Vb, which 242 Squadron had inherited from 611 Squadron. Later in the day, a number of these aircraft took part in formation flying and two sections were scrambled to patrol over St Abb's Head, but had no luck.

The next day, training continued with cloud flying, formations, and 'circuits and bumps'. The high spot of the day was an operational scramble by Red Section comprising two Spitfires (Mk Vb). Some 60 miles east of Drem they made contact with a Ju 88 at 2,500 feet. Plt Off. Byford launched the first attack, followed by FS Portz. The enemy returned fire, but failed to hit either of the fighters. The Junkers was last seen trailing black smoke and losing height over the sea:

> It was first claimed as 'damaged', later changed to 'destroyed' and eventually to be made only 'probable'. As far as the squadron is concerned we consider it 'destroyed' so that's that! High jinks in both messes and dispersal points.[15]

The squadron's claim to having shot the Junkers down was likely to have been true, as the German records show that a Junkers Ju 88 of 3(F)/122 failed to return from a sortie to the Scottish coast on that date.

Red Section was scrambled again on 6 June, but this time drew a blank. Four days later, three Spitfires were detached to RAF Ouston, near Newcastle, to assist with 'readiness cover'. During June, training encompassed dog fights, height climbs, formation flying, night flying and air-to-air firing at a target towed by one of the squadron's Spitfires. An entry in the log book for 20 June reads: 'Little flying today, pilots in need of a rest'. On 1 July 1942, a convoy patrol was flown and five Spitfires went to RAF Peterhead for an exercise. There were a number of uneventful scrambles during this month. Training intensified, with over 150 hours flown in just the first four days. There was much air-to-air firing, camera gun attacks and low flying, with pilots instructed not to fly below 300 feet over the control tower. By the end of the month, 242 Squadron had notched up 1,000 flying hours, which included thirty-two on operational flights and thirty-five on night flying.

During the first few days of August, the Spitfires participated in 'Dryshod', a large exercise with the Army. Low-level attacks were made on motorised transport and tanks. Shortly after this exercise, 242 Squadron was informed they would be leaving Drem. The log recorded that the 'whole Squadron [were] very happy about going south'. On 10 August, two Harrows flew some of the personnel to RAF North Weald, near London. In the evening others travelled by road and rail. Their aircraft left the following day, including some Spitfires (Mk Vb) on loan from 222 Squadron, which had arrived at Drem the previous day. No. 222 Squadron (twenty officers, 131 airmen, and eighteen Spitfires) had left RAF North Weald on 4 August, flying north to RAF Winfield in Berwickshire, where it had spent several days participating in 'Dryshod'. On 5 and 6 August they 'attacked' camouflaged tanks and large columns of transport.

On 14 August, just when the squadron had begun to settle at Drem, it was ordered to return south to RAF Biggin Hill, near London. From this now famous Battle of Britain airfield and numerous other bases close to the Channel coast, large numbers of fighters were to provide air cover for the commando raid on Dieppe in Northern France. No. 222 Squadron commenced operations on 17 August with Spitfire Wings patrolling the area. The seaborne assault ended in disaster with the Allied ground forces suffering heavy casualties, and 222's Spitfires (Vb) returned north to Drem on 20 August, to routine flights and one convoy patrol.

On 6 September, B-Flight was ordered to proceed to RAF Ayr, but this order was later cancelled. At 11.20 a.m. there was a scramble to intercept two Me 210s of 16/KG6 heading for the British coast. No contact was made with these long-range fighter bombers, but both were later shot down over Yorkshire by 1 Squadron Typhoons. A week later, Blue Section Spitfires were scrambled to investigate a report of an unidentified raider some 20 miles off St Abbs Head. They had chased the aircraft down to sea level, and were about to attack when they realised it was a Blackburn Botha, an obscure RAF twin-engined bomber adopted for training purposes.

While at Drem, 222 Squadron suffered two crashes, both resulting in the death of the pilot and each thought to be due to structural failure. On 18 September 1942, Sgt York, an American, crashed 6 miles north-east of Abbotsinch airfield, near Bardowie Farm. On 1 October, another foreign member of the squadron, Sgt Millington's Spitfire Vb AD235 crashed at 10.55 a.m., 2 miles south of Dunbar. B-Flight moved to

RAF Ayr on detachment a few days later. The remainder of 222 Squadron then joined it on 22 October and its stay at Drem came to an end.

One of the few squadrons that actually formed at Drem was 453 Squadron, Royal Australian Air Force (RAAF). The pilots were Australian with the exception of a Canadian and three Poles (the only pilots with operational experience), who were able to render valuable assistance to the trainees. The commander and the ground crew were British. Its first eight Spitfires (Vb) arrived on 23 June 1942 and flying commenced on the afternoon of 26 June after acceptance inspections. Flying was limited because six of the aircraft were new and it was necessary to stagger the hours so that all the aircraft would not be due for inspection on the same day. Delivery of the remaining aircraft was fairly rapid, but there was a shortage of tyres meaning aircraft were frequently grounded. A number of senior NCOs posted to the unit were not technically qualified and Forms and Air Publications (technical manuals) were also in short supply.

Until the middle of July, training consisted of formation flying and air-to-air firing. At first, a Westland Lysander shared with 242 Squadron towed the drogue, limiting the amount of air-to-air firing. One of the squadron's Spitfires was then equipped for the task, increasing the time available. Different coloured lithographic ink was used on the bullets, so that as many as three pilots could shoot at the target on a single trip, greatly accelerating training. When the weather was bad, there were lectures and practice on the Link Trainer, an early form of flight simulator.

On 10 July, 453 Squadron started to provide operational readiness alongside 242 Squadron. No operational flights were flown during the month, but some 748 hours were notched up on routine and training missions. There were eighteen Spitfires (Mk Vb) and one Miles Magister on strength, along with eight Australian officer aircrew and fifteen other ranks.

The squadron experienced its first fatality on 1 August when Plt Off. Charles Riley, an Australian, spun in from 15,000 feet and crashed into Cairns Place Farmhouse, near Crail, in Fife. The building's occupants were not injured. Just before the accident the pilot had been performing aerobatics above the cloud. Surprisingly, enough of the Spitfire survived to permit a thorough examination, but no mechanical fault could be found. Riley was buried at Leuchars, in Fife. The first Australian ground crew arrived on 5 August. Rain and mist hampered flying training, and when conditions improved there was another accident, fortunately not fatal. Sgt G. Whiteford was carrying out practice attacks on other Spitfires at 3,000 feet some 3 miles off the coast, when he lost oil pressure. He made a forced landing in a field near Cockburnspath, Berwickshire, demolishing a stone wall. Whiteford, having undone his safety harness and jettisoning his canopy while descending, in case he had to use his parachute:

Was thrown out on landing and having being airborne for about 15 yards landed on his head on a heap of stones. It says much for the quality of skull issued to this airman that beyond a slight concussion and a cut on the scalp which necessitated two stitches he received no injury. Examination of the aircraft showed there was a crankshaft bearing failure.[16]

Members of 222 Squadron pose for their photograph in October 1941. (*RAF Museum*)

Pilots of 453 Squadron pose for their photograph in front of one of their Spitfires. (*East Lothian Museum Service/SCRAN*)

The following day, 12 August, the 453 Squadron flew its first operational flights. At 9.20 p.m. Sgt Furlong and Sgt Leith as Red Section were ordered to patrol Dunbar at cloud base. Arriving on station, they were given a vector to intercept two enemy aircraft, flying west some 25 miles away. The fighters were taken over by the GCI (ground-controlled interception) radar and climbed to 13,000 feet, when they became separated in thick cloud. A short time later Sgt Furlong caught sight of the enemy aircraft, but it disappeared into the cloud. Two Spitfires of Yellow Section were then scrambled, but Sgt Ford had to return to base with a non-functioning radio. Arriving over the field he discovered that the runway lighting was off and he had to signal the control tower using his upward identification light. Soon the flare path was turned on and Sgt Ford successfully touched down. Just as his Spitfire finished rolling, Ford heard an explosion followed quickly by three more He instinctively ducked as an aircraft passed just 20 feet overhead. It was a Ju 88, one of the enemy aircraft the Spitfires had been attempting to intercept. On examination, Ford's Spitfire was found to have holes on the left side of the fuselage, in the tail, and at the left wing root.

On 14 August there was a visit from the press, with practically every newspaper in Australia and most of those in Scotland being represented. A squadron formation was flown for the benefit of the journalists, who then spent the afternoon interviewing the pilots. Not much flying was done between 15 August and 22 August, as a large number of 453's Spitfires had been lent to 222 Squadron to provide fighter cover for the Dieppe raid. On 21 August, two Spitfires were scrambled to intercept an enemy aircraft at 15,000 feet. At this height, they were flying above thick cloud, which they assumed the enemy aircraft had escaped into, as nothing was sighted. Early next morning, and again on 26 August, six Spitfires provided air cover to a convoy sailing through the area.

Two days later, 453 Squadron lost another of its pilots; Sgt D. Steele, an Australian, was practicing dog fighting and steep turns with Sgt Leith at 30,000 feet. The weather was fine, but haze reduced visibility. The two pilots were climbing in line astern with Leith leading, when he noticed that Steele's aircraft had disappeared. Witnesses saw the aircraft dive almost vertically from around 20,000 feet, and crash into the Lammermuir Hills, some 5 miles south-east of Garvald Village. There appeared to have been no effort by Steele to pull out of the dive. An Air Investigation Board inquiry was requested, but refused. On 30 August two Spitfires were scrambled to intercept a 'hostile' approaching the airfield at 6,000 feet, but it was discovered to be an RAF Coastal Command aircraft.

Full advantage was taken of the early September fine weather. Aircraft serviceability was high and many squadron and battle formations were carried out. On 6 September, Flt Lt Harrington and Plt Off. Thornley were scrambled to intercept a 'bandit'. There was considerable excitement on the airfield when a loudspeaker announcement was made that an enemy aircraft was approaching from the south-east at 6,000 feet:

> Everybody rushed outside and peered up at the sky in spite of the fact that there was cloud at about 2,000 feet. The same cloud defeated the section which was trying to intercept and it returned to base after being airborne for 25 minutes. The bandit turned out to be a Blenheim.[17]

Training continued throughout the month, with particular emphasis on gunnery practice—17,000 rounds being expended one day. Instructions came that 453 Squadron was to move to RAF Gravesend, near London, but this was later changed to RAF Hornchurch. Most of the ground crews and equipment departed by rail on 24 September and the rear party left the following day by air. The seventeen Spitfires (Mk Vb) were delayed by bad weather and finally left for their new deployment on 26 September.

Heading in the opposite direction was the 65 East India Squadron. The instruction for them to leave southern England to join 13 Group was received 'with universal despondency'. The squadron commander, René Mouchotte, had hoped to be posted to Malta: 'Another six months in Scotland! I think I shall leave the Air Force'. He had previously served in Malta with the 340 Free French Air Force Squadron. No. 65 Squadron's seventeen Spitfires flew north from RAF Gravesend and arrived at Drem at 2.30 p.m. on 26 September. The next day, a number of Sector reconnaissances were flown. René Mouchotte recorded in his diary that 'nothing has changed here but the faces are nearly all different. Temperature noticeably cooler than in London. The nights are beginning to be icy'.

News arrived on 1 October that 65 Squadron was to return south in a rapid concentration of units in 2 Group. Although the reason for the move was given as an

Pilots W. Waldron and W. de Crozier of 453 Squadron, both from Tamworth, New South Wales. (*Museum of Flight, National Museums of Scotland/SCRAN*)

A line-up of Spitfires of 453 Squadron on 14 August 1942 preparing to take-off. (*Museum of Flight, National Museums of Scotland/SCRAN*)

exercise, only René Mouchotte and the station commander knew its true purpose. On 2 October, the squadron leader took off from Drem followed by the entire squadron of eighteen Spitfires. To prevent the Germans detecting this large-scale movement, the order stated that on no occasion were the aircraft to fly above 650 feet:

> Thus it was practically by leap frogging over trees, skating down and skimming up mountain slopes that we covered the 435 miles between Drem and Lympne [in Kent, near Hythe].[18]

On 7 October the AOC, Leigh Mallory, presided over a meeting of all squadron leaders involved, as well as some wing commanders. He informed them that their mission had been to provide air cover for a mission similar to the earlier commando raid on Dieppe. However, it had been postponed until the following year because of the weather. No. 65 Squadron's time at RAF Lympne was not altogether wasted, as it escorted a Flying Fortress raid on Lille in Northern France.

No. 65's Spitfires returned to Drem on 11 October. The following day, two of them were scrambled, but the aircraft turned out to be friendly. White Section were scrambled on 14 October and vectored at 5,000 feet. Sgt Long's engine failed 5 miles out to sea, north of Dunbar, although he managed to nurse his machine back to the coast and crash landed in a small field north of Dunbar. He was unhurt, but the Spitfire was badly damaged. Meanwhile René Mouchotte was not enjoying his stay in Scotland, as related in his diary (published in book form in 1956):

> A lot has happened in the theatre of war between 10 October and 30 November 1942 but my life at Drem has been troubled by violent and recurrent desires to throw my hand in and offer my resignation as Squadron Leader. The spirit prevailing among those who command the station at Drem is characteristic of 13 Group and it has got it a sorry and unenviable reputation. Administration is all here and turns the tiniest regulation into a rut. The sergeants are dead keen on meeting the whims of their superiors, they turn advice into compulsion, rules into tyranny. The pilot is made for the station and not the station for the pilot.[19]

Training, which included instrument flying, dog fighting, GCI co-operation flights, and camera gun practice, continued throughout the remainder of the month. René Mouchotte did not think much of the RAF training procedures, complaining that they were organised along rigid lines, with more concern for report writing than developing individual's skills. October drew to a close with two crashes, the first involved Fg Off. Kon, a Pole, who crashed on landing after a night flying exercise. His Spitfire was repairable and he was unhurt. The second also involved a Pole, Sgt Karasinski, who also damaged his machine while landing.

On 5 November, despite intermittent bad weather, two big squadron formations were flown. A week later, twelve aircraft performed GCI co-operation flights. During the middle of the month, Sqn Ldr Mouchotte, in full French dress uniform, was presented with the Distinguished Flying Cross by Air Vice-Marshal Andrews at a special parade.

On 20 November, another Pole was involved in a flying accident, this time fatal. Fg Off. Strozak took off from Drem in the morning on a flight to Blackpool. Contact was lost while he was flying over hills in Cumbria. Nothing further was heard until late in the evening when it was reported that his body had been discovered along with the remains of his aircraft near Ullswater, close to the town of Penrith. The aircraft had flown into a hill in misty weather.

As November drew to a close, a long night-flying programme involved eight pilots. A Polish pilot survived a crash-landing uninjured and the machine was repairable. No. 65's Spitfires continued to perform the occasional scramble and convoy patrol. Three sections of two aircraft patrolled over a convoy on 2 December 1942. The next day there was a further convoy patrol, as well as an exercise involving camera gun 'attacks' on RAF Hampden bombers.

On 12 December, Acting Flt Lt C. R. Hewlett DFC took one of the Spitfires up for a test flight. As the aircraft was circling in preparation to land it suddenly broke up, its wings falling in a field. Hewlett was seen descending by parachute, but when members of the squadron reached him they found him to be dead, his neck broken. His parachute had opened due to a tear in its case, apparently caused by the plane breaking up. René Mouchotte rushed there in his car and was one of the first on the scene. He described what he found in his diary, depicting the true horror of such flying accidents not often conveyed in official records:

> When I got to the spot I found that he was dead and appallingly mutilated. I listened to his heart, it was no longer beating. His small, very young face, so full of hope, the eyes which had always shone with such ardour, his fine curly hair were all unrecognisable, soiled with earth and blood.[20]

The subsequent accident report, based on the examination of the wreckage, concluded that the aircraft was travelling at high speed and at over 5,000 feet when it disintegrated. The Spitfire Mk Vb, AD 115, had suffered structural failure of the right wing under severe pressure or by rigging discrepancies, which resulted in the ailerons riding up at speed. The mechanics were instructed to immediately check the tension on the aileron cables of all Spitfires on base. The investigation also had looked into the possibility of sabotage, but no evidence was found.

Training continued over the next couple of weeks, despite interruptions due to the winter weather. As with other squadrons, there was a large turnover in pilots, which caused much frustration to those who remained and had to teach new arrivals from scratch.

Fighter Command Headquarters informed 65 Squadron that it had been selected to operate the naval version of the Spitfire (the Seafire) from aircraft carriers. This was the first time in the Second World War that an RAF unit had been detailed for such a task, probably because the pilots had more experience at providing fighter cover than those of the Fleet Air Arm.

René Mouchotte selected sixteen pilots for Seafire training and part of Drem airfield was marked out with white lines to simulate an aircraft carrier deck. A RN officer gave lectures on carrier procedures and acted as the batsman on the mock flight deck, signalling to the pilots if they were approaching at too high or too low an angle. On the first day of training, Sgt Robertson crashed while attempting to land. This activity continued unabated, even on Christmas Day. The weather had turned very cold and René Mouchotte complained that his office, which had seven windows, resembled a glacier.

At the end of December, 65 Squadron was flown in a Dutch transport to the Fleet Air Arm station of HMS *Condor*, near Arbroath, which had special facilities for training pilots in operating from aircraft carriers. Mouchotte was impressed with the base, which he recorded had far more comfortable accommodation than Drem with a mess like a grand hotel, complete with waiters. His pilots, however, had numerous accidents while practising landings using arrester hooks. The final stage of their training was aboard the aircraft carrier HMS *Argus* in the Firth of Clyde. Such was the importance given to their mission that they were given priority over all other pilots under instruction. After a week on this ship, during which each pilot made six landings, the group returned to Drem on 10 January 1943.

It had been thought that, once trained to operate from aircraft carriers, 65 Squadron would participate in some form of special operation similar to the raid on Dieppe. However, the skills they gained in this field were never put to any use.

A short time later Mouchotte was posted to RAF Turnhouse to assist in the formation of 341 Free French Air Force Squadron. Later in the year, he achieved his ambition to fly combat missions against the Germans. On 28 July 1943, he disappeared over Northern France, while protecting a large formation of flying fortresses that were under attack by Focke Wulf 190s.

Although 65 Squadron spent much of its time over the winter in training, it was still responsible for providing fighter cover at Drem. On 20 December, Red Section was scrambled in the morning. In the afternoon, Blue Section spent a long time being vectored onto a 'bandit', which turned out to be a Liberator. While many of the pilots were undertaking training at HMS *Condor*, 124 Squadron, equipped with the Spitfire Mk VI and based at RAF North Weald, was called in to plug the gap—'[...] another move for the Squadron, aircraft and pilots only proceed to Drem for an unknown period, a rather sudden and mysterious move'. No. 124 Squadron arrived in Scotland as the year drew to an end. The squadron log book records that 'the year made a poor opening, even allowing for the Scottish climate and bad weather prevented flying'. The following day, J. C. Nelson, an American experienced in high-altitude flying, took command of the squadron. On 3 January 1943, the Spitfires engaged in dog-fighting against 197's Typhoons. Flt Lt Kilburn DFC suffered an engine failure, but glided the 2 miles back to Drem to land safely. Three days later, the squadron carried out exercises with a destroyer off St Abb's Head in the afternoon after a snow-bound morning. On 7 January 1943, ten aircraft took part in a 'Jumbo' exercise to Glasgow. Not long after this, 65's pilots returned to Drem to relieve 124 Squadron of readiness duties:

> We all were itching to get back to the south and more activity. Exile was not at all popular.
> 65 Squadron were no doubt glad to see us go, since they had to maintain both their own

and our aircraft. The Squadron did local flying whenever the weather permitted which was infrequently as fog and rain predominated.[21]

No. 124's Spitfires departed on 17 January for RAF Catterick in Yorkshire. They remained stranded there for several days as their base, RAF North Weald, was fog-bound. Until the end of the month, normal training—air-to-air and air-to-ground firing—was resumed. Squadron formations were flown, including 'Wing' practices with 222's Spitfires (Mk Vb), now based at RAF Ayr. There was another fatality when Sgt M. Robertson, a New Zealander, took off on 16 January at 3.40 p.m. for a practice flight, but did not return. The aircraft, with the pilot's body still in the cockpit, was discovered four days later on the Lammermuir Hills, near Westruther, Greenlaw in Berwickshire.

Over 500 hours were flown by 65 Squadron in February. Bad weather did not prevent a varied training programme, which included a GCI co-operation exercise in the neighbourhood of Rosyth. Sqn Ldr J. Storrar led the squadron to RAF Ayr for a demonstration of formation flying on 7 February. Locally based Hurricanes took the opportunity to carry out mock attacks on the visiting Spitfires. On the return to Drem, a close formation was flown over the airfield, 'which aroused grudging admiration from our colleagues and compatriots on the station'. Further mock aerial combat sorties were flown against two Typhoons of 197 Squadron. It was concluded that 'the Typhoons would have done considerable execution upon 65 Squadron had they not been shot down (in theory) during their first attack'. A particularly busy day, 13 February had A-Flight of 65 Squadron flying convoy patrols in the morning, followed by Spitfires flying high-altitude standing patrols 40 miles off the coast, between Leuchars and Berwick; nine aircraft then took off from Drem and patrolled over Edinburgh for half an hour that night, at stepped altitudes from 1,000 to 21,000 feet. The object of this exercise was to ambush 'a weather willie', an enemy weather reconnaissance aircraft that had been regularly plotted in this area. In the latter stages of the war, often the only enemy activity over northern parts of Britain was these flights gathering meteorological information essential for planning future ground and air operations in Continental Europe. Congratulations were received from 13 Group upon the squadron's timing and the professional way this exercise was undertaken.

On 14 February, six Spitfires of A-Flight performed a formation flight in the afternoon, during which they were 'bounced' vigorously by a Hurricane from RAF Annan. The pilot afterwards landed at Drem and spent the night there. Two days later, 65 Squadron paid a return visit to RAF Annan, where they were again 'attacked' by Hurricanes from 55 OTU. The tactical flying recently practised proved most effective against the Hurricanes. Later in the month, RAF Mustangs based at RAF MacMerry acted as attacking fighters. Finally, several mock attacks were staged on army units in south-east Scotland. The most notable was performed on 17 February by Sqn Ldr Storrar and Flt Lt P. Tripe, who made low-level attacks on dispersed troops and motor transport in the Coldstream area:

What was believed to be a staff car was last seen removing itself from the scene of operations at a computed ground speed of no mean order![22]

On days when no flying could be undertaken, the pilots practised on the Hunt and Link trainers and tested their knowledge of aircraft recognition:

A-Flight took their bi-monthly recognition test. Any form of dishonest co-operation being inconceivable in the Squadron, it was remarkable what heights of coincidence or possibly thought transference phenomena were reached during this test.[23]

Training continued into the following month. Proceedings were enlivened on 12 March when three 65 Squadron Spitfires were scrambled at 1.10 p.m. and vectored by Dirleton GCI radar onto an enemy aircraft flying at 35,000 feet off the Farne Islands, Northumberland. They took over from 197's Typhoons (also from Drem), which had initially been detailed to intercept. Once the fighters had closed to within 1,000 feet, the Ju 88 began to draw rapidly away. Two of the Spitfires opened fire with both cannon and machine guns, but no apparent damage was done to the Junkers before it disappeared. The previous night, fifty-one German bombers had attacked Newcastle-upon-Tyne, and the aircraft was probably on a reconnaissance mission in connection with this raid. When the fighters returned to Drem, Sgt Watt was unable to lower his wheels and circled for fifty minutes. He eventually landed safely with only 3 gallons in his tank.

The following day, Sgt Austin and Sgt Smith, both New Zealanders, succeeded in flying the squadron's Tiger Moth into 197's dispersal. Neither was hurt, but the biplane was completely destroyed. On 14 March, 65's Spitfires flew to RAF Ayr, where they rendezvoused with 222 Squadron and 341 Squadron from RAF Turnhouse. The three squadrons then flew as a wing towards Northern Ireland at low level. They climbed to cross the Irish Coast and then flew a considerable distance inland. No. 65 Squadron refuelled at RAF Ayr before returning to Drem.

Towards the end of March, an instruction was received that 65 Squadron was to move to RAF Perranporth, near Newquay, in Cornwall. An informal farewell party was given at North Berwick 'at which the squadron's gratification at the early prospect of operational activity was made abundantly clear'. The main party left by train on the evening of 28 March. Two Harrows arrived the following day to airlift the remaining personnel, but due to bad weather one could only fly as far as RAF Northolt, London. Those on board had then to complete their journey by train.

Travelling in the opposite direction was 130 Squadron. 65 Squadron had left their Spitfires (Mk Vb) behind at Drem for the incoming squadron:

The aircraft left for us were in a very poor condition and a great deal of work was anticipated in bringing them up to the standard always maintained by this squadron.[24]

Despite this handicap, some of B-Flight's aircraft were pronounced serviceable on 1 April and were able to perform readiness duties in the afternoon. Plt Off. Graham

A rare aerial view of the western edge of RAF Drem in 1944. The control tower is visible in the lower portion of the picture with several aircraft dispersals behind it. (*Wilhelm Ratuszynski*)

fell foul of the bad runway surface and became bogged, slightly damaging the tips of his propeller blades. Over the next few days, formation flying and air-to-ground firing training was carried out. On 4 April, two Spitfires participated in a 'woodcock' exercise, with one aircraft acting as an attacking aircraft on a large convoy and the other as its protector. The latter Spitfire was given vectors onto the 'hostile' aircraft by the escort vessels. A similar exercise was flown four days later in conjunction with convoy 'Status'. A-Flight had its first scramble on 10 March, but the 'hostile' turned out to be a 'friendly'. Earlier on the same day, two of 130's Spitfires 'carried out an optimistic patrol over the North Sea in the morning in the hope of finding a Hun but they got no joy'. During April, 130 Squadron carried out 'attacks' on army convoys and 'beat up' tanks, a welcome break from normal training. Other training was in gun camera attacks, dog fighting and air-to-air firing of cannon and machine guns. At one stage, the armament officer became worried at the rate his ammunition was being used, 'but the pilots agreed that despite his concern it was the type of practice most needed and that they could not have too much of it'. The second half of the month saw scrambles become more frequent. On 16 April, one section was at readiness from first light. At 12.35 p.m. the aircraft were instructed to intercept a possible enemy aircraft, but it was far to the south, travelling very fast, and they were unable to catch it. Three days later, A-Section got off the ground promptly in response to an alert, but were soon recalled as the aircraft was identified as 'friendly'. In the afternoon there was another scramble and this time the enemy aircraft was a Typhoon near Holy Island. An entry in the squadron log book bemoans: 'We are beginning to become rather sceptical of these Scottish scrambles'. On 20 April, a further false alarm resulted in a Wellington being intercepted near St Abb's Head. No. 130 Squadron mounted a patrol on 22 April in an effort to put an end to the frequently sighted 'weather willie' Me 210, but the pilots saw no sign of it. The next day their luck changed. FS Saunders and Sgt Hill of Blue Section were scrambled at 1.20 p.m.:

> They climbed through cloud and after a series of vectors found their prey. It was a Messerschmitt Me 210. The Hun obviously disliked the Spits and turned for home but Blue Section got after him and although handicapped by the comparative slowness of their Vbs got near enough to have a bang. The pilots attacked from astern and from the quarter at extreme range and caused the Hun to jettison what appeared to be a long-range tank. The Hun was diving for home and despite the fact that both pilots of the Squadron pressed the tit [gun firing button] it continued to gain on them and they were forced to abandon the chase. When they landed, Drem was agog with excitement. It was the first Hun anyone had shot at for months and almost everyone turned out to get the 'gen'. Literally fighting his way through the crowd, the Intelligence Officer got to the pilots and got his story but no claim could be made.[25]

The Me 210 was produced in limited numbers and was rarely encountered in British skies. After another scramble next day, two Spitfire pilots recognised the 'enemy' aircraft as friendly but did not know the type, much to the annoyance of the intelligence officer. After being shown a recognition book, they identified it as an Armstrong Whitworth Albemarle, an obscure twin-engined transport, originally designed as a bomber.

On 26 April, the squadron was advised it was to move to RAF Ballyhalbert, in Northern Ireland: 'Everyone cursed this for it had been decided that if the squadron was to spend some months out of operations, Drem was a first class place for a rest'. On 28 April, most of the pilots turned out for duty in the morning with a hangover acquired at the squadron farewell party the night before. Many of the personnel left by train later on that day, after being given the traditional send off 'by the Station Padre—an adept at that peculiar Scottish instrument—the bagpipes'. Due to poor weather the Spitfires were unable to leave until 30 April. Padre Sutherland also gave them a musical send off as the squadron swept over Drem in formation and set course for Ballyhalbert. The remaining pilots and ground crew were transported in two 'Sparrows' (Harrow transports).

No. 340 Free French Squadron was then deployed to Drem for the summer of 1943, departing in November (see Chapter 9). No. 485 Squadron, a unit mainly composed of New Zealanders, replaced it. It had operated as part of the Biggin Hill Wing and then the Hornchurch Wing for just one month. Its Spitfires (Mk IXb) arrived at Drem on 8 November 1943 and flew a handful of scrambles during the closing part of the year.

On 22 December, Fg Off. John Dasent was flying in a co-operative role with the Royal Navy when he misjudged his height and his radiator hit the water. A sudden loss of glycol caused the engine to fail shortly afterwards. Dasent tried to gain height, but was only a few hundred feet above the water when he jumped from the aircraft. The parachute opened as he hit the water. His attempt to escape the aircraft had been hindered by the experimental 'G-suit' (the Franks Flying Suit), which the squadron had been given the responsibility for testing. Some twenty minutes later, the destroyer HMS *Vivien* arrived on the scene, but found Dasent had died.

In January 1944, only one scramble was flown. The number of operational flying hours for this month was just three with just six hours of night flying. The non-operational hours total was a more impressive 254.

The squadron became busier in February. Two Spitfires were scrambled on the morning of 2 February to escort a Catalina in difficulties and, later in the month, a Liberator. No less than ten aircraft provided protection for a convoy on 21 February. At the end of the month, the squadron returned to RAF Hornchurch, its Spitfire Mk IXb having been replaced by the Spitfire Mk Vb. When back at its old base, 485 Squadron was transferred to the 2 Tactical Air Force, which would be responsible for air operations in support of the invasion of Continental Europe.

The next Spitfires to arrive, on the evening of 7 March 1944, were those of 91 Squadron, formerly at RAF Castle Camps in Essex. The squadron had just been re-equipped with thirteen new Spitfires (Mk XIV) and had been moved to Scotland for training. Entering service in January 1944, this was one of the fastest RAF fighters at that time, fast enough to shoot down the V-1 flying bombs. The squadron went on to destroy 184 of them. Training commenced on 10 March. The first accident followed just two days later when FS Sayer failed to return from a late afternoon scramble with two other Spitfires to assist a Liberator find its way back to its base. His burnt-out and deeply buried aircraft was later found 2 miles east of Carstairs, in Lanarkshire, but there was no trace of the pilot. A search was organised that involved aircraft from Drem, and the next day, after the site had been excavated, Sayer's body was found in the cockpit.

On 17 March, there was a practice squadron formation comprising eleven Spitfires (Mk XIV) and one Spitfire (Mk XII). No. 91 Squadron flew its first night flights later on the same day, and 'everyone was pleasantly surprised to find how nice the Mk XIV were to fly at night, no trouble at all was experienced by exhaust fumes'. Cannon tests, dusk flying and height climbs to 40,000 feet with practice interceptions at that altitude, were among the other training activities that took place over the next few weeks. After some flights on 1 April, 'weather down to the deck' prevented any further activity for a week. The following day conditions improved and ten pilots were able to carry out early evening moonlight flying. On 23 April the Squadron left for RAF West Malling in Kent. Their Tiger Moth was reluctant to depart, suffering engine failure on take-off. It had to make a forced landing in an adjoining field, damaging its undercarriage and right wing. With German aircraft now rarely venturing into the Scottish skies, the days of Drem playing host to several RAF fighter squadrons at the same time had come to an end. For much of the remainder of 1944, a single squadron of obsolete Hurricanes maintained the security of the skies over the mouth of the Firth of Forth. It was not until the following year that another Spitfire Squadron was based at Drem—this was 603 Squadron mentioned elsewhere in the text.

A small number of Mk V Spitfires were used by the SCR-584 (Signal Corps Radio No. 584) Training Flight. The SCR-584 was a trailer-mounted early warning radar that came from the USA in early 1944 and was used to automatically control heavy AA-guns in the campaign against the V-1 flying bombs being launched against London. The exact function of this unit is still unclear. It was formed at RAF Milfield in Northumberland and then moved to Drem on 1 January 1945. Its personnel consisted of around ten officers, sixty-three other ranks and fourteen WAAFs. Records show that instructions were given to set up a VHF mobile station to communicate with aircraft employed on SCR-584 training at Musselburgh dive-bombing range. Hence it is probable that the role of this unit was to train pilots to attack ground targets, particularly shipping, with the assistance of this ground-based radar. SC-584 Training Flight departed for RAF Manston, Kent, at the end of May 1945.

A mural depicting RAF Drem on the outside of the building that once housed the short-lived Drem Museum in 2006. It has since been painted over. (*Malcolm Fife*)

The Hawker Hurricane Squadrons

At the outbreak of the Second World War, the Hawker Hurricane was held in the same esteem by the general public as the Supermarine Spitfire, but with the passage of time the Spitfire stole the limelight. A number of factors contributed to this, principally the decision by the RAF to concentrate on developing the Spitfire as its main fighter, ensuring a long career in the service. It was thought that the airframe of the Spitfire was more suited to future development, particularly as it could be adapted to house more powerful engines. Propaganda also played a part in boosting the aircraft's image, as Britain wanted to impress the Americans with its technological achievements, of which the Spitfire was one.

The Hawker Hurricane (introduced 25 December 1937) was the first operational RAF aircraft capable of exceeding 300 mph, but it could not match the Spitfire's (introduced 3 August 1938) speed and rate of climb. By the outbreak of war, 497 Hurricanes had been completed out of an order for 3,500. It was robust and manoeuvrable, capable of sustaining massive combat damage before write-off. Unlike the Spitfire, it was a go-anywhere do-anything fighter. It has been estimated it accounted for around 80 per cent of all enemy aircraft destroyed between July and October 1940.

During the Battle of Britain, the Hurricane was credited with destroying around 860 enemy aircraft as opposed to the Spitfire's 485, but there were far more Hurricanes in service.

The first Hurricane Squadron to be based at Drem was 111, which arrived on 7 December 1939 from RAF Acklington, in Northumberland: 'The whole squadron moved in two hours down to the last man and lorry'. No. 111 had been the first Fighter Command squadron to operate the Hurricane, receiving its first aircraft in late 1937. For the rest of December 1939 its Hurricanes (Mk I) flew sorties over the area, including dawn and dusk patrols. On 17 December, Red Section was patrolling Drem at cloud base and was vectored onto an unidentified aircraft heading towards the airfield. It turned out to be 'friendly'. The squadron records for 21 December note:

Big raid reported coming in from the North Sea. Both Spitfire Squadrons sent up to intercept. Raid turned out to be 24 Hampdens returning from raid on Germany.[1]

Two of the Hampdens were shot down by 603's Spitfires. This incident is related in greater detail in the chapter on Bombers. During the course of the month a number of new pilots joined 111 Squadron and fighter attack training was carried out on 24 December. The Hurricane pilots also flew several flights to enable anti-aircraft gunners to practise and on 29 December three aircraft were detailed to carry out mock attacks on two CH (Chain Home) radar stations.

The year 1940 began with poor weather hindering flying activities. Green Section carried out simulated attacks on CH sites at Drone Hill and Douglas Wood, near Dundee. On 7 January 1940, the squadron was 'at available' status from 8 a.m. to 12 p.m., then 'at readiness' from 12 p.m. to 5 p.m. The weather was very bad with thick fog.

On 9 January, instructions were given to maintain standing patrols for the whole day from May Island to Berwick-upon-Tweed for a distance of 20 miles out to sea. This was in response to enemy attacks on convoys that, after a lull, had recommenced the same day. Although patrols were maintained for a further two days, due to the appalling weather no interceptions were made. At 9.42 a.m. on 13 January, Spitfires of Red Section were directed to intercept an enemy aircraft detected flying at 20,000 feet in the vicinity of Crail. Along with Spitfires of 602 Squadron, Red Section attacked a He 111 (of 1(F)122), which came down in the sea 15 miles north-east of Fifeness. One crew member was picked up in a dinghy, the other three perished in the air battle.

For the remainder of January, regular patrols were flown by 111's Hurricanes over south-east Scotland. On 30 January, Blue Section sighted a He 111, and one of the Hurricanes engaged it for about three seconds before the aircraft disappeared in cloud over May Island. The same day, Plt Off. Walker made a forced landing due to engine failure. Heavy snow fell on the last day of the month and the squadron was released from duty.

Four Hurricanes managed local flying on 1 February, but the weather conditions remained poor throughout much of the month with the airfield being frequently unserviceable. To add to the problems, seven officers came down with influenza. Despite these handicaps, the Hurricanes still maintained the state of readiness and, on the 22 February, Blue, Green, and Red Sections all took off to intercept a Heinkel reported to be approaching the airfield. No contact was made. The following day, 111 Squadron was ordered to start standing patrols at 6.30 p.m. and to continue through the night. At 10.30 p.m. this instruction was cancelled.

Several exercises were carried out with anti-aircraft gunners, including one on 16 February involving four Hurricanes operating in the Forth and Clyde Valleys. Convoy patrols were also flown during that day and the next. These involved the provision of air cover for HMS *Cossack* on its way to Leith with 229 Allied prisoners liberated from the German supply ship *Altmark*, intercepted in then neutral Norwegian waters. Training in conjunction with the radar stations also took place, as did attack practices. On 19 February, 'tea relief instituted today as the days are much longer'. How long this arrangement lasted is not known, as on 27 February 111 Squadron departed to a place where the days were somewhat shorter than those experienced in Central Scotland at this time of the year. They would be based at Wick in the far north for the next six weeks and return to Drem later in the year.

A Luftwaffe aerial reconnaissance photograph of RAF Drem taken on 22 July 1940. (*Luftwaffe Collection, RCAHMS/SCRAN*)

May 1940 saw the arrival of two Hurricane Squadrons. The first was 245, whose motto was 'I Put To Flight—I Do Not Flee', that arrived on 12 May from RAF Leconfield. The main air party of Hurricanes (Mk I) arrived at Drem almost simultaneously with the ground party. All personnel worked until well after nightfall, unloading and transporting equipment from the railhead. The following day, the unit became operational with A-Flight on standby until sunset. Three Hurricanes were scrambled at 4.30 p.m. and vectored to St Abb's Head, but no enemy was sighted. Two days later, an order was received that one flight was to be made ready to proceed to France. This was cancelled, then reinstated the next day, with A-Flight and six pilots leaving with their Hurricanes at 2.05 p.m. In the evening, the maintenance crews left Drem on board three unusual transport aircraft—former Sabena Airlines three-engined low-winged Savoia-Marchetti S.73s, acquired prior to the occupation of Belgium. There was also an accident on that day involving Plt Off. C. Carlson, who crashed his Hurricane N2559 1 mile south of Dirleton after taking off. The aircraft was written off and the pilot was admitted to Edinburgh Castle Hospital with multiple injuries. A-Flight's stay in France was short-lived and it returned on 21 May.

B-Flight maintained normal patrol activity without incident until 28 May, when fifteen Hurricanes and thirty-six airmen left for RAF Hawkinge (in Kent) to cover the evacuation from Dunkirk. The following day, a further two aircraft joined them. On

30 May, nine of 245's Hurricanes provided air cover for Allied forces on the French beaches. Two pilots were reported missing on 1 June after their aircraft were in combat with Bf 109s. The last patrol was flown on 3 June. On 5 June 245's personnel moved to RAF Turnhouse, the Hurricanes flying directly from England.

No. 605 County of Warwick Royal Auxiliary Air Force Squadron was brought south from Wick to take part in the air battle over Dunkirk. Although the squadron was at RAF Hawkinge for only ten days, it destroyed eleven enemy aircraft. At the end of May, the squadron, its commanding officer, and several other pilots having been killed in action, was withdrawn to Drem to refit and re-equip. On 30 May, a handful of pilots touched down in their Hurricanes (Mk I). One aircraft did not even make it—Sgt Ralls made a forced landing near Selkirk in the Scottish Borders. The Hurricane turned over onto its back and Ralls was badly burned. The next day there was yet another loss; Plt Off. Dini was killed taking off from RAF Hawkinge for Drem, when he attempted a forced landing and crashed: 'The few remaining pilots in the unit were scattered all over the country collecting aircraft'. Early June was taken up with aircraft collection and leave and rest for the pilots. The entry for 6 June in the squadron diary records:

> The heat wave continues and so does the peace of the squadron. It is hoped pilots will be posted soon, so that work can recommence [There were only five personnel at Drem on 5 June]. Idleness is grand but not conducive to winning the war. We must reform as soon as possible and be ready to fight again.[2]

Sqn Ldr Churchill was appointed 605's CO in mid-June, having previously been in charge of 3 Squadron. He stepped up the number of training flights and is credited with much of the subsequent success of the unit when it returned to action. By the time the squadron arrived at Drem, it had lost all its original Auxiliary pilots, many of whom had been posted elsewhere, but the ground crews were still largely pre-war reservists from Warwick.

> [By 15 June, night flying] was progressing satisfactorily, perfect weather for practice. Sgt Allen parked an aircraft very heavily and did a certain amount of damage—little experience. It is unfortunate that pilots from the Flying Training Schools cannot have previous experience on types before coming to a squadron, or failing this unit's case, a Miles Magister to be supplied for dual practice before going off in a Hurricane. A certain number of accidents could be avoided.[3]

Nineteen pilots were now on strength. Tragically, Barry Godwin was killed on 24 June when his Hurricane Mk I was seen to dive and crash five miles south of Dunbar from about 6,000 feet. The accident was attributed to the gun panels loosening and detaching. Four days later, Sgt Ritchie managed to put a Hurricane on its nose, causing considerable damage to the machine, but not to the pilot. On 30 June, he had another accident in similar circumstances. Despite these mishaps, 605 Squadron was declared operational on 31 July 1940. Total flying time during the month was 657 hours

'[...] from which has developed a grand body of pilots. There is complete harmony everywhere and the results should fully justify the hard work'.

Unfortunately, the squadron was about to suffer another setback. On 8 August, the CO was returning from a patrol with Plt Off. Passey and Sgt Ritchie when Ritchie's Hurricane L2103 plummeted from 15,000 feet. The aircraft hit the sea at 4.45 p.m., 1 mile from the shore due east of Dunbar. Sgt Ritchie's body was picked up by the motor patrol vessel *Eunmara* and returned to Drem. It was thought that he had been asphyxiated by fumes caused by a glycol leak.

A few days later, 605 Squadron was given the opportunity to inflict some casualties on the enemy. Shortly after noon on 15 August 1940, radar operators at Anstruther plotted what they thought was a large-scale raid heading for Edinburgh over the North Sea. It was discovered to be a diversionary formation of eighteen German seaplanes. A main bomber force of sixty-three He 111s of KG26 took off from airfields around Stavanger, Norway, thirty minutes later. The Heinkels flew in a broad front accompanied by twenty-one Bf 110 long-range fighters. The mission was to attack RAF airfields near Newcastle-upon-Tyne, possibly as far south as Hull or, failing that, to bomb the major towns.

This flank attack from the east was intended to saturate British air defences, allowing fleets of bombers to attack targets on the south coast relatively untroubled. The Germans thought the RAF had moved most of its fighters to the south of England for the Battle of Britain, being ignorant of Fighter Command's newly introduced practice of rotating squadrons between the now dangerous skies of south-east England and the more placid ones further north. The Germans had hoped to lure the fighters north to attack the seaplanes, but due to a 3 degree navigation error, the Heinkels instead converged on the decoy formation. They belatedly changed course and flew south, parallel to the Northumberland coast. Unluckily for them this brought them close to RAF Acklington, were twelve Hurricanes of 79 Squadron were scrambled. No. 72 Squadron, also flying from RAF Acklington, observed around 100 German aircraft heading towards the coast, thirty miles off the Farne Islands. Its Spitfires fell on this large formation, shooting down three enemy aircraft. Drem was alerted and six Hurricanes were airborne at 12.25 p.m., flying south towards Northumberland:

> A red letter day, 605 Squadron ordered off at 12.15, B-Flight from 'available' were in the air within 10 minutes. Big air battle off Newcastle in which it is understood about 150 enemy aircraft were involved.[4]

Five minutes after 72 Squadron had been action, 605's Hurricanes attacked the Heinkels just to the north of Blyth. At 1.12 p.m., two formations of enemy aircraft were sighted approaching at 12,000 feet, the first a formation of some sixty to seventy machines and the second made up of twenty to twenty-five aircraft. Blue Section Hurricanes attacked the larger formation, while Green Section, led by Plt Off. Christopher Currant, went after the smaller group. A He 111H-4 (1H+GH) fell victim to Currant's guns, which put its starboard engine out of action and forced it to break formation. Fg Off. C. Passey and Fg Off. J. Muirhead then proceeded to finish off the Heinkel by disabling its other engine, causing the doomed aircraft to spiral down through cloud into the sea. Remarkably, all five of its crew survived and clambered aboard their dinghy to be subsequently rescued by a Fisheries Patrol boat. A further three Heinkels were destroyed in the same air battle by five Hurricanes of 605 Squadron. Shortly after, the remaining enemy bombers headed back home across the North Sea. Around the same time, there was a raid further down the coast by a formation of about fifty Ju 88s flying from Denmark. This resulted in the destruction of ten British bombers at RAF Driffield.

The day after the air battle the 605 Squadron diary states:

> The correct figures for yesterday were 4 confirmed, 4 probables and 3 damaged—a brilliant performance by the flight. No definite news at present of Plt Off. K. S. Law in hospital at West Hartlepool, it is hoped he was not badly injured when making his forced landing at Hartlepool Railway Station. Plt Off. Passy had to force land his aircraft within a mile of Usworth Aerodrome (Sunderland). He returned safely to his unit.[5]

According to 13 Group Fighter Command Operations Record Book, participating pilots made claims amounting to thirty-one enemy machines 'destroyed', twenty-two 'probably destroyed', and fourteen 'damaged'. Most of the German aircraft were destroyed over the North Sea, so there was no way of authenticating the losses. The initial claims by the RAF fighter pilots were somewhat overstated. The Luftwaffe's records for losses during this operation were eight He 111s and eight Bf 110s. Nonetheless, it was a decisive blow against bombing raids over Northern Britain and there would never be a daylight raid against this part of the country on this scale again. In fact, unknown to the RAF, the Germans withdrew some of their bombers based in Scandinavia to strengthen units in France and the Low Countries. Had Fighter Command been aware of this, it may have also redeployed some of its fighter squadrons to protect the south coast of England.

On 23 August, three of 605's Hurricanes and two Blackburn Skuas from the Fleet Air Arm staged an 'invasion' from the Black Rock, Leith, for the benefit of the Duke of Gloucester, who witnessed the proceedings. Night flying for the month amounted to 118 hours, a squadron record. On 7 September, the unit was ordered south to RAF Croydon, London's pre-war commercial airport, to relieve 111's Hurricanes, who would be travelling in the opposite direction. At 2.15 p.m., eighteen of 605's Hurricanes (Mk I) took off in two flights of nine aircraft. Thirty-two maintenance crew followed in a Harrow and a Bombay.

During 605's final weeks at Drem, it was accompanied by 145 Squadron's Hurricanes, previously in action over Dunkirk and in the Battle of Britain at the height of the fighting. It was intended to briefly withdraw the unit to Scotland, where it would rest and reform while its Headquarters and maintenance flights remained at RAF Tangmere, situated next to RAF Westhampnett. At 6.15 p.m. on 13 August, two Harrows left RAF Westhampnett bound for Drem carrying the ground crews for twelve Hurricanes. RAF Tangmere was bombed three days later. The remainder of 145 Squadron headed north as well. One of the pilots who flew the remaining

Hurricanes north had a bandaged wound sustained during the Battle of Britain. On 19 August, six new pilots arrived at Drem. To replace the lost aircraft, new Canadian-built Hurricanes were delivered to the squadron and training flights flown over the next few days.

No. 13 Group ordered that one flight should be declared operational on 22 August and it was not long before 145 Squadron was again involved in combat. In the small hours of 27 August, Flt Lt Boyd was on patrol east of St Abb's Head when he saw a concentration of searchlight beams and bomb bursts. He proceeded to investigate and caught a glimpse of a He 111. He fired six short bursts, but no damage was seen and the bomber disappeared into the darkness. No. 145's stay at Drem was to be short-lived, as on 29 August orders were received for A-Flight to move to RAF Montrose and B-Flight and Headquarters to RAF Dyce, to provide fighter cover for north-east Scotland. This move was completed by the end of the month, except for the maintenance flight which remained behind.

No. 111 Squadron returned to Drem for a second stay on 8 September 1940. In the intervening period it had been stationed at various airfields close to London and had been heavily involved in the Battle of Britain. Sadly, many pilots who had previously flown from Drem in the days of the Phoney War had since perished. Between May and early September no less than fourteen pilots were killed in thirty-four actions against the enemy. The 111 Squadron diary for early September narrates:

> The Squadron through losses in action rendering its operational strength far below par is being used at the moment for training purposes, with the idea of posting pilots when trained to 11 Group Squadrons [responsible for the air defence of south-east England] as and when required. A nucleus of experienced pilots is being retained in the squadron for training purposes and operational flying duties in this sector are being undertaken with the squadron personnel as at present constituted as they are considered operationally trained for fighting purposes in this group.[6]

During September many new pilots, several from training units and three from 600 Squadron, were posted to 111 Squadron at Drem. On 5 October, Sqn Ldr Biggar became CO. After a stay of just over a month, A-Flight's Hurricanes were instructed to proceed to RAF Montrose, north of Dundee. If the airmen had expected to be spared the air attacks suffered by airfields around London, they were in for a shock. About two weeks after their arrival, RAF Montrose was attacked at dusk by four He 111s. Six men were killed and a further twenty-one injured; several aircraft on the ground were damaged and two hangars were destroyed. Four of 111's Hurricanes were scrambled and gave chase. One Heinkel was located and fired on, but managed to make its escape. When A-Flight deployed to RAF Montrose, B-Flight went to RAF Dyce. The squadron remained at these two airfields until July 1941, when it departed again for southern England. The maintenance section had to remain at Drem due to lack of accommodation.

Two weeks later, another Hurricane squadron put in appearance at Drem. No. 232 Squadron had been based at RAF Castletown, Caithness, northern Scotland, until

13 October 1940. It then moved briefly to RAF Skitten (in the same county) before heading south on 24 October with all eleven aircraft flying in formation. Other air crew and essential stores were ferried in two transport aircraft, while two officers and fifty-three men travelled by train. The mission of 232 Squadron was to provide fighter cover, but its stay at Drem, like that of several of the previous Hurricane squadrons, was very brief. 263 Squadron was also based at Drem, but had only a small number of Hurricanes and was in the process of re-equipping with Westland Whirlwinds. It was intended to temporarily combine machines from both units to form one operational squadron that would share duties with two fighter squadrons based at RAF Turnhouse. A Blenheim squadron was also present at Drem for night patrols.

On 31 October, one section of 232 Squadron, comprising four pilots and four machines with ground crew, moved to RAF Acklington as a temporary measure to provide night fighter cover. Two days prior, Sgt E. Redfern attempted to lower his undercarriage for an hour and twenty minutes, before crash-landing on the airfield under instructions from the air traffic controller. He escaped without injury, but his Hurricane V6848 was damaged beyond the squadron's ability to repair it. This was the only incident of note while 232 Squadron was stationed at Drem.

On 11 November 1940, 232 departed back north to RAF Skitten. An entry in the Squadron's diary written on this date complains that 'there is nothing whatever to record this month—the time has been uninteresting from an operational point of view'. As soon as 232 Squadron left, its place was taken by 607 County of Durham Royal Auxiliary Air Force Squadron. Its Hurricanes (Mk I) made the short hop from RAF Turnhouse (Edinburgh) where they had spent most of the previous month. Flying training occupied much of the time, with some operational patrols. Unlike the City of Glasgow Squadron, 232 had not adopted the practice of using just two machines on patrols to save wear and tear on both pilot and aircraft and instead frequently used three Hurricanes.

Exactly a month after it had arrived, 607 Squadron departed for RAF Usworth in north-east England, its home base in pre-war days. Early the following year it returned to Scotland, initially being based at RAF MacMerry, just west of Drem. 607 was the first operational squadron to fly from this former civil airfield. On 2 March 1941, 607's Hurricanes flew the short distance to Drem, where they spent the remainder of the month.

Plt Off. B. Pollitt was killed on 10 March when his aircraft crashed 1 mile south of Harperigg Reservoir, on the edge of the Pentland Hills. The next day, three Hurricanes along with ground personnel proceeded to RAF Leuchars for ten days concentrated fighter tactical training. By the end of March the squadron had notched up the following flying hours for the month:

	Day	Night
Operational	176 hours	Nil
Non-operational	282 hours	12 hours

Operational flying consisted of two- or three-aircraft patrols. Nothing of any interest was sighted. On 16 April, 607's Hurricanes (Mk I) departed for RAF Skitten, near Wick.

No. 258 Squadron, detailed to fill the gap left by the departure of 263 Squadron at the end of November, had reformed at RAF Leconfield in November 1940, but had no aircraft. After a brief stay, it moved to RAF Duxford, Cambridgeshire. The move to Drem on 4 December 1940 involved three sergeant pilots, five other sergeants and ninety-two other ranks travelling north by train. Seven others made their way in private transport.

Most of the nine 'clapped out' Hurricanes (Mk I) left behind by 263 Squadron were taken over by 258 Squadron. An additional seven new Hurricanes (Mk I) arrived from 27 Maintenance Unit on 5 December. A further Hurricane and three pilots from other squadrons arrived two days later. The ground crews began overhauling and painting the new aircraft at the dispersal points in very cold weather—so cold that the engines had to be periodically warmed up throughout the night to ensure that they would start again at daybreak. The ground crew also had to clear the snow from the runways.

The first flights by the newly formed 258 Squadron took place on 8 December, when four more Hurricanes arrived. A full day of operational flying followed. A few days later, the squadron was instructed to move south to RAF Acklington, and on 14 December most of its personnel travelled the short distance to Northumberland by train, the remainder in service transport or in private vehicles. With the weather improving slightly, Sqn Ldr Clouston lead twenty-one aircraft in seven 'vics', line astern, to the new base on 15 December. Only sixteen aircraft made it, the remaining five being forced back to Drem by the weather.

Beginning 18 December, 258 Squadron, using every available aircraft, carried out intensive operational training at RAF Acklington. The squadron was eventually posted to the Far East, where Japanese paratroopers overran its airfield. Many of the squadron personnel were killed or died later in prison camps.

No. 43 Squadron and its Hurricanes (Mk I) arrived on 12 December 1940. Unlike most of the other fighter squadrons that lasted only a few weeks, 43 Squadron were there for almost ten months, the longest stay by any squadron at Drem during the Second World War. Like many of the Hurricane squadrons that arrived in the closing months of 1940, 43 Squadron had suffered grievous losses in the Battle of Britain. It was removed from the frontline on 8 September, retiring north to RAF Usworth with just twelve operational pilots and twelve aircraft. In just the previous two weeks at RAF Tangmere, Sussex, four of its pilots had been killed in action and a further seven hospitalised. No. 607 Squadron replaced 43 Squadron in the front line, flying south from RAF Usworth at first light. No. 607 lost more aircraft and pilots in the first five days in action than 43 Squadron had lost in as many weeks. Both units eventually returned to Drem to recover and regroup.

At around this time, Lord Dowding (Head of Fighter Command) reorganised his resources by dividing the squadrons into three classes—A, B, and C. Those in the thick of the fighting, mainly in south-east England, were considered Class A and received priority access to resources. Class B, fewer in number, were on the fringe of the battle and were available at short notice to replace any Class A squadron that had suffered serious losses. Like many of the other fighter squadrons operating from Scottish airfields, 43 Squadron had been relegated to Class C. Having only a handful of operational pilots, the Class C squadrons' main role was to provide experience for recently graduated pilots before they were put in the front line. They were also to defend north and west Britain, where they were likely to encounter only small scale raids or reconnaissance aircraft.

During December 1940, 43's Hurricanes patrolled in groups of three, generally in hour-long sorties. B-Flight, with four Hurricanes, was based at RAF Prestwick from 12-19 December, when it returned to Drem. On Christmas Day, three pilots flew operational flights. One particularly busy day of practice included cross country flights, local formation flying, air combat flying, practice air firing, aerobatics and formation flying at 25,000 feet. There was a single accident when, on 15 December, Plt Off. Malarowski's Hurricane (Mk I) R4227 crashed into the sea near May Island while on patrol with two other aircraft. The uninjured Malarowski was picked up by a Royal Navy destroyer. Unfortunately for him, the ship's first port of call was Scapa Flow in the Orkney Islands.

To add to Britain's woes, the first few years of the Second World War saw a succession of harsh winters. To ensure the maintenance of fighter cover, some of 43's Hurricanes were moved to the still operational Fleet Air Arm airfield at Crail, in Fife: 'The squadron had left Drem for Crail on the 22nd February, as severe snowstorms at Drem had rendered the runways useless'. As both Turnhouse and Drem were unserviceable at the time, leaving the sector entirely undefended, Sqn Ldr Morgan volunteered and obtained permission to attempt to take off from a snowbound, roughly prepared, short and narrow runway. In addition, there was a bad boggy patch at the half-way mark, which made it absolutely necessary to be

Two Hurricanes (Mk I) taking off from RAF Drem in spring 1941. The Garleton Hills are visible in the background. (*RAF Museum*)

airborne in a very short distance. Using full throttle, all twelve pilots, led by Sqn Ldr Morgan, managed to take off. After making the short flight to Crail, they became operational immediately:

> The intelligence officer together with F/Sgt. Kay joined the pilots at Crail and our stay there was made most enjoyable by the Captain and Officers of HMS Jackdaw [the Crail Fleet Air Arm Station]. Everything was done to make us as comfortable as possible and the whole station was most helpful in providing us with anything we wanted.[7]

The weather improved and the squadron returned to Drem on 1 March, only for winter to return on 8 March. One section of Hurricanes (Mk I) returned to Crail and operated there for twenty-four hours, returning the next day. As well as maintaining operational patrols throughout the winter, 43 Squadron flew numerous training flights to enhance its pilots' skills. An entry in the squadron records for 30 April 1941 records:

> In spite of bad weather during what has been one of the hardest and worst winters for many years, the squadron has been able to do a monthly average of 330 hours by day and 26 hours by night practice flying in addition to any operational flying.[8]

The training exercises were not without incident. In early February, Sgt Stoker was posted as missing when his Hurricane Mk I L1968 crashed into the sea during air-firing practice at RAF Acklington. About a month later, Sgt Richardson's undercarriage gave way when landing, but he was fortunately uninjured. On 24 March, Plt Off. West was forced to land his Hurricane near Drone Hill when his engine failed through fuel starvation. West had not switched from the main tank to the reserve quickly enough.

With improving weather on the advent of spring, the Luftwaffe stepped up its offensive. In the first three months of 1941, 43 Squadron made just one inconclusive contact, when Blue Section engaged a German aircraft on 20 January 1941 over the sea near Aberdeen. The next encounter was on 9 April 1941, when Plt Off. du Vivier, a Belgian, and Sgt Scorer intercepted a Ju 88 flying very low over the sea to evade radar detection, 2 miles east of North Berwick. The two Hurricane pilots expended all their ammunition in a series of synchronised attacks. Bullets were seen hitting the Junkers, but it was last seen fleeing east, apparently undamaged. The squadron's log for April notes:

> Nevertheless in spite of bad weather during what has been one of the hardest and worst winters in many years, the Squadron had been able to do a monthly average of 330 hours by day and 26 hours by night practice flying, in addition to any operational flying. The squadron has also had larger number of operational and training pilots, night trained than any other Squadron in 13 Group.[9]

Beginning on 19 April, the delivery of eight- and twelve-gun Hurricane Mk IIs boosted the squadron's potency. Powered by a Merlin two-stage supercharged engine, this model was 20-mph faster than the previous version. It would not be long before the squadron was given the chance to test the effectiveness of the new planes against the enemy.

Until the middle of March 1941—when there were large raids on Glasgow and Clydeside—the cities of Scotland had not suffered raids on the scale that had wrought destruction on London and other southern cities. On the evening of 5 May, an aerial armada of 460 long-range bombers took off from Continental Europe for Glasgow and Clydeside. Between 12.25 a.m. and 3.40 a.m., the shipyards and industrial districts were attacked by 103 aircraft. A further eighty hit Greenock and others dropped their bomb loads over the north bank of the Clyde, including Dumbarton. The Germans did not confine their activities to the west coast of Scotland, as ten aircraft bombed Leith. Although skies were clear that night, a further eight crews could not find this target and instead dropped their bombs on Edinburgh.

On this fateful night, 43 Squadron carried out fourteen patrols. The Hurricane, like the Spitfire, was unsuitable for night fighting as the pilot had the dual task of both flying and searching for the enemy. It was very rare for any enemy bomber flying under the cover of darkness to fall victim to the guns of single-seat fighters. Specialised night fighters, such as the Defiant and Blenheim, had two crew members and many were equipped with a primitive form of airborne radar. The Hurricane pilot's job was even more difficult, since condensation on the windscreen and reflections off the spinning propeller severely reduced forward vision at night.

This made the achievements of 43 Squadron on the night of 5 May all the more remarkable. A-Flight sent five aircraft on a 'Fighter Night' (a patrol over the bombers' target area by individual aircraft, each at a different height). Nothing was sighted but the burning buildings below. B-Flight patrolled the approaches to the Firth of Forth across the line of attack of bombers flying from Norway. Sqn Ldr Tom Morgan shot down no less than three in the space of twenty-four hours. Witnesses in the coastal town of Anstruther saw the sky illuminated by a burning aircraft which spun into the sea, breaking into pieces on impact. Morgan had just claimed his first victim, a Ju 88. Wasting no time, he flew back to Drem to rearm and refuel. Just two hours after his first encounter, he saw an unidentified aircraft which was too big to be an RAF fighter and opened fire. A patrol boat off Fifeness reported an aircraft crashing into the sea. Plt Off. Harries flew two patrols on that night. On the first he intercepted a He 111, but he could only chase it for a short time as he was running short of fuel. Several other pilots flying over Glasgow saw enemy aircraft silhouetted against the fires, but no interceptions took place as the fighters were too high.

The following night, the Germans returned with 232 long-range bombers to press home their attack on the Clyde Valley. The area between Greenock and Dumbarton was attacked by 155 aircraft, resulting in severe damage to shipyards and factories. Eleven Hurricanes of 43 Squadron took off into the darkness, but again it was only Sqn Ldr Tom Morgan who met with any success. At 1.35 a.m., while in the locus of St Abb's Head, he glimpsed a Ju 88, and managed to fire a six-second burst from his twelve machine guns. This was enough to send the bomber crashing into the sea. One Hurricane managed to get lost after its radio failed. Its pilot, Sgt Haley, parachuted to safety at Barnard Castle, County Durham, just a few miles north of Yorkshire.

By 7 May, the raids on Glasgow ceased and were followed by a number of reconnaissance missions to assess the results. At 4.05 p.m., two Hurricanes of 43 Squadron flown by Plt Off. Cotton and Sgt Lister, intercepted and opened fire on a Ju 88 snooping over the mouth of the River Tay. Pieces were observed falling from the Junkers, but it disappeared into cloud before the outcome was clear. Later that same afternoon, the Royal Observer Corps post at St Abb's Head saw the same Junkers Ju 88 heading south, struggling to remain airborne and then diving into the sea. A short time later another reconnaissance Ju 88 was spotted by the St Abb's Head post. Flt Lt du Vivier and Plt Off. Mize (an American trainee) were on a practice flight and ordered to intercept the intruder. This Junkers put up more of a fight than its predecessor. Its rear gunner scored several hits on du Vivier's Hurricane before the fighters pressed home their attack and sent the stricken Junkers into the sea. No. 13 Group acknowledged 43 Squadrons achievement in destroying five German aircraft, offering the 'warmest congratulations on your good show these last two days'. A short time later, the War Cabinet sent a message of appreciation. Sqn Ldr Tom Morgan was awarded the DFC and du Vivier appropriately received a Belgian *Croix de Guerre*.

But their work was far from over. On 10 May, Flt Lt du Vivier and Plt Off. Hutchinson were on a training flight when they intercepted yet another reconnaissance Ju 88 over the Pentland Hills, near Edinburgh. It was on its way home after photographing the Clyde area. The two Hurricanes gave chase. With their quarry disappearing in and out of cloud, they pursued it across much of the Scottish Borders. It was last seen, with smoke pouring from its right engine, disappearing out over the North Sea at Berwick-on-Tweed. The Junkers was claimed as 'damaged' by 43 Squadron, but a reliable witness later stated he saw the crew parachuting from the crippled machine before it crashed into the sea a long way from shore.

There was a change of duty on 28 May; fifteen Hurricanes flew to RAF Prestwick to provide cover to the battleship *Prince of Wales*, returning home after sinking the German battleship *Bismarck* a few days earlier. While on the west coast of Scotland, du Vivier and Plt Off. Czajkowski were scrambled to intercept a Ju 88 at 24,000 feet. It was eventually brought down on the other side of the country at Newcastleton, in the Scottish Borders. Two of its crew were killed and two injured, but the pilot escaped unscathed. He informed his interrogators that 'every time the Hurricane fired, large pieces of the Junkers fell off'. The squadron returned to Drem on 29 May. No pilots had been lost due to enemy action during that month, but several were injured in flying accidents. On 4 May, the American, Plt Off. Mize, experienced engine trouble while practising high-altitude climbs and sustained minor injuries in the forced landing. Four days later, Mize was involved in a tragic accident at RAF Acklington. His taxiing aircraft hit and killed a man working on the edge of the airfield. Mize was charged with manslaughter, but was exonerated at a subsequent inquiry.

At the beginning of June, Plt Off. Czajkowski was returning with other Hurricanes from an operational patrol at only 600 feet due to bad weather, when he made a sharp turn and crash-landed in a field 2 miles south of North Berwick. The Hurricane was destroyed and Czajkowski was so seriously injured he could not be questioned about the cause of the incident.

A more positive note was struck a few days later when, on 8 June, Sqn Ldr Tom Morgan claimed his fourth enemy aircraft while stationed at Drem. This was perhaps his most incredible victory. At first he did not see the Ju 88 flying low over the sea at around 100 feet, only its shadow on the moonlit water. He dived from 2,000 feet, opening fire from about 200 feet behind the target. The first burst had no effect, then on the second attack bullets were seen hitting the cupola of the enemy aircraft. The Junkers dived into the sea and broke up some 15 to 20 miles off St Abb's Head. The squadron's log book for June 1941 gives the following summary of its activities:

> During this month 15 new pilots have been posted to the squadron from Group Training Units and 15 posted away. The squadron has done 37 operational trips by night and the total number of hours flown during June were 805 of which 91 were by night. This total, so far as is known, is the highest ever recorded in any single month by 43 Squadron. Comment has been made by 13 Group Headquarters regarding the squadron's cine camera gun training in the returns of which 43 Squadron took the largest number of feet of film. In 13 Group's letter dated 2nd July it is stated 'It is noteworthy that in spite of the low state of camera serviceability, 43 Squadron expended 3,287 feet of film, the highest figure for squadrons in the Group'. The squadron also did well with regard to air firing training of which 60 practices were made during the month with a large percentage of the pilots securing hits. These details are recorded here to show that quite apart from the operational flying, the squadron's training of new pilots and keeping the old pilots up to scratch continues unceasingly.[10]

Shortly after midnight on 11 July 1941, Sqn Ldr Tom Morgan took off with orders to investigate an 'X raid', east of the Bell Rock. When he reached the location, he observed two He 111s above a northbound convoy. In the light of a full moon, one of the hostile aircraft begun to make an attacking run on the ships at about 200 feet. Morgan's Hurricane gave chase and attacked twice from behind at very close range. The Heinkel took no evasive action and did not return fire. After the second attack, it crashed into the sea, and its destruction was confirmed by the convoy. Radar coverage was poor in this area and the enemy believed they could operate here with little chance of interception. It would not be long before Tom Morgan was in action again. On the afternoon of 24 July 1941, he took off with Plt Off. Bourne for a practice interception flight. No interception instructions were received from the controller, but after some twenty-five minutes a Ju 88 (A6+BH of 1F/120) was spotted, flying low over the sea, east of May Island. The enemy aircraft turned east and the two Hurricanes followed. Within three minutes Morgan's aircraft had closed to about 3,000 feet, the engine then began to malfunction and the cockpit filled with white smoke. The Merlin of that era had a design weakness—when set at high boost pressure in combat situations, the ethylene glycol coolant could find its way into the cylinders. Nonetheless, Morgan managed three attacks. After the second, the Ju 88 right engine slowed. Plt Off. Bourne then joined in and the Ju 88 was hit in the fuselage and wing before crashing into the sea. Morgan's engine then failed completely. Due to the low altitude, he was forced to crash-land, tail down, into the sea. He managed to escape from the sinking aircraft and clambered into his dinghy. Du Vivier arrived to relieve Plt Off. Bourne and then guided HMS *Ludlow* to Morgan's position. The warship rescued him after he had spent about two hours in the sea. Other than knocking his front teeth into his palate on the aircraft's gun site, Tom Morgan was uninjured. He was discharged from hospital on 1 August and given twenty-eight days leave from 15 August. Flt Lt du Vivier assumed command of the squadron in his absence.

August was a quiet month for operational flying. There were many postings in and out of the squadron and, at one time, the number of fully operational pilots was reduced to a bare twelve. The pilots, including those undergoing training, came from a variety of countries including Australia, Belgium, Czechoslovakia, Canada, India, Ireland, South Africa, Poland, Norway, and New Zealand. Several Americans had passed through the unit during that summer and had gone on to form the Second Eagle Squadron. At the end of the month there were a couple of flying accidents. On 23 August Plt Off. Bourne was making practice attacks in the squadron's Miles Magister. He lowered the flaps to reduce speed, but then found he could not retract them. Bourne flew around for half an hour trying unsuccessfully to free the flaps, eventually making a forced landing with his wheels up, slightly damaging the aircraft. A few days later Plt Off. Vosburg, who was on his second trip with the squadron, had to make a forced landing due to the perennial problem of an internal glycol leak.

September 1941 got off to a bad start when Sgt J. Welling crashed west of the Tay Rail Bridge on a practice night patrol in clear skies. The cause of the accident was

A Hurricane (Mk IIB) of 43 Squadron with ammunition belts laid out on the muddy ground—1941. (*RAF Museum*)

never proven, but it was assumed the pilot lost control. Just four days later, on 5 September, Plt Off. David Bourne, leader of Black Section, was killed near the Fleet Air Arm airfield at Donibristle, in Fife. His Hurricane crashed into a wood on a hillside after making a sharp turn. He apparently lost control and was unable to recover from a spin. The area was covered by thick low cloud at the time. Bourne had been with 43 Squadron for a couple of months. On 7 September, twelve pilots were instructed to take off for RAF Valley on the Isle of Anglsey to cover an interchange of squadrons there, but bad weather delayed their departure until 10 September. They returned home a week later, having spent most of the time flying convoy patrols.

Flying hours for 43 Squadron for this month were badly down because of ten days on which conditions made any flying impossible. Poor serviceability of the aircraft did not help either. There was great difficulty in obtaining spare parts and, on one occasion, eleven out of a total of twenty Hurricanes were unserviceable, waiting on rubber hose connectors to come from the manufacturers.

Sqn Ldr Morgan scored his sixth night victory on 2 October. During a raid on Tyneside, he was given permission to patrol the southern part of the sector south of the Forth. Interpreting his instructions somewhat liberally, he left the designated patrol area altogether. Flying at 10,000 feet, 20 miles south-east of the Farne Islands, Morgan caught sight of a Ju 88 flying 2,000 feet below him. He dived on his prey from astern and opened fire. The top upper gunner on the enemy aircraft shot back, but with little effect. With the third burst from the fighter, a wing of the Junkers Ju 88 caught fire and the crippled aircraft plummeted into the sea below. This brought Tom Morgan's score to sixteen, all with 43 Squadron, seven of them while based at Drem. Just two days later, the squadron departed for RAF Acklington where it was to be responsible for providing air defence for the sector where the Junkers had been intercepted by Morgan:

> Ten months at Drem ended abruptly and the move brought more sorrow than delight. Such is the inbred cussedness of men that even those who initially had most heartily abhorred the place and had hinted in a dark and confidential manner of the dreaded 'Drem-doom', a disease which allegedly drove to madness any who tarried there too long, were now ready to admit that lots of places were much worse. Indeed, survive and surmount the easterlies that funnelled up the Forth and the equal acerbity of Station Warrant Officer Copping, and there were few places better, never forgetting that only eighteen miles away was unequalled as an off duty centre for servicemen [referring to Edinburgh].[11]

The period that 43 Squadron was stationed at Drem was the longest it had been at any station since the outbreak of the war, and it saw many changes amongst the personnel. During the stay at Drem, eleven enemy aircraft were destroyed by squadron pilots of which seven were credited to Sqn Ldr Tom Morgan, eighty-six pilots were trained of which ten remained with the squadron when it moved to RAF Acklington and three pilots were killed in flying accidents.

At 11 a.m. on 4 October, a special train pulled into Drem Station to transfer the squadron personnel to their new posting. On the footbridge over the tracks stood the

Reverend Jock Sutherland, Minister of the Parish of Dirleton, Padre to RAF Drem, playing the lament 'Will ye no come back again?' on his bagpipes. The squadron never did return to Drem, but it did come back to Scotland in 1969 when it was based at RAF Leuchars on the opposite side of the Firth of Forth, its F-4K Phantoms frequently flying over East Lothian and its war-time base.

The newly formed 260 Squadron spent its early days at Drem. It was reformed at RAF Castletown on 22 November 1940 before moving to RAF Skitten, where it received the Hurricane Mk I during December. In anticipation of its deployment overseas it moved to Drem on 16 April 1941, where the squadron was made up to overseas establishment strength and as much leave as possible was given to all ranks:

> The aircraft were fitted with long distance tanks and all pilots were busy getting in as much practice of flying the aircraft as possible. Several pilots, posted to us had very little experience of Hurricanes and these also put in a considerable amount of flying. Everything was ready for the move by 15th May.[12]

The pilots left by rail on 16 May for embarkation at Scapa Flow in the Orkneys. They were followed on 19 May by the ground personnel, who departed for embarkation at Liverpool on the SS *Christian Huygenes*. No. 260's final destination was Haifa, in Palestine.

6

Whirlwinds and Typhoons

At the outbreak of the Second World War, all modern RAF fighters were single-engined types—the Supermarine Spitfire, the Hawker Hurricane, and the Bolton Paul Defiant. Additionally, there were a small number of a fighter version of the twin-engined Bristol Blenheim, originally designed as a bomber. A purpose-built, twin-engined, single-seat fighter—the Westland Whirlwind—had been under development since 1938.

The Hurricane and Spitfire were household names, but the existence of the Whirlwind was a closely guarded secret. It employed many technical innovations, including four 20-mm Hispano cannons grouped together in the nose to provide a heavy concentration of firepower and a bubble-shaped cockpit hood to give excellent all-round visibility.

No. 263 Squadron, decimated when the aircraft carrier HMS *Glorious* was sunk evacuating it from Norway, was reformed at Drem on 10 June 1940. It was meant to be the first squadron to receive the Whirlwind, but deliveries were delayed by development problems. Instead, Hurricanes (Mk I) were supplied as an interim measure. No. 263 Squadron left for RAF Grangemouth at the end of June 1940, where it continued re-equipping and training.

It was imperative that the Whirlwind enter service as soon as possible, so the first off the production line were to go directly into the front line. The first was flown north on 6 July by Sqn Ldr Eeles, the new commanding officer. He landed *en route* at RAF Disforth, Yorkshire, to avoid risking the aircraft in the heavy thunderstorms reported over Scotland. The next day, he continued to RAF Grangemouth, landing at Drem on the way. A further two aircraft were delivered in the following weeks. On 2 September, 263 Squadron returned to Drem with a mixture of Hurricanes and Whirlwinds. The next day Sir Archibald Sinclair, Secretary of State for Air, visited the airfield and two Whirlwinds put on a demonstration for him. Such was the interest in this new twin-engined fighter that a few days later a similar flying display was arranged for the Duke of Kent.

On 15 September, a flight of three Whirlwinds flew north to RAF Losssiemouth for exercises with 21's Blenheims. On their return they flew up the River Dee and across Ballater, much to the alarm of the locals on the ground. Balmoral Castle was close by and there were fanciful rumours that one of the duties of 263 Squadron was to protect this Royal retreat against enemy attack. In fact, Air Chief Marshal Dowding had informed Sqn Ldr Eeles that the prime role of his squadron was to defend the Royal Navy base at Rosyth, particularly as the battleship *King George V* would shortly berth there for fitting out.

The Westland Whirlwinds were not cleared for night flying when mine-laying enemy aircraft were most active, but they could perform most other duties and pilots often swapped between Whirlwinds and Hurricanes as need dictated. Much of the operational flying fell to B-Flight, which was still using Hurricanes.

Throughout September there were numerous uneventful scrambles and patrols over the mouth of the Firth of Forth, but this changed in October. During the afternoon of 2 October, a section of 263's Hurricanes were seen by an observer corps post to be flying near a Ju 88, which had reportedly flown over RAF Turnhouse at an altitude of 3,000 feet. Visibility was very bad and no interception was made. On 18 October, a Ju 88 dropped a bomb off North Berwick and then flew to the other side of the Firth of Forth to drop two bombs on Crail in Fife. A short time later, Plt Off. Ferdinand in a Hurricane caught a momentary glimpse of the Junkers, but it disappeared into thick cloud.

Despite appalling weather, further patrols were flown in the next few weeks. This devotion to duty was acknowledged after a patrol over the mouth of the Firth of Forth on the afternoon of 22 October, when 13 Group sent a message complimenting Blue Section on the way in which it had carried out operations in such conditions.

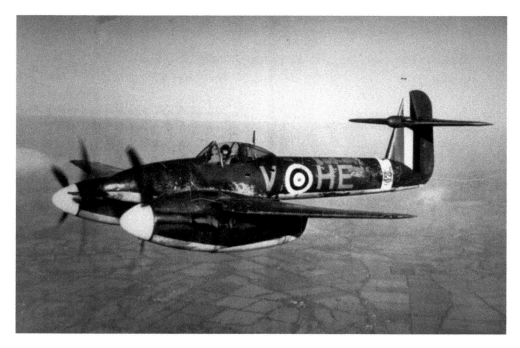

Westland Whirlwind twin-engined fighter, 263 Squadron. (*Museum of Flight, National Museums of Scotland/SCRAN*)

A-Flight, now equipped with eight Whirlwinds, was still non-operational. The prototype had been returned to its makers. A Dragon Rapide was used to ferry spare parts from the Westland Factory at Yeovil in Somerset to keep the Whirlwinds airworthy, enabling training to continue.

On 8 November, B-Flight and its Hurricanes moved to nearby RAF MacMerry, an unsatisfactory and short-lived arrangement. A short time later, eight Hurricanes deployed to RAF Prestwick to provide protection for the aircraft carrier *Formidable* in the Firth of Clyde. Several dusk patrols and a convoy patrol were flown before the detachment returned to Drem on 27 November, where the pilots were informed that the squadron was to move to RAF Exeter to operate solely with Whirlwinds: 'It was with great regret that leave was taken of the Hurricanes'.[1]

On 28 November, ten Whirlwinds departed Drem for their new home. The only other operational unit to receive the Whirlwind was 137 Squadron, which put in a brief appearance at Drem between 2 and 11 August. Resources were concentrated on producing Spitfires and Hurricanes, while development of the Whirlwind was neglected. Although it had been designed as a fighter, it had now been relegated to the role of ground attack as its engines performed poorly at altitudes above 20,000 feet. There were other technical problems, which could possibly have been rectified, but for a variety of reasons, were not. While based at Drem, 137's Whirlwinds participated with Spitfires and twin-engined Bostons in exercise 'Dryshod', but, due to bad weather, flew few sorties. When they did manage to get airborne, they made mock attacks on tanks, guns and troops. At the conclusion of the exercise, 137 Squadron returned to its base at RAF Matlaske in Norfolk. The squadron log book records the following comment about the brief excursion to Scotland: 'The change of scenery was appreciated by the Squadron and the operation turned out to be a welcome rest for everyone'.[2]

This was the last time a Whirlwind squadron was based at Drem, but there is a postscript to East Lothian's association with this aircraft. A short distance to the south and just east of Haddington was RAF Lennoxlove satellite landing ground, which served as a secret location for the storage of replacement aircraft. When withdrawn from service, many of the Whirlwinds ended up there. Later in the war, Westland developed the Welkin, a high-altitude fighter designed to combat German reconnaissance aircraft equipped with pressurised cabins. The Welkin was a development of the Whirlwind, but was not a successful design. Only sixty-seven were built, as it was found stripped-down Spitfires could perform the high-altitude role. After only a brief period of service, the Welkins were withdrawn and placed in storage at RAF Lennoxlove during the summer of 1945.

Another aircraft that was developed as a fighter, but ended up as a close support aircraft, was the Hawker Typhoon. Originally designed to replace the Hurricane and the Spitfire, the prototype flew in early 1940. It was hoped that it would be in squadron service by summer, but the first production aircraft were not delivered until the following year. Early examples were plagued by numerous problems, including engine unreliability and carbon monoxide leaks into the cockpit, though more serious were structural weaknesses. Whole tail units were becoming detached in flight, usually with fatal consequences. Of the first 150 Typhoons delivered, over 100 were involved in accidents attributed to failures of either engine or airframe. Eventually many of these problems were overcome. For instance, the cause of the tail failure was traced to a bracket on the elevator that caused it to flutter violently.

No. 197 Squadron was formed to operate the Typhoon on 21 November 1942. RAF Duxford, initially intended to be its home, was later replaced by RAF Turnhouse. This proved unsuitable for Typhoons, so the squadron moved to Drem on 25 November. The first Typhoons arrived four days later. The squadron was commanded by Sqn Ldr L. Prevot, who was in the Belgium Air Force at the beginning of the war and had escaped to Britain via Morocco. James Kyle joined the squadron on 1 December and later wrote about his experiences in his book *The Typhoon Tale*. When Kyle arrived at Drem, a number of brand-new Typhoon 1A aircraft were standing at dispersal, devoid of markings and tied down to the ground in a howling gale. Further pilots arrived throughout December, which included three Canadians, three Belgians, two New Zealanders, two Poles, one Southern Irish, and, 'two tough, extrovert Australians with the verbal delivery of a machine gun, enough for any British squadron'.

A Miles Master aircraft was allocated to the squadron for testing pilots with limited flying experience. On 12 December, Sqn Ldr Prevot made one of the first flights in a Tempest (the improved version of the Typhoon), which had to be cut short because of fumes entering the cockpit. Further Typhoons arrived during the month, making a total of ten serviceable machines on strength by 19 December. The first accident was not long in coming. Just before Christmas, Plt Off. R. Bokobza landed very heavily in DN371, causing the undercarriage to collapse—the 'lack of experience and carelessness being contributory factors'. There were also some heart stopping take-offs by the less experienced pilots. As the Tempest's tail lifted, the aircraft would swing sharply to the right; to avoid loss of control, the pilot had to apply hard left rudder.

During the closing days of December, several formation practices were flown, including one with nine aircraft formating in threes. By the end of the month, 197 Squadron had twenty pilots on strength and thirteen serviceable aircraft, despite a shortage of the appropriate tools for maintenance.

New Year 1943 started wet, curtailing most activities. A mock gas attack was made on the airfield at the beginning of the year and, on 4 January, three new sergeant pilots managed to make their first solo flight. Three days later, nine Tempests were involved in formation flying: 'Everyone feels that the Squadron is at last now taking shape'. RAF East Fortune was used for cannon firing tests as there were no suitable butts at Drem. The aircraft were tested to 25,000 feet on 10 January, an altitude the Tempests had no difficultly in reaching. The pilots reported that the cockpit remained quite warm and they felt no discomfort. Air-to-air and air-to-ground firing practice, interceptions, dogfights, and a small amount of night flying by moonlight were all undertaken in January. One flight of Tempests was declared operational as of 1 p.m. on 27 January and was immediately placed 'at readiness'. Two sections were scrambled on the last day of the month to investigate an enemy raid, but were recalled after half an hour when the aircraft were identified as 'friendly'. On 20 February, 197's Typhoons were ordered to keep a patrol between Arbroath and Dunbar at 15,000 feet, replacing Spitfires in a detail lasting about three hours. At the start of 1943 there was no certainty that the Allies would win the war, and Drem was not about to let down its guard.

At the beginning of March, the squadron was declared fully operational. This had not been without cost, as several pilots had died in training. The first fatal accident occurred on 24 January 1943 when Plt Off. Gould perished on a non-operational, cross-country flight between Drem and RAF Ayr. His Tempest DN364 flew into a hill in cloud some 6 miles from Lochwinnoch, near Paisley. Only a short time later, on 28 January, the tail came off Tempest DN364, killing its pilot Sgt C. Beechey. The stricken aircraft fell into a potting shed in Kingsburgh Gardens at East Linton, killing John McDonald, who worked there. The aircraft was flying at 2,000 feet at the time and was seen to break in two by some of the squadron's pilots at Drem. The entire tailplane had broken away from rest of the aircraft. During the following month, two pilots died on a single day in comparable incidents. On 14 February at 10.30 a.m., Plt Off. R. Bokobza's Typhoon IB DN313 was carrying out a camera gun exercise when it flew into high ground in the vicinity of Halls Farm, Lothian Edge, in East Lothian. That afternoon, Typhoon DN366 struck a hill close to Ferresay Cottage, also in East Lothian, killing its pilot Sgt J. Bowler. On 23 February, Plt Off. McNair-Taylor and Sgt Richardson crashed a Tiger Moth; the former had to be taken to hospital for treatment.

Further training—cross-country formations, air-to-sea firing, instrument flying, and weather patrols—continued in March. Night flying commenced on 14 March. There were occasional scrambles, most of which were false alarms and RAF Mosquitoes were often the culprits. On 12 March, Red Section was scrambled to intercept a Ju 88, but was recalled almost immediately, as the Junkers was too high; Spitfires of 65 Squadron were ordered up instead and eventually intercepted the enemy aircraft at 36,000 feet over the Farne Islands. After a brief burst from the fighters, the Junkers managed to give them the slip. James Kyle recounts in his book that he was scrambled to intercept a Ju 188 (a development of the Ju 88) approaching the east coast at high altitude. His aircraft and another Typhoon climbed to 30,000 feet, but there was no sign of the solitary German aircraft—'a common occurrence at this latitude and an anti-climax'.[3] This is the only reference to Drem-based fighters involved in trying to intercept this type of aircraft.

In the middle of March, an order was received that 197 Squadron was to move to RAF Tangmere: 'Never was so little news received by so many so cheerfully'.[4] The advanced party left by train on 20 March. All the pilots stood by their aircraft, but were unable to take-off because of the poor weather, a regular occurrence for squadrons departing Drem. It was not until 27 March that conditions improved enough for 197's nineteen aircraft to fly south. Of the forty-three original members of 197 Squadron (formed at Drem in December 1942) only ten survived the war.

A second Typhoon squadron, 186 (Army Support), received its first personnel on 27 April 1943, and by March approximately 120 men had been posted in addition to the No. 3120 Servicing Echelon complement. On 6 May, Fg Off. W. H. King, the squadron adjutant, was the first officer posted. Preparations were then made for the arrival of aircraft and pilots, but during the next couple of months a large number of personnel were detached to other units in 13 Group, pending delivery of the Typhoon. On 3 August, 186 Squadron moved to RAF Ayr, leaving twenty-five technical personnel to assist 488 Squadron. Due to continued delays with deliveries of the Typhoons, Hurricanes (Mk IV) were delivered to 186 squadron at Ayr as an interim replacement, but the first were not received until November.

That was not the end of Drem's association with this type of aircraft. No. 486 Squadron was scheduled to become part of 148 Airfield Headquarters based at Drem, but shortly before it moved north from RAF Beaulieu, in Hampshire, its newly delivered Tempest Vs were transferred elsewhere. No. 486 received Typhoons as interim replacements, which arrived at Drem on 28 February 1944. The unit also received four Spitfires (Mk VI) for high-level interception, but these were unserviceable.

The only operational flight flown by 486 while at Drem was a convoy patrol by eight aircraft. After a stay of little more than one week, 486 was moved to 149 Airfield Group at RAF Castle Camps, Essex, where they would eventually receive new Tempests. This location was deemed more suitable than Drem for the introduction of the successor to the Typhoon as it was much closer to Hawker's factory, providing easy access in case of teething troubles.

In the later stages of the war, the organisation of Fighter Command underwent a number of radical changes. Increasingly fighters were used in offensive operations across Nazi-occupied Europe rather than the defence of Britain. A number of wings were set up, each having several squadrons. The wing had the advantage of being an integral unit, able to move at short notice between airfields. No. 148 Airfield Headquarters was formed at Drem on 23 February 1944:

> To fulfil its operational role, the Airfield is to be fully equipped and established to carry one night fighter squadron and one day fighter squadron and capable of servicing a third squadron.[5]

No. 29 Squadron (Mosquito XII and XIII) and 486 Squadron were originally assigned to this role but the latter was replaced by 91 Squadron (Spitfire XIV). Many of its officers were transferred *en masse* from Drem Station Headquarters. Among them was Wg Cdr Sheen, the station commander, who now took charge of 148 Airfield Headquarters:

> The initial issue of equipment was made by the Air Ministry and has arrived in vast quantities throughout the month.
>
> The allotment of motor transport far exceeded the capabilities of the Section to collect. In the middle of March, the Section was faced with some 70 vehicles to collect from points as far distant as Stafford and only 6 drivers on strength. The gap was filled by experienced drivers in civilian life.
>
> A requirement exists for the training of over 130 drivers capable of all aspects of convoy driving and beach landing. An additional 260 drivers are required as second and reserve drivers.[6]

Several days of rain and the soggy state of the camp site had necessitated postponement of the move from 1 April to 8 April 1944. All 148 Airfield Headquarters slept under canvas, but officers remained in buildings and meals continued to be taken in the station messes: 'The rain continued over the next few days completely water logging the tent site and necessitating its removal to a new location'.

At the end of the month, 148 Airfield Headquarters were given instructions to move to RAF West Malling to become 148 Fighter Wing. The main road party left Drem on 27 April, followed by most of the other personnel on a special train at midnight. No. 29's Mosquitoes had flown south earlier that day. Sqn Ldr P. Ottewill assumed command. The station strength was reduced to a holding establishment only, which meant that difficulty was experienced in obtaining personnel for the normal administrative routine jobs.

Drem was now becoming a ghost of its former self.

The Twin-Engine Night Fighters

At the outbreak of the Second World War, air raids were confined to daylight hours, so once the sun had set there was little need of protection from German aircraft. Responding to its daytime losses, Germany switched to operating under the cloak of darkness, and became a formidable adversary. The first large-scale night raid was on 28 August 1940, when 160 bombers attacked Liverpool.

In late 1939, RAF Fighter Command's Achilles heel was its inability to defend the country at night. Hurricanes and Spitfires, without airborne radar, were of little use after dark. There were also seven squadrons of twin-engined Bristol Blenheim fighters, of which there were around 111 in front-line service. The Blenheims had been converted from a bomber into a long-range fighter by the addition of four machine guns mounted in a pack under the fuselage. They required a crew of two or three and were deemed most suited to the role of protecting the night skies.

To the great relief to 602 Squadron, whose Spitfires had hitherto been responsible for maintaining air cover at Drem around the clock, the twelve Blenheims of 29 Squadron arrived on 4 April 1940. Maintaining radio silence, the aircraft flew up the east coast in formation from RAF Martlesham, near Ipswich. A former Imperial Airway's ensign transported the essential stores and ground crew.

The first operational patrol was flown the next day over Methil Bay, the area used for assembling convoys bound for destinations as diverse as the south of England and Murmansk. On 7 April, the Blenheims provided protection for a convoy sailing some 10 miles off the east coast. The section, led by Flt Lt Adam, escorted the ships from Inverbervie to Kinnairds Head. Instructions were received to return to base, but these were subsequently cancelled and the section was instructed to investigate unidentified aircraft proceeding west. Before contact was made, the Blenheims were again ordered to return to Drem, landing in failing light and low cloud. The unidentified aircraft were believed to have been carrying out a raid on Scapa Flow.

Standing patrols were flown over convoys assembling in Methil Bay throughout the month, and on the 9 April numerous daytime patrols were flown in protection of shipping. Three Blenheims escorted four Royal Navy cruisers in the Firth of Forth. Most patrols were uneventful, although on 17 April Blenheim L1375 had to abort its patrol due to a loose rear escape hatch. On 18 April, there were two uneventful

A preserved example of a Bristol Blenheim (Mk I) at an air show at East Fortune. (*Malcolm Fife*)

scrambles and on the 23rd three Blenheims were sent to check out an aircraft near St Andrews, but it was identified as a 'friendly'.

At the end of April and the beginning of May, 29's Blenheims participated in radio direction-finding exercises, which involved flying 60 miles out to sea from St Abb's Head, near Drone Hill Radar Station. On 9 May, taking off at 4.35 a.m., three Blenheims patrolled between Crail, May Island and North Berwick, but no enemy were sighted. Around midday, three aircraft took off to intercept three unidentified aircraft flying some 40 miles east of May Island, but were recalled when the aircraft were reported to be 'friendly'. In the meantime, three more Blenheims scrambled to locate another enemy aircraft east of May Island, with no result. There was yet another alert at 4.50 p.m., when a section of three took off to intercept a supposed enemy aircraft east of May Island. This patrol was recalled no sooner than it had left the ground. The day ended when Blenheim L1327 struck an obstacle on landing at 11.05 p.m. The lone pilot was unhurt, but some structural damage was sustained.

The following day, 10 May, Fighter Command ordered 29 Squadron to deploy to RAF Debden, in Essex. As was usual at Drem, this was effected almost immediately. Thirteen Blenheims and crew flew south in 'vic' formation in sections arriving at their new base at 5.45 p.m. One officer and seventy-nine airmen left by rail at 7.30 p.m., arriving at Debden at 9 a.m. on 11 May. With the long days and short nights experienced in Scotland in summer there was not a present need for specialised night fighter squadrons, so the Hurricanes and Spitfires reverted to providing both day and night patrols. In the autumn (24 October), as the nights began to draw in, 600 (City of London) Royal Auxiliary Air Force Squadron, based at RAF Catterick, dispatched a small number of its Blenheims to Drem. B-Flight remained at Drem throughout the winter months and were joined by the remainder of the squadron in March 1941.

Following the departure of 29's Blenheims from Drem, a new twin-engined purpose-built night fighter—the Bristol Beaufighter—entered service in September 1940. It was powerfully armed with 20-mm cannon and six machine guns. Most significantly, it incorporated the effective short range, high precision AI Mark IV air-to-air radar.

The radar network was further improved. 'A' network ground-controlled interception (GCI) stations were established and were the first to use radar screens with the 'rotating clock face'. This display enabled the ground controller to accurately direct the night fighter to the enemy's position. The new GCI stations worked in co-operation with the older Chain Home Radar stations, such as Drone Hill. Chain Home would raise an alert and the fighters would be scrambled. The medium range GCI radar would then direct the fighters to within a short distance of the enemy bombers. The radar operator in the night fighter would then use the A1 air-to-air radar to close in and attack its target.

Dirleton ground-controlled interception station came into operation in April 1941. Initially the transmitter was housed in a three-ton trailer with the receiver in a second trailer. The operations room was fitted on another four-wheeled trailer, but this arrangement was replaced in the summer of 1942 by wooden huts. These in turn gave way to a large brick structure located on the north side of the village, not far from the road to Yellowcraigs Beach. With this facility, Drem gained a reputation as a training establishment for night fighter pilots and the Royal Navy had a training squadron permanently based there during the latter part of the war. Beaufighters with the OTUs based at nearby RAF East Fortune also made extensive use of the Dirleton GCI station to familiarise themselves with the techniques of interception directed by radar controllers on the ground.

The winter weather restricted operational flying in early March 1941 for 600 Squadron at its base at RAF Catterick, Yorkshire, and its detachments at RAF Prestwick (A-Flight) and RAF Drem (B-Flight). New Beaufighters were being delivered to replace the Blenheim IV and some daylight practice with the A1 radar had been undertaken. On 13 March, squadron headquarters was instructed to move to Drem. That same evening, Glasgow and Clydeside were attacked by 263 aircraft of Luftflotten 2 and 3. The conflagration, involving warehouses along the river and other industrial installations, could be seen miles away. A Drem-based Blenheim of 600 Squadron, flown by Plt Off. Gordon Denby and his operator Plt Off. Gilbert Guest, succeeded in shooting down a He 111 south of Glasgow at 9.51 p.m. The enemy aircraft was operated by KG 100, an elite pathfinder unit, whose function was to locate the targets for the main bomber force. The Heinkel was the Squadron's first definite kill. On succeeding nights, nature again restricted 600 Squadron's flying activity:

The moon waned and the weather closed in again with the result that bad weather state succeeded bad weather state with almost monotonous regularity.[1]

'C Watch' of Dirleton ground-controlled interception unit at their billet during July 1944. The group is composed of men and women, either serving in the Royal Air Force, Womens Royal Air Force, or Womens Auxiliary Air Force. Most were conscripts who had to serve for the duration of the conflict. (*East Lothian Museum Service/SCRAN*)

A vertical photograph of East Fortune airfield that was built originally as a satellite for Drem and subsequently served to train night-fighter crews. However, it still continued to be used by aircraft from Drem. (*Royal Commission on the Ancient and Historical Monuments of Scotland/SCRAN*)

A further three Beaufighters were delivered that month, and by the beginning of April the number of pilots in the unit had increased to nineteen. However, there had been little improvement in the weather:

> An English Spring may be something to write lyrics about but the Scottish variety seems little different from the winter with its attendant bad weather states and for the first week of the month scarcely any flying took place.[2]

The moon came up on the night of 6 and 7 April. Flt Lt Hayes was on patrol in the vicinity of the Bell Rock at 14,000 feet, when he caught a glimpse of a He 111, which immediately opened fire. The reflector gun sight in the Beaufighter vibrated so badly that Hayes was unable to sight properly, so he fired one long burst, emptying the four ammunition drums. The Heinkel dived away steeply and disappeared. Hayes claimed it as a probable kill, but this was later disallowed. The following night, Wg Cdr Stainforth, 600's CO, fired on a Ju 88 at 13,000 feet over the Pentland Hills. After a short burst, during which the Junkers was seen to falter, the Beaufighter's cannon jammed. The Ju 88 returned fire, then dived steeply into cloud. Again, this was claimed as a probable kill, but was disallowed as no wreckage was found:

> Excitement died down as the moon waned and we were frequently compelled to operate from Acklington owing to weather conditions at Drem without, however, having any luck.[3]

Wg Cdr G. A. Wood arrived at Drem on 18 April. He was anxious to study night fighter operations at first hand, but during his stay there was little activity. With the approach of spring and shorter nights, AM Douglas felt that there would be an increase in attacks on southern Britain. In anticipation of this, on 24 April he sanctioned the transfer of 600 Squadron to RAF Colerne, near Bath. The Beaufighters and the few remaining Blenheims completed their move by 28 April. The squadron was less than impressed with the new base:

> … we arrived at an aerodrome which seemed a mass of unfinished buildings, unfinished roads, unfinished everything, perched on a hill top of 800 feet above sea level, but this does not matter as we understand Huns come over as in the old days at Redhill.[4]

As the nights lengthened at the end of 1941, 141 Squadron provided a small detachment of Beaufighters (Mk I) to Drem from its main base at RAF Ayr. The two aircraft flew only two patrols during the whole of October 1941. Early in 1942, this squadron moved its main base to RAF Acklington, but the detachment at Drem remained. Four all-night individual patrols were flown in January 1942, but no contact was made. The small number of missions flown is surprising, as enemy activity continued along the north-east coast. A handful of operational patrols were flown in succeeding months, the only incidents of note being two accidents. The first occurred on 16 March when FS Henderson, pilot of Beaufighter X7566, had trouble with his landing gear. His two crew members, FS Chard and FS Hogg, baled out safely near Drem. Henderson belly landed at the airfield and escaped injury. On the night of 25 March, Plt Off. Benn and his radio observer Sgt Hall in Beaufighter X7576 also experienced undercarriage trouble. They baled out successfully on the orders of the Drem station commander. A month later, a Beaufighter was scrambled to intercept a single enemy aircraft, but the crew were unable to make contact. The detachment came to an end in June 1942 when 141 Squadron left for a posting in the south of England.

At the beginning of September 1942, two crews from A-Flight and three crews from B-Flight of 219 Squadron's Beaufighters (Mk 1F) from RAF Acklington, acted as guardians of the night sky from Drem. Their first patrol took place on 9 September and the last on 29 September, all flown at night. No. 219's Beaufighters left RAF Acklington on 21 October for RAF Scorton, Yorkshire. The following year, 409 Canadian Squadron operated a similar arrangement. Its main force of Beaufighters (Mk VI) were also stationed at RAF Acklington, but a small number flew from Drem.

Equipped with the Beaufighter II, 488 Squadron, composed of New Zealanders, reformed at RAF Church Fenton at the end of June 1942 then moved to RAF Prestwick to complete its training at the beginning of September. A small number of its aircraft were detached to Drem to provide night fighter cover during the forthcoming winter. Initially, it was only one Beaufighter, but on the instruction of AOC 13 Group this was soon increased to an entire flight. During October 1942, there were a number of scrambles. On 2 October, a Beaufighter at readiness was scrambled at 6.45 p.m. to intercept an enemy aircraft 80 miles north-east, flying south, only to be recalled as the target turned east towards Europe. There was another alert on 11 October when a Beaufighter took off at 9.15 p.m. in response to an enemy raid in the vicinity of Newcastle. After forty-five minutes in the air, its radio failed and it had to return to base. A second Beaufighter took over, but no contact was made. At 9.50 p.m. on 24 October, Sgt Boulton was ordered to investigate a report of an unidentified aircraft which was identified shortly after take-off as an RAF Wellington—the second time that evening that an 'enemy' aircraft turned out to be a 'friendly'.

Towards the end of the month a 'gun saturation' exercise was arranged with 36 AA Brigade at Turnhouse, North Berwick and Linlithgow. Four Beaufighters of A-Flight took off at 10 a.m., but very bad weather forced them back to Drem after only twenty minutes. Little operational flying took place in November. A Beaufighter was damaged on landing and a visiting machine (X7931) from 125 Squadron overshot and ran into a dispersal pen in bad visibility.

During the first half of 1943, 488 Squadron remained at RAF Ayr with a small detachment of its Beaufighters at Drem. On the evening of 13 January 1943, an aircraft was scrambled to investigate an unidentified aircraft flying south, some 120 miles north-east. It was later identified as 'friendly'. In January and February, Beaufighters assisted in three Air Sea Rescues. At 2 p.m. on 12 February, a Beaufighter was scrambled to patrol in the vicinity of May Island with no result. Ten days later, Sgt N. Knox and Sgt Ryan patrolled over Leuchars and 20 miles out to sea to search for a downed Beaufighter, but were recalled when Air Sea Rescue took over.

Perhaps the most testing day for the detachment at Drem came on 12 March when German aircraft were reported to be bombing Newcastle. One Beaufighter was dispatched and flew south to Northumberland, but encountered no German planes. No. 488 Squadron sent three additional Beaufighters from its base at RAF Ayr to reinforce Drem. WO Reed and FS Bricker's Beaufighter had no sooner landed at 9 p.m. than it was scrambled and instructed to fly south-east at 12,000 feet. They were given a vector by GCI to the enemy aircraft, now some 4,000 feet away and 40 degrees below. Reed realised he was overtaking it, so he slowed to 150 mph and lost height. After descending to 8,000 feet, the enemy aircraft was now 12,000 feet away and 10 to 15 degrees to the right. Immediately afterwards, it was lost. More vectors were given by GCI, but there was no further contact and the crew landed at 11.15 p.m. The following day the detachment at Drem was again strengthened by four Beaufighters flown in from RAF Ayr, which returned the following day without being scrambled.

During May and June, many of 488's aircraft deployed to RAF Middle Wallop in southern England, from where they flew frequent missions over France, destroying numerous trains. Little of note happened back at Drem, with the Beaufighters there assisting in the occasional air-sea rescues. A signal was received from 13 Group Headquarters on 1 August to move the entire squadron from RAF Ayr to Drem. Beaufighters were at a state of readiness from 5.30 p.m. two days later.

The career of the Beaufighter Mk VIF with 488 Squadron was nearing its end. The first two Mosquitoes (Mk XII), equipped with the new centimetric AI Mark VIII radar, arrived on 8 August, with a further three machines being delivered a few days later. A 'circus' of several aircraft equipped with these new radar sets arrived on 13 August, under the Command of Sqn Ldr W. Green, to provide aerial instruction on the equipment. The previous day, a Beaufighter was sent to investigate an 'X' raid to the north of Peterhead. After receiving various vectors, it was ordered to orbit at 1,000 feet to search the sea for a raider thought to have crashed. After fifteen minutes it descended to sea level to investigate a light, which was found to be a light buoy, at which point the Beaufighter was recalled.

There was concern that there would be further enemy activity in the Aberdeen/Peterhead area. Wg Cdr P. R. Burton-Gyles DSO DFC flew a daily patrol over the area, but, as the enemy did not put in an appearance, this duty was discontinued a few days later.

Plt Off. N. Knox and his radar operator Plt Off. T. Ryan were training for single-engine flying in one of the newly delivered Mosquitoes (Mk XII), when one prop refused to unfeather. The engine over-revved and the aircraft lost height from 2,000 feet to 400 feet over the sea, some 25 miles from Drem. Knox kept the machine airborne and eventually Ryan managed to unfeather the prop. They landed safely. Four days later, on 21 August, there was another narrow escape; Plt Off. G. Reed and his radar operator Plt Off. R. Bricker were taking off on a radar exercise when they flew into a flock of seagulls. The right wing hit one of the birds, causing a hole close to the engine. They completed the exercise and returned safely to base.

At the end of August, violent riots and a wave of sabotage swept Nazi-occupied Denmark. The Germans dismissed the civil government and imposed martial law. Some

Danes managed to flee and, on 30 August, Drem received information that a flotilla of fishing boats were heading towards the coast. In the early morning, two Beaufighters (Mk VI) and two Mosquitoes of 488 Squadron mounted an unsuccessful search. Two other Beaufighters (Mk VI) continued the search and were given a pin-point location in the North Sea, roughly 200 miles east of Drem. At 9.40 a.m., a Mosquito and a Beaufighter spotted the fishing boats spread over a 20-mile area. In rain and clouds down to 700 feet, the two aircraft circled the boats as they made their way slowly westwards in the heavy seas. The refugees recognised the aircraft as friendly and waved sheets. The aircraft remained with the Danes until low fuel forced their return.

The month ended in tragedy for 488 Squadron. Pilot FS S. Gordon and Plt Off. L. M. Rawlings were killed when their Mosquito MkXII HK183 flipped over and crashed from 500 feet, within sight of Drem at Congleton Farm, near Kingston. The aircraft had flown through the wake turbulence of a Beaufighter from nearby RAF East Fortune.

On 3 September, 488 Squadron was ordered to move to RAF Bradwell Bay in Essex. Six Mosquitoes and seven Beaufighters left the same day, with the ground crews following by rail later. The next day, ten Beaufighters of 96 Squadron arrived to convert to the night fighter version of the Mosquito. To assist with the training, a dual-control Mosquito Mk III HJ864 was delivered from RAF Ayr. On 9 September, three aircraft were dispatched to RAF Peterhead to provide protection against enemy night bombers. From 6-19 September, Fighter Command Navigator (Radio) Conversion Flight was based at Drem to familiarise 96 Squadron personnel with the new equipment. C-in-C, Air Marshal Sir Trafford Leigh-Mallory, met all aircrew at the dispersal and afterwards dined in the mess with all officer air crews:

> He told us he was very sorry for the way the Squadron had been treated in the past and he also stated that as soon as the Squadron is re-equipped we will move down south where there will be more activity.[5]

Some operational missions were flown during the squadron's stay in Scotland. Not long after midnight on 22 September, one Beaufighter took off from RAF Peterhead to investigate a report of a raid off Aberdeen. Fighters from Drem also patrolled the mouth of the Firth of Forth, but nothing was sighted.

A few days later the detachment at RAF Peterhead was withdrawn and replaced by 409 and 604 Squadrons, each supplying two Beaufighters fitted with Mark VIII AI radar. There were several attempts over the next few weeks to intercept German high-altitude weather reconnaissance aircraft. On 30 September, two 96 Squadron aircraft took off at first light but saw nothing. This was repeated on October 1, 2, 3, 7, and 8. Five days later, an aircraft was sent to investigate a report of an 'X' raid, but the culprit was an RAF Halifax.

On 18 October, two of 604's Beaufighters, based at RAF Scorton in Yorkshire were attempting to intercept a 'weather willie' reconnaissance aircraft, when bad weather forced them to land at Drem. They later departed, but made it only as far as RAF Charterhall in Berwickshire, as the poor weather persisted over Yorkshire.

On 7 November, FS McLardy crashed while making a single-engine landing in Mosquito HK373, injuring his observer Fg Off Hankins. The next morning, 96 Squadron's stay ended when its Mosquitoes took off for RAF West Malling. The squadron would go on to great success, claiming some twenty enemy aircraft in the coming months. Drem did not have to wait long for its next Mosquito deployment, as the following day 307 Squadron arrived (see Chapter 10).

The final night fighter squadron to operate from Drem was 29 Squadron, which arrived on 1 March 1944 to become part of 148 Airfield Wing. Coincidentally, this unit had been the first twin-engined night fighter squadron based at Drem. It had long since given up the Blenheim and now flew the potent Mosquito Mk XIII with the Mark VIII airborne radar. Training commenced shortly after the Squadron's arrival, and on 4 March, six Mosquitoes committed fifty-six 'murders' on some 300 Allied bombers flying from bases in England to Northern Scotland. Towards the end of the month two Mosquitoes performed a low-level patrol off Peterhead in a fruitless search for 'a low flying Hun which comes over on reconnaissance on most nights'. March closed with GCI training, cine-gun practice, air-to-air firing, and cross-country flying.

There were now thirty crews, probably more than ever before. Among them were several Americans. The pilots were initially housed in Greywalls House, Gullane. An order that the personnel should move into tents on 1 April was greeted with little enthusiasm. Due to howling gales and heavy rain, the move did not take place until 8 April.

> [The bad weather continued and] the squadron almost became waterborne for the first time in its history, owing to the flooding of the camp sites. A popular move to drier ground was undertaken, the airmen displaying notable glee on finding that their new site was adjacent to the camp cinema.[6]

Poor weather curtailed the training programme until 6 April when an improvement enabled six aircraft to carry out air-to-air firing practice and, later, low-level daylight interceptions and cross-country flying. A Ju 88 was reported overflying Peterhead at dusk on several occasions and on 23 April, two of 29's Mosquitoes made an unsuccessful attempt to ambush the marauder. The following day, a further mission was flown in the hope the Junkers would turn up, 'but the Jerry would not play'. At 2.15 p.m. on 27 April, two Mosquitoes were scrambled to investigate an unidentified aircraft reported flying towards Peterhead, but it was later identified as a 'friendly'. This would have been the last opportunity to intercept the elusive Ju 88, as the squadron then moved south to RAF West Malling with the rest of 148 Airfield Wing. Ground crews departed on 30 April, followed by the Mosquitoes the next day. B-Flight formed up over Drem at about 8.30 a.m., followed shortly afterwards by A-Flight. At its new home the squadron was to be housed in tents, so its Scottish experience was not wasted.

The Bolton Paul Defiant Squadrons

While most of the specialist night fighter squadrons that flew from Drem were equipped with twin-engined Blenheims and Beaufighters, there were two exceptions—141 and 410 Squadrons, which operated the single-engined Bolton Paul Defiant. One feature it had in common with the twin-engined night fighters was that it had a crew of two, but it was there that any similarity ended.

Superficially, the Defiant was not unlike the Hurricane and Spitfire. The press in the early months of the war often mentioned the Defiant with the same reverence as the other two. Instead of having the early Hurricane and Spitfire's eight wing-mounted Browning machine guns, the Defiant relied on a four-gun powered turret at the rear of the cockpit. In many ways this was a throwback to the fighters of the First World War and the inter-war years, when the only threat to Britain was envisaged to be unescorted enemy bomber formations.

In the 1930s it was thought that the defensive crossfire from large formations of enemy bombers would be lethal against conventional fighters attacking from the rear. The rear-turreted Defiant, would attack by flying below, ahead or to one side, where the bombers could not provide protective fire. Had the Defiants been based in Scotland when the first air raids of the war took place, they may have had the same success as the Spitfires and Hurricanes. Most German bombers over Scotland were unescorted as German fighters at the time did not have the range. However, during the Battle of Britain, the Germans rarely dispatched their bombers without escorts. The Defiants suffered heavily and, as losses mounted, it was decided in August 1940 to switch them from daylight operations to night.

On 19 July 1940, six Defiants of 141 Squadron were destroyed by Bf 109s near Folkestone, Kent. Three days later, the squadron was moved from the front line to Scotland, and was initially based at RAF Prestwick and RAF Grangemouth. On 30 July, three Defiants flew to RAF Drem to patrol at the mouth of the Firth of Forth but no enemy were encountered. On 30 August, 141 Squadron moved to RAF Turnhouse, where it commenced training as a night fighter squadron. On 5 September, Plt Off. Constantine and air gunner Plt Off. Webber in Defiant N1566 of A-Flight were on night patrol from RAF Turnhouse. They briefly sighted an enemy aircraft in the searchlights over St Abb's Head, but it managed to escape. At this time the

Bolton Paul Defiant V1110 night fighter of 410 Squadron on a winter's day at RAF Drem. (*IWM HU64553*)

Defiants were without AI radar, so the aircrew had only their own eyesight, aided by searchlights or anti-aircraft gunfire, to spot an enemy aircraft. Moonlight was greatly favoured.

Night-flying training continued from 12 September to 15 October when the squadron moved to RAF Drem. Operational flights by the Defiants commenced the same night, but the squadron's stay was short-lived, as instructions were received on 20 October that A-Flight and Headquarters were to move to Gatwick to join B-Flight. The following day, transport aircraft arrived to take the operational crews to Gatwick, but the departure of the transports and the Defiants was prevented by bad weather. A train left late at night with the airmen and equipment and arrived at Horley Station in Surrey at 4 p.m. the following day. The final leg to Gatwick was by road.

The Defiants and transports remained weather-bound at Drem until 23 October. They managed to reach RAF Church Fenton in Yorkshire for refuelling, but were prevented from continuing their journey, again due to bad weather. The following day the Defiants managed to take off, but had to divert to Farnborough and Reading airfields. Most of them finally arrived at Gatwick on 25 October. Undercarriage problems and damage when landing at RAF Cottesmore meant Plt Off. Edwards had to complete his journey by train.

It was ten months before another Defiant squadron deployed to Drem. The Defiants had now been equipped with AI radar, enabling effective night interceptions. During the winter of 1940–41, it had the highest number of 'kills' per interception of any night fighter type. On 1 August 1941, 410 squadron was ordered to move most of its headquarters and aircraft to Drem, and on the 6th, nine aircraft of B-Flight left RAF Ayr. On arrival, the undercarriage of Defiant I T4120 failed to lower and the pilot, Sgt S. Lewis, made a crash-landing and escaped unscathed. The following day, Defiant I N100 crashed making a night landing. The pilot, Sgt Brooks, was also not hurt. One operational flight remained at 410's base, RAF Ayr. This Royal Canadian Air Force Squadron, whose motto appropriately was 'Wandering by Night', was formed at Ayr on 30 June. A further six Defiants were also ordered to move to RAF Acklington to provide night fighter coverage for north-east England.

On 18 August, Sgt W. A. Du Perrier lost control of his Defiant V1125 in cloud. He instructed his passenger, Cpl Jenkinson, to bale out of the gun turret. A few moments later Du Perrier regained control and landed safely back at Drem, minus his passenger. Throughout the month of August, 410's Defiants flew numerous daylight training flights.

Given the long daylight hours experienced by Scotland in the summer, night flying had to take place at unearthly hours and no doubt deprived local residents of a good night's sleep. For example, between 12.55 a.m. and 1.45 a.m. on 9 August four aircraft practised circuits and landing. Training recommenced at 2.10 a.m. and continued to 4.10 a.m. On 31 August, no less than ten aircraft were involved in night flying between 9.10 p.m. and 5.15 a.m., with each airborne for an hour or so. Two aircraft flew to RAF Montrose on 15 August and on 18 August eight aircraft flew to the squadron's former base at RAF Ayr.

Towards the end of August, four pilots of B-Flight completed training and were declared operational. By the end of the month, 13 Group Headquarters declared 410 Squadron operational. Not all members of the unit displayed equal dedication. AC2 C. Holman (ex-Sgt Gunner) was arrested by civil police at Fort William as he was absent without leave. On his repatriation to the squadron, he was sentenced to twenty-eight days detention by Wg Cdr H. West, Drem's O/C.

The month ended on a low note. While night flying, a Defiant I crewed by Sgt D. W. Hall (pilot) and Sgt D. Cresswell (air gunner) crashed into the top of Bleak Law Hill, approximately 4 miles south-east of Gifford. At daybreak, six Defiants took off to search, but the crash site was not found for some time due to its remote location. The aircraft had been totally wrecked and both men had perished. A service funeral was held for Sgt D. Hall at Dirleton on 2 September.

This was not the only fatal accident involving a Defiant in East Lothian during August 1941. The recently opened airfield at East Fortune, situated approximately 3 miles to the south-east of Drem, was home to 60 OTU, specialising in instruction in night fighting. It had over thirty Defiants on strength and they often flew the short distance to Drem to practise landings and take-offs. On 15 August one of their aircraft (N1692) hit a farm building while attempting to make a forced landing near the airfield. The gunner managed to parachute to safety but the pilot, Sgt F. Westray, was killed.

Now the squadron was operational, training flights declined and scrambles became routine. By September the unit was responsible for providing night fighter coverage to south-east Scotland. During the course of the month there were several uneventful alarms. Other duties included a single Defiant participating in searchlight co-operation exercises.

A Miles Magister aircraft (T9874) was acquired from RAF Turnhouse on 9 September for transport and training purposes. Just three days later, it made a forced landing at Mount Lothian, near Penicuik, due to engine failure. Both occupants were uninjured and the aircraft was repairable. No. 410 Squadron would often be let down by this Magister. On 5 October, it made a forced landing at Drem, again due to engine failure. Neither crew member was hurt. On 20 October, a signal was received from 13 Group:

> [To] reduce 410 Squadron's detachment at RAF Ouston to six aircraft and air crews with minimum essential ground personnel. Air crews are to be exchanged between Drem and Ouston as Squadron decides but minimum stay at Ouston should be 14 days. Readiness 2 flights at thirty minutes. Drem state one flight at readiness.[1]

Relatively little night flying was done by the squadron during October. The total number of hours flown (including Defiants based at RAF Ouston) were:

	Daytime	Nightime
Non-operational hours	296	66
Operational hours	nil	23

There were several scrambles during October, the most notable on 2 October when no less than nine Defiants took off shortly after 8 p.m. As in the previous month, all proved uneventful. Non-operational flights included further searchlight co-operation exercises, GCI flights and one flight to test the petrol consumption of a Defiant. Drogue towing to provide a target for live firing was performed by a single aircraft on 25 and 26 October.

As winter approached and the nights lengthened, there was increasing dependence on the skills of the night fighter pilots. No. 410's Defiants participated in a small number of scrambles, but, as on previous occasions, no contacts were made. Air-to-air firing exercises utilising a Defiant towing a drogue target were now frequent. On 25 November, no less than seven Defiants were involved in air-to-sea gunnery practice. Between 11.25 p.m. and 1.10 a.m. on the same day, a searchlight co-operation exercise was flown.

On the morning of 19 November, Defiant N3385, after completing camera-gun practice, landed at Drem in fog and struck one of 611's Spitfire (P8248) on the west side of the airfield. The Defiant was wrecked but the crew escaped unhurt. By the end of November 410 Squadron had eighteen Defiant Mk I and one Magister on strength. The composition of the personnel was:

	Aircrew	Ground Crew
RCAF Officers	1	4
RCAF Airmen	11	70
RAF Officers	10	2 (incl. 1 Belgian)
RAF Airmen	23	124 (incl. 1 Canadian)
RAAF (Australian)	3	0
Total	48	200

On 2 December, Air Cdr L. Stevenson, AOC RCAF, paid a farewell visit to the squadron prior to his return to Canada. A few days after this morale boosting visit, the squadron suffered a severe setback. On 8 December, pilot Flt Lt Day and his rear gunner FS Townsend scrambled Defiant V1137 after an enemy aircraft was reported. They were unable to locate it and were instructed to return. The weather and visibility were poor, so the aircraft was taken over by ZZ (a ground-controlled blind landing system). At approximately 7 p.m., on approach with its undercarriage down, the Defiant hit the top of a clump of trees south-east of North Berwick some 6 miles short of the runway. It lost its wings, engine, and Perspex from the pilot's cockpit and turret cupola and was finally stopped when it struck and demolished a large tree. Flames soared to 12 feet from the engine and forward part of the fuselage, but did not endure as the petrol tanks had fallen out on the initial impact. Townsend managed to crawl out of the turret and release the harness of the pilot, who was suffering from severe head injuries, but was conscious. His feet were jammed in the rudder pedals, but he was eventually pulled clear.

James Ferguson of Blackdykes farm then arrived and assisted Townsend to inflate and invert the plane's dinghy to serve as a bed. They wrapped Day in his parachute for warmth. Townsend was suffering from a cut above his eye and from shock to such an extent that he collapsed twice. Flt Lt Day was taken at first to Edinburgh Military Hospital and then, due to the seriousness of his injuries, to Bangour Hospital. Three days later, he was still seriously ill, but showing signs of improvement. The accident was considered a severe blow to the squadron as Flt Lt Day was an original member and was the commander of B-Flight. The actions of FS Townsend were highly praised and his name put forward for the George Medal.

While most of the crashes could be attributed to pilot error, the state of serviceability of the Defiants with 410 Squadron was causing concern. By 20 December, the squadron strength was down to seventeen effective aircraft.

On 21 December, a signal was received from Headquarters 13 Group, instructing four of 410's Defiants to deploy to RAF Dyce, near Aberdeen, to protect shipping during the fading hours of daylight and at night. This lead to the unpopular cancelling of all New Year's leave for B-Flight. The maintenance party of thirty airmen with one officer headed for Dyce on Christmas Day. The four Defiants arrived on 27 December after a weather delay. While at Dyce, Sgt W. Du Perrier was sent up soon after midnight in poor weather to find a Coastal Command Lockheed Hudson that had got lost returning from Norway. He was vectored in the vicinity of the bomber by controllers at Dyce and after some minutes, sighted the aircraft. The Defiant gunner signalled to it and, despite the failure of their radio, the Hudson crew were able to acknowledge the Defiant and follow it to Dyce where both machines landed safely. During their stay, 410's aircrew were impressed with the effectiveness of the special control equipment at Dyce:

Such equipment and operators for it, if installed at Drem, would give 410 Squadron a real chance to make the most of the few bandits which approach the sector.[2]

Operational flying for the squadron for December was limited to occasional patrols and scrambles with no interceptions. Night flying consisted mainly of sector reconnaissance and GCI practice and calibration. Flying during daylight hours comprised mainly of gun-camera and air-firing exercises and aircraft tests.

The toll among Defiant aircrew flying from East Lothian was further increased as 1941 drew to a close. On 30 December, 60 OTU Defiant N1680, while on circuits in deteriorating weather, struck the ground 150 feet west of Drem railway station, killing the pilot.

On 8 January 1942 the four Defiants returned from their detachment at Dyce: 'We have received a message of appreciation from the fighter sector controller at Dyce. We have, in fact, been invited to go up there again'. The normal state was resumed at Drem the next night. Two aircraft were at immediate readiness, with a further two each at thirty-minute and sixty-minute availability. The Magister (T9874) departed on 10 January to RAF St Athan to be equipped for night flying practice. A few days later, a party of twenty-nine Canadians arrived to join 410 Squadron: 'These airmen have only just disembarked and have hardly got their land legs yet'.

Flying training was hampered by the winter weather. On 17 January, there was another accident. At dusk (6.30 p.m.), Sgt M. Montgomery was returning to Drem in Defiant N1565 after an air test when he attempted to land down-wind and overshot. He ground looped to avoid the airfield boundary and the undercarriage collapsed. The damage was repairable and the relatively inexperienced pilot was uninjured. The poor weather continued. On 22 January there was heavy fall of snow, melted by rain the following day. Instructions were again received to send two Defiants to RAF Dyce, this time for convoy protection duties to commence on 26 January, but due to the weather the aircraft were unable to depart until 28 January. They managed to fly within sight of Dyce but found the airfield snowbound and were forced to return. The maintenance party for the detachment which had travelled by surface transport had managed to reach Dyce, where they were kept occupied clearing the snow. On 2 February the maintenance party was recalled as the allotted Defiants were still stuck on the ground at Drem. By this stage the squadron had a total of twenty Defiants on strength of which eighteen were serviceable. Personnel now included around 60 per cent Canadians:

	Aircrew	Ground Crew
RCAF Officers	4	4 (incl. 2 Americans)
RCAF Airmen	11	113 (incl. 1 American)
RAF Officers	16	2 (Incl. 1 Belgian)
RAF Airmen	21	82
RAAF Officers	1	0
RAAF Airmen	2	0
Total	55	201

On 8 February, 410 Squadron acquired a Blenheim (L8549), which had been left behind by 141 Squadron. It appears this was done on the initiative of the squadron's officers:

We intend using the aircraft for training pilots on twins, in the hopeful anticipation that our new re-equipment with twin engined aircraft (Beaufighters seems to be the popular choice) will not be long delayed. All our pilots are keen on the idea.[3]

The Magister (T9874) also returned fitted with night flying equipment. Little flying was done in the first part of the month due to the poor weather, but by 11 February it had began to improve. At 7.35 p.m. on 12 February FS E. King was scrambled to locate an alleged enemy aircraft, but was unable to locate it and returned. 15 February proved an eventful night for 410 Squadron. A Defiant on local night flying practice was vectored by ground control onto an aircraft some 60 miles off Arbroath. The pilot recognised it as a RAF Beaufort and proceeded to follow. The Beaufort crew 'got the wind up' when they realised they were not alone in the sky. They fired off recognition flares, but selected the wrong colours and then headed at great speed for the airfield at RAF Leuchars.

At 3.45 p.m., on the same day, Sgt P. Brook was on a night-flying test with Sgt E. Malony as air gunner in Defiant AA287. At 800 feet a severe grinding noise developed in the engine, which began emitting fumes and clouds of white smoke. Climbing to 1,000 feet, Brook instructed Malony to bale out. This he promptly did, landing safely in a field near Aberlady. Sgt Brook eventually made a normal landing at Drem. When the Defiant was examined, it was found that the engine had several holes punctured in the sump. Sgt Brook 'has been highly commended for his fine effort'. There was plenty of activity in the early part of the following night. A 'record' number of enemy aircraft were reported to be in the sector. No. 410 Squadron was permitted to have only two operational aircraft airborne at any one time, but a number of crews turned up anyway in the hope of chance of engaging the Germans. A Defiant already airborne was instructed to fly to St Abb's Head, but low cloud over the coast made it too dangerous to descend to look for the quarry. When the pilot was about to land at Drem, he was given another vector following a report of a German aircraft over Dunbar. This mission proved equally unfruitful. No. 410 Squadron Defiants were scrambled again later the same day:

The result of the night's operations was disappointing to say the least, the fact that 141 Squadron (equipped with Beaufighters) got a Hun is simply piling on the agony. Still more opportunity will come our way in the future, so we'll just keep hoping in the meantime.[4]

At 11.30 p.m. on 17 February, a Defiant piloted by Plt Off. Barker was ordered to take off immediately to escort some Allied bombers to Drem. While taxiing, Barker was blinded by flares and collided with the airfield's Chance Light (a portable self-powered flood light) that was obscured by the smoke from the flares mingled with a low-lying mist. The Defiant tipped on its nose, sustaining damage to its undercarriage, mainplane, and centre section, although neither of its crew were hurt. The following night, while on patrol along the Fife coast, FS Williams saw a bomb burst on the edge of RAF Leuchars, but was unable to locate the hostile aircraft, believed to be flying at low level. Only seventeen hours had been flown on operational flights during the month. Training hours flown (some with the Blenheim) were 219 daylight and 116 at night.

On the afternoon of 1 March, the Commander of RAF Drem, Wg Cdr P. Townsend, took one of 410's Defiants for a local flight. On his return he said he found the machine slow and heavy compared to the Hurricane, which he used to fly; 'Just prejudice we call it', comments the squadron's diary. On 3 March, a Defiant crew were informed of an enemy aircraft in the sector, but the plot faded before an interception could be made. Flying operations had been hindered by snow at the end of February and on 5 March winter returned with a vengeance. Some parts of the airfield had 6 foot snow drifts. All 410 Squadron ground personnel billeted outside the station were brought into the camp. Every nook and cranny was occupied, including the Squadron headquarters. Two days later, the sun broke through and 410 Squadron had the distinction of being first in the air.

Early in the evening of 12 March there were two operational flights, but again no actual engagements. In the first, an Australian pilot in Defiant N1613 was vectored towards Arbroath. He chased what his air gunner thought may have been a Dornier 17. It was too fast for the Defiant and escaped in the direction of Norway. The second sortie was scrambled at 8.15 p.m. and patrolled over May Island in the vain hope of intercepting one of the three enemy aircraft reported. Despite this fleeting appearance by the Germans, the 410 Squadron diary for 13 March records the following with a tone of frustration: 'Another quiet night for both flights including Ouston ... Where is the much vaunted Hun these days?'

Another entry complains:

What with the night state getting later and later (19.54 hours last night), the absence of Huns in the Sector, and bad weather, we are not getting much in the way of operational flying these days.[5]

The Magister carried out instrument training during the month. Despite a recent engineering check, it once again managed to disgrace itself. On 15 March, the engine cut out at 30 feet shortly after take-off and its pilot, FS Du Perrier, was forced to land straight ahead into a barbed-wire boundary fence. The right undercarriage collapsed and the wings were damaged. This was the fourth time the Magister had crash-landed due to engine failure. Again, neither crew member was hurt. Subsequently, it was determined that the cause was a foreign body lodged in the main *carburettor* jet, causing petrol starvation. The following day, Plt Off. I. Constant and Plt Off. W. Lewis were killed when their machine (V1183) crashed at Dissington Hall, Northumberland, after a high-speed stall while undertaking unauthorised low flying.

The 26 March, 'a beautiful night at Drem, which led to some practice flying in the early evening'. By 10 p.m. things had quietened down, when there was a report that a Beaufighter of 141 Squadron (which had previously flown Defiants at Drem, and was now based at RAF Acklington) had crashed. The observer had parachuted safely, but there was no trace of the pilot. Three of 410's Defiants were unable to find any trace of the crashed plane and returned to base at 1 a.m. Some time later the pilot phoned from near Gifford, East Lothian, to say he was safe.

The following night was also eventful; three Defiants were patrolling over a convoy that was steaming north off Berwick-upon-Tweed. Sgt Haines in Defiant N3364 was instructed to take off and loiter above the base in the expectation of raiders. Nothing more was heard until a message was received that Haines had ordered his gunner, FS Pelletier, to bale out. The gunner was uninjured despite having to jump out of the steeply diving aircraft at a height of only 800 feet over the Farne Islands. The aircraft's radio receiver and blind-flying instruments had failed. At 2 a.m. it was learned that Sgt Haines, a Canadian aged only nineteen, had been killed when his aircraft crashed 6 miles north-west of Morpeth at Beacon Hill, Northumberland. Two of the other Defiants that had been airborne that night had to orbit Drem for twenty minutes. All the runway lights had been switched off, as it was believed that the Germans were bombing Dunbar.

By the end of March 1942, the squadron had eighteen Defiants, one Magister, and one Blenheim on strength. The career of the Defiant as a night fighter was drawing to a close. It had already been superseded by the Beaufighter in several other squadrons. On 2 April, 410 Squadron took delivery of its first two Beaufighters (Mk II)—T3387 and T3152. An additional Blenheim IV (Z5880) was received from 289 Squadron to speed up the training of pilots on twin-engined machines. Around the same time, the detachment of A-Flight at RAF Ouston was withdrawn and returned to Drem, the first time the entire squadron had been at a single base since 6 August 1941. Headquarters was moved from the cramped conditions of Rose Cottage, on the domestic side of the camp, to a hut at the dispersal point. A new beam-approach system was installed. This proved so troublesome that Sqn Ldr Lipton was called on to test it. It was not the only piece of equipment giving trouble in early April. There were numerous complaints about the state of 410's Defiants, which were 'getting very old and decrepit and all the time small pieces of equipment and radio are going u/s'. Fortunately, the Beaufighters were due to become operational in the forthcoming months.

On 11 April, the squadron suffered yet another tragedy. Sgt R. Smith (RCAF) with gunner Sgt P. MacKinnon took off from Drem in the late morning for a sector reconnaissance. Shortly before midday the aircraft was seen to dive out of low cloud and hit the water while flying in the vicinity of Aberlady Bay, East Lothian. Naval vessels arrived promptly, but could find no trace of the crew and only a small amount of wreckage. On 25 April, four enemy aircraft were reported in the Sector. At 11.25 p.m., a patrol was dispatched and orbited Drem at 8,000 feet, but the alert was called off as the enemy aircraft had never approached near enough to be engaged. On 28 April, two Defiants were scrambled to intercept a raid reportedly coming in from the north-east. As with many other scrambles, no contact was made. Before returning to base, one Defiant flew over Edinburgh at midnight to inspect the blackout.

By the end of April 410 Squadron had received a total of nineteen Beaufighters (Mk II). There were still ten Defiants on strength as well as two Blenheims and the Magister. The majority of its personnel were now Canadian:

	Aircrew	Ground Crew
RCAF Officers	13	5
RCAF Airmen	37	116
RAF Officers	8	1
RAF Airmen	8	72
Total	69	194

On 3 May at 10.50 p.m., after a dusk training flight, Defiant V1110 touched down and swung around to taxi to the dispersal. An undercarriage leg snapped causing the entire undercarriage to collapse. The 5 May was the last night 410's Defiants were on readiness. The aircraft 'behaved exemplarily on this, their last night on operation'. The next evening, two Beaufighters were on standby for night operations. FS Brook could not lock down the port oleo leg and had to land Beaufighter T3374 with its wheels up—the crew were unhurt. The probable cause was thought to be that on take-off the undercarriage struck rising ground while retracting. The runway in use at the time was uphill with a 20 foot rise, and very rough. As more and more pilots became operational on the Beaufighter, some of the Defiants were disposed of, including six that were dispatched to 277 Squadron.

The course to convert pilots from the single-engined Defiant to the twin-engined Beaufighter took the following form:

1. Elementary dual instruction and then solo on the Oxford and Blenheim.
2. Conversion and experience on the Beaufighters. The first two stages involved flying in daylight hours only. After going solo on the Beaufighter, the pilot was teamed with a radio operator/observer and undertook a further 25 to 30 hours flying. Many of 410 Squadron's gunners who operated the gun turret on the Defiant now found themselves redundant and were posted to other units or retained as radio operators/observers.
3. Dusk and Night Flying. This involved circuits and bumps at dusk followed by 5 to 15 hours night flying.[6]

Intensive training continued throughout May, including a successful exercise with night equipment. However, there were a further two crashes involving 410's aircraft. On 22 May, Sgt L. M. Jones (RCAF), in Blenheim IV (L9257) with another Canadian pilot as a passenger, crashed on take-off—the culprit was a blown tyre. The aircraft was badly damaged but both occupants were uninjured.In the second incident, on the 30th, Plt Off. Johnston (RCAF) and Sgt Dawson belly landed their Beaufighter II (T3389) after a complete failure of its hydraulic system. Again, there were no injuries.

By June, 410 Squadron's strength was two Defiants, nineteen Beaufighter II, one Oxford, one Blenheim, and one Magister. Two Beaufighters were flown to Preston at the beginning of the month for a major inspection. After receiving instructions that it was to move to RAF Ayr, the squadron continued training, including live air-to-sea firing. On 11 June, the officers held a farewell dance at Greywalls House, Gullane, with the station orchestra in attendance. A farewell party for the sergeants was held in their mess on 14 June, after which they visited the officer's mess at the invitation of the squadron commander.

On 15 June many of the ground personnel departed for RAF Ayr by rail. The last group marched out of the camp early the next morning. Sqn Ldr Wardle, the Administrative Officer made a speech in which he thanked the personnel of 410 Squadron for their 'splendid work'. At Drem railway station they were given the traditional send-off, with the Station Padre, Sqn Ldr Sutherland, playing his bagpipes as they boarded. Beaufighters departed in the afternoon, leaving behind a detachment of five Beaufighters, six operational crews, and some ground crew. This flight was ordered to maintain a night state of two aircraft at readiness with a further one at thirty minutes availability.

On 22 June the squadron's last Defiant took off for RAF Desford, Leicestershire. Reluctant to leave its old home, it developed oil trouble and had to return. It was made serviceable again and taken on a test flight by Plt Off. R. Ferguson. This time it developed trouble with the hydraulic system and crash-landed back at Drem. The pilot was unhurt and the aircraft was repairable. The following month, one of the detachment's Beaufighters was taking off from RAF Ayr when the machine blew a tyre. Arriving over Drem, the pilot circled and asked those on the ground if his tyres

A preserved example of a Miles Magister. This type was used as a station 'hack' at RAF Drem. Several fighter squadrons also had one or two for transport and training duties. (*Malcolm Fife*)

appeared undamaged. The answer was affirmative, so he came into land. On touching down the Beaufighter swung to one side, causing the starboard undercarriage to collapse. The aircraft was repairable and the crew were unhurt.

No. 410's detachment remained at Drem throughout most of the summer of 1942. Its aircraft were rarely scrambled and operational flying remained at a minimum. The exception was on 12 August, when two Beaufighters were scrambled to meet an incoming 'bandit'. One got within 400 yards of the enemy bomber, but could not make visual contact. In any case, the Beaufighter could not have opened fire as its weapons had failed to operate. A short time later, a Ju 88 dropped a few bombs on Drem airfield. Fortunately, little damage was caused. For the remainder of their time the pilots carried out high and low evasive exercises, air-to-air firing, cross-country flights, GCI, and army co-operation exercises. No. 410's Oxford and Magister were utilised in August to give air cadets flying experience.

At the beginning of September, the detachment of Beaufighters departed Drem for their new base of RAF Scorton, in Yorkshire, where they were joined by the rest of 410 Squadron from RAF Ayr. Within a few days, the Beaufighters were in action against enemy bombers attacking Middlesborough. One Beaufighter succeeded in damaging a Ju 88, the squadron's first victim.

The Free French Air Force

The first Free French Air Force squadron (340) was formed at RAF Turnhouse, Edinburgh, on 7 November 1941:

> On paper, only we haven't, so far, got even the paper. What we have got to date is a CO, who went off this morning in a stray Spitfire to collect his flying kite from RAF Benson, a British Adjutant, a British Intelligence Officer and one small dispersal hut for Squadron HQ.[1]

Over the next few days more and more French pilots arrived to join the new unit, including Lt René Mouchotte, who had risen from obscurity at the beginning of the war to become one of the great leaders of the Free French Air Force. He had escaped from Oran (North Africa) to Gibraltar in an unserviceable plane and a short time later enlisted in the RAF.

The new squadron had not made much progress by 12 November 1941, with the following comment being recorded in their squadron diary:

> No serviceable aircraft, no dispersal points, no tools, no engineers but any amount of good temper and patience and a stubborn conviction that Guinness in the end will be good for us.[2]

By 15 November, they had received just two Spitfires. Lt Mouchotte described them:

> [They were] so old that exhaust pipes are dropping off, the undercarriages won't retract and more serious won't let down. In the air they are in the tin can or flat-iron category. Add to this that fog and cold are giving us a lot of trouble.[3]

The pilots were joined by French ground crews, many of them from the *Aéronavale*, the French 'Fleet Air Arm'. An exotic touch was added by a small group of Tahitians who felt the cold very badly. By 16 November, the squadron had three aircraft flying. The unit also suffered its first casualty when Capitaine Duperier's black Scottie dog was run over in the dark outside the mess. The following day there was a rumour that the squadron was to move to Drem in the near future:

It won't break anyone's heart to leave Turnhouse (and probably won't break anyone's heart to see us go, we were rather young and rather noisy for Turnhouse, which is rather elderly and rather prim), but we shan't want Drem either for too long. The whole squadron's heart will be broken if we don't fairly soon go south, where there's war on.[4]

Similar sentiments were expressed by many of the pilots posted to Drem, but no more so than by Lt Mouchotte, who had few positive things to record in his diary about his stay in Scotland. The 'Paris Squadron' was the intended name, but in the end 340 Squadron adopted the title '*Isle de France*'.

At 9 a.m. on 29 November, the squadron was declared operational, just a fortnight after it had received its first plane. At 12.55 p.m. on the same day, the six Spitfires (Mark II) of A-Flight provided fighter cover. Their duty was to be at readiness for a twenty-four hour period for one day in three. On the other days, 611's Spitfires would be on alert.

At the beginning of December A-Flight practised air-to-air firing. The target was towed by a Lysander, which flew some 3 to 4 miles out to sea between Dunbar and St Abbs Head: 'A certain number of the pilots contrive to miss not only the target but the Lizzie too'. On 8 December Gen. Valin paid a visit to A-Flight at Drem. Five days later there was an alert when a Ju 88 was reported to be approaching the coast near St Abbs:

Sirens screaming in Edinburgh, sirens screaming (you could hear them from Drem) in North Berwick (where it's the only sort of siren they stock, according to A Flight which has been attending a round of kindly-meant parties in North Berwick and coming home with longer faces every time).[5]

Despite the efforts of several of A-Flight's Spitfires, the Junkers escaped for home after dropping one bomb.

On 20 December, the remainder of 340 Squadron moved to Drem from RAF Turnhouse. Lt Mouchotte, at Drem since the beginning of the month with A-Flight, recorded the following in his diary:

First impression of the mess at Drem, a huge room, comfortably furnished, as is the anteroom. In the middle is a deep fireplace, very wide, above which stands an enormous copper goblet, taller than a bucket but a little narrower. The name of some generous donor is inscribed on the base. Once or twice a week some volunteer comes forward, fills the cup to the brim, which represents more than twenty full pints and makes a point of drinking the lot before going to bed. I have never been able to see the humour of this joke. To judge by the pallor of his complexion I suspect the hero does not either. I shall not be a candidate for it.[6]

The squadron suffered its first fatal accident when Daligot's Spitfire was lost over the North Sea. Air-Sea Rescue launches and squadron Spitfires looked for it in vain. On 21 December, Sqn Ldr Loft's machine sprung a glycol leak when he was searching 30 miles out from the coast. Fortunately, he was at a height of 10,000 feet, enabling the machine to be nursed down to the closest airfield at Arbroath. There were three major landing accidents at Drem in the second half of the month. In the first, a 340 Squadron Spitfire overshot the runway, 'which you wouldn't think possible on a field as big as Drem', and completely demolished a brick latrine:

> There wasn't one brick left standing on another, which gave rise to a chorus of vulgar remarks as to the advisability of leaving one's machine outside whatever one's hurry.[7]

The pilot was fine, but the nose and port wing were badly damaged.

Just before Christmas, Sgt Caron's Spitfire was stood on its nose, damaging its propeller. On 28 December, Capt. Bechoff, who had only joined the squadron a few days earlier, overshot the landing ground:

> [He] smashed his Spitfire to quite small pieces and got a bump on his forehead, poor chap. His chances of total extinction were probably at least 1,000 to 1, what saved him from burning at least was that his motor flew out and landed four yards away.[8]

On 1 January 1942, 340's Spitfires (Mk II) departed in formation, as the squadron was moved to RAF Ayr to replace 312 Squadron. They would return to Drem for a longer stay in the following year. René Mouchotte also came back at a later date, but this time as 65's Commander. The French were not impressed with RAF Ayr:

> It is an exceedingly unpicturesque site where only the runways are useable and the rest is a quagmire, the noise of the frogs must be deafening in the summer months. The accommodation is disconcerting and represents war at its grimmest. At least that's the way it strikes us, fresh from the happy Sybaris of Drem. [Sybaris was an ancient Greek colony in Southern Italy, notorious for its luxurious living].[9]

In March 1943, 340 Squadron returned to Scotland from RAF Biggin Hill. Unusually, the pilots made their way to by road, their Spitfires (Mk IX) having been left behind for 341 Squadron, another Free French unit. At Turnhouse, they were allotted largely unserviceable Mk Vbs.

A large scale raid on the night of 24–25 March 1943 involved an attack on south-east Scotland by around thirty Ju 88 and Do 217 of KG2 and KG6 from bases in Holland. Fourteen aircraft dropped high explosive and incendiary bombs at random, none of which came close to the intended target of Edinburgh. The enemy's plans were thwarted by bad weather and nil visibility at 600 to 3,000 feet. The forecast had been for clear skies over the target. Due to this low cloud, the fighters based at Drem and Turnhouse had little opportunity to attack the enemy bombers, but anti-aircraft guns shot down one Ju 88A, which crashed at Balerno near Edinburgh. Two Do 217 flew into high ground on the Cheviot Hills, Northumberland. A further Ju 88A crashed near Earlston, in the Scottish Borders, having been shot down by a 409 Squadron Beaufighter based at RAF Acklington.

No. 340 Squadron moved from Turnhouse to Drem on the 30 April 1943, although training flights had taken place from there before this date. The Spitfires were placed on readiness and operational flights were flown in protection of numerous shipping convoys steaming to or from the Firth of Forth. In the evening of the 19 May, Red Section provided air cover for convoy *Queen*. On 25 May B-Flight flew patrols over a southbound convoy *Force*, while four sections of A-Flight covered a northbound convoy *Paddle* between the Firth of Forth and the Firth of Tay. A similar duty was performed on 28 May for a southbound convoy, *Dimple*.

With German air power in decline, less RAF fighter squadrons were needed to defend British airspace. Many were now given an offensive role in anticipation of the invasion of Continental Europe. No. 340 Squadron was no exception. Numerous exercises with the Army were held throughout the summer including, on 17 May, successful 'attacks' on the 10th Armoured Division.

Broad Sands (locally known as Dirleton Sands) air-to-ground firing range was situated at East Fortune close to Drem. It was used principally by 132 Squadron aircraft based at RAF East Fortune to the south. The targets were located on the sand dunes to absorb the projectiles shot at them. There was also another range a short distance to the north of Ferrygate farm, east of Dirleton. The fields under the practice run to the targets produced a crop of cannon shell cases for many years after the war.

An exercise of a different nature took place on 24 May in which three sections of A-Flight each made two runs at 11,000 feet over the centre of Glasgow. They were playing the role of bombers as part of a concentrated daylight 'attack' on the city to afford practice for control and ground defences.

Formation flying was carried out during 'Wings for Victory Week'. After flying over Edinburgh, 340 Squadron refuelled at RAF Acklington, then formatted with two other squadrons over the Newcastle area. Unusually, 884 Fleet Air Arm Squadron's Seafires Mk II took up readiness at Drem while the Spitfires were away. One section was scrambled, but soon recalled. Near the end of the month the squadron put up another formation over Edinburgh, including the '*Croix de Lorraine*'.

On 5 June Spitfires landing in the evening sent up showers of mud and water. A few days later, aircraft scrambled to patrol the base at 30,000 ft. The alarm was caused by a friendly aircraft and the Spitfires recalled. The official records make frequent reference to how cold the French pilots found it when they had to fly at these altitudes. On several occasions during June practice interceptions were performed on Wellingtons and Whitleys in near perfect weather. During the afternoon of the 22 June Sgt Rosa, on a camera exercise at 6,000 feet, was alerted by another Spitfire pilot that his engine was on fire. He managed to crash-land with a terrific impact in a field near East Fortune. Sgt Rosa luckily escaped with nothing more than a cut on his forehead. A similar incident took place only three days later, during formation practice; thick white smoke, attributed to a glycol leak, began pouring from Sgt Le Goff's Spitfire. He tried to glide to RAF East Fortune but missed the runway and the aircraft ended on its nose—Le Goff was unhurt.

Exercises with the army continued throughout the summer. At 7.30 a.m. on 6 June, three sections of B-Flight made a surprise 'attack' on troops waiting to be embarked from a beach near Reed Point, Cockburnspath, retreating from an assault on a viaduct. The Spitfires flew in from the sea, but the high cliffs made a low-level attack impossible. The troops retreated to the base of the cliff where they were almost completely hidden from the pilots. Great satisfaction was expressed by the Army authorities at the result of the exercise. Later, an invitation to co-operate in an invasion exercise against the base had to be turned down as the runways at Drem were too wet for flying except for operational patrols. On 8 June, Blue Section took off to 'attack' a convoy of vehicles, but could not locate their target due to low cloud. A further exercise on 13 June was no more successful. Green Section took off to make dummy attacks on a train load of tanks leaving Kelso station in the Scottish Borders. After flying round the area for half an hour, the mission had to be abandoned as the train had not left the station. On another day fourteen pilots flew to RAF Findo Gask, near Perth, for enemy tank recognition practice. Some of the Spitfires then 'beat up' infantry crossing Hedderwick Range. The following month on 5 July, six Spitfires carried out mock attacks on a southbound vehicle convoy.

No. 340 Squadron did not neglect its fighter skills. Air-to-air firing practice was frequently undertaken. During one such exercise, one of the Spitfires collided with the cable towing the drogue. Despite damage to the starboard wing, the pilot managed to land safely back at Drem. On 5 July, just three days later, Adj. A. Pottel had difficulty in lowering his undercarriage despite activating the emergency blow-down bottle. The undercarriage collapsed on landing, causing slight damage to the airscrew and one wingtip. Ten days later, Lt P. Kennard had to make a forced landing near Blackford, Perthshire, due to a glycol leak. Luckily he escaped without injury, but his aircraft was badly damaged; an Anson of 281 Squadron flew him back from RAF Findo Gask.

The pilots were kept busy during July. Yellow Section carried out a practice scramble, becoming airborne in just two minutes. They were vectored on to a formation of Whitleys before returning. The following day, 11 July, six Spitfires carried out a similar sortie with bombers from RAF Kinloss OTU. On 13 July a further fighter affiliation exercise with Whitleys was carried out at 8,000 feet, with a practice scramble and interception under Turnhouse Control. The Whitleys afterwards landed at Drem and the crews discussed the exercise with the pilots concerned. More unusually, on 17 July, some of 340's Spitfires performed an affiliation exercise in cloudless skies with fifteen Stirling bombers. This is the only mention of this type of aircraft ever being involved with any of the units based at Drem. At the end of the month, 226's Mitchells arrived at the airfield for ten days of training with the squadron. This episode is related in the chapter concerning bombers at Drem.

Training was not only carried out with bombers, but also with other fighter squadrons. On 18 July, ten Spitfires participated in combat training with 63 Squadron's Mustangs from RAF MacMerry. No. 64 Squadron, based at RAF Ayr, sent a section of Spitfires to maintain readiness at Drem.

Low-level formation flights with three to eight aircraft were also added to the training syllabus to provide experience in low-flying and cross-country navigation. They proved to be very popular with the pilots. On 20 July, despite low cloud, four Spitfires of B-Flight and three Spitfires of A-Flight flew in opposite directions over a

150-mile route. The two Flights are recorded as meeting each other half way around the course with about 300-foot separation.

A small number of operational missions did take place in July. At the beginning of the month one aircraft was ordered to shoot down a drifting barrage balloon, but it had disappeared in cloud. Red Section scrambled on the afternoon of 16 July to investigate an X-raid (unidentified aircraft). Directed by the sector controller, then GCI, they intercepted two Fulmars, Albacores, Swordfish, and a Master near RAF Leuchars. On 23 July, the 'enemy' aircraft was identified as a Mosquito. Several uneventful patrols were flown over the convoys *Transfer*, *Usage*, *Might*, *Boldrock*, and *Tinsmith* and two battleships were escorted northbound in the Firth of Forth on 9 July.

At the beginning of August, 340 Squadron sent five Spitfires on detachment to RAF Ayr to replace 64 Squadron. The unit also received orders to move into the new dispersals on the north-west side of the airfield, recently vacated by 186 Squadron. The remaining aircraft carried out further flying in conjunction with the Mustangs from RAF MacMerry:

> It is felt that these practice attacks with aircraft of a different type are extremely beneficial.[10]

There was a further co-operation sortie with Whitleys from Kinloss OTU. On 11 August, five Spitfires carried out practice attacks and interceptions under GCI control, in co-operation with 784 Fleet Air Arm squadron, also based at Drem:

> The success of the exercise was somewhat marred by the fact the naval boys were operating on the same [radio] channel and took advantage of this.[11]

Group declared that 'night readiness state' was no longer necessary, but 340's CO decided that some night flying would still be beneficial. On 12 August, Blue Section was instructed to proceed to Bell Rock Lighthouse and then far to the north, but saw nothing. While returning from another mission to investigate a 'bogey', the Spitfires were diverted to escort a Mosquito flying on one engine. Its pilot successfully made landfall. At 1.25 p.m., on 25 August, there was a scramble to patrol over Drem at 20,000 feet when a high-flying raid was reportedly coming down from the north. No. 340's Spitfires were recalled when the radar tracks became confused with those of friendly aircraft. The same day a Spitfire hit a rut on the strip and the starboard undercarriage leg collapsed. The previous day, Sgt Filliol suffered a pneumatic system failure, then found himself without flaps or brakes and overshot the south-west corner of the landing ground. He was fortunately unhurt. Two Spitfires' wings touched while flying in formation, but little damage resulted. Earlier in the month, the squadron's Tiger Moth DE922 came to grief when it crash-landed at Nethershiel Farm, approximately 3 miles north of RAF Kirknewton, near Edinburgh. The aircraft was totally burnt out. The two crew survived, one receiving minor injuries. The final scramble of the month was on 28 August, when two Spitfires went in search of two Ju 88s. Visibility nil, cloud very low, no enemy aircraft seen.

Throughout September there were further fighter affiliation exercises with two Whitleys. On 25 September, Number One Section attacked both bombers, thus ruining Second Section's practice. A few days later, two sections of Spitfires bounced 63 Squadron Mustangs, which were attacking B-Flight's aircraft.

There were a small number of scrambles throughout September. On 19 September, two Spitfires investigated an unidentified plane near Montrose which turned out to be 'friendly'. Two Spitfires landed at RAF East Fortune after night flying on a moonlit night. Adj. Oury struck part of the lighting equipment on the runway, damaging his aircraft's propeller. At Drem, there were anxious moments when an undercarriage wheel fell off a Spitfire when lifting off. The pilot made several circuits then, to the relief of the watching crowd, held the aircraft steady until almost the end of the landing run, upon which it leaned gently over onto its port wing, causing little damage to his machine and none to himself.

On a more positive note, on 22 September, 340 Squadron received the first of its new Spitfires (Mk Vb), the version designed as a fighter bomber, and suitable for low flying. Re-equipment was almost complete by the end of the month. A-Flight returned from RAF Ayr during the month.

Autumn begun with gales and rain, curtailing flying activities. A heavy flying programme on 6 October included a squadron battle formation. Three Spitfires beat up the airfield by permission of the CO. A few days later, a squadron formation was flown and the CO co-operated by flying his Miles Master aircraft for interception practice. At 10.30 a.m., on 19 October, the squadron's Spitfires took off in formation to perform practice attacks on the airfield. Shortly take-off, Adj. Pottel was seen to be experiencing engine trouble very low over the sea near Bass Rock. His aircraft crashed into the sea and rapidly disappeared under the waves. A large patch of oil was seen, but the crews of the air-sea rescue Walrus and Anson were unable to find any trace: 'The loss of this experienced pilot who had been with the squadron since 24 September 1942 was very keenly felt'. A gale force wind blew all that afternoon.

On 22 October, one section investigated a report of a boat firing on an aircraft. It was discovered to be an anti-aircraft practice. For the rest of the month, 340 Squadron was involved in exercise 'Goliath' with Army units based near Perth. On the first day the Spitfires carried out a sweep over 'enemy territory' and 'attacked' a large moving convoy of vehicles. The next day, 25 October, a bridge was 'destroyed', then B-Flight made a low-level attack while A-Flight provided cover. Some opposition was encountered and a general dog flight developed. In the early evening a target in the River Tay was attacked.

Low cloud and bumpy conditions prevailed the following day. The first sortie involved successful 'attacks' on a convoy of vehicles moving between hills. A second sortie was postponed due to weather and an obstruction on the Drem runway. Eventually, at 1.50 p.m., 'attacks' were made on a pontoon bridge over the River Earn. At 3 p.m., the Spitfires made low-level 'attacks' on 'enemy' headquarters and troop concentrations.

On 27 October the poor weather persisted with 10/10 cloud cover down to less than 1,000 feet. After 'attacks' on heavy concentrations of 'enemy' troops and vehicles north of Kinross, a second sortie was cancelled. After lunch and the Spitfires 'attacked' concentrations of troops and vehicles on roads between Alloa and Dollar. Many 'attacks' were pressed home, though the troops concealed themselves well after the preliminary beat up. Further operations were cancelled so local flying in the vicinity of Drem airfield was undertaken. Tragedy struck during a camera gun practice when two Spitfires collided in mid-air at about 1,000 feet over Dirleton. Both aircraft spiralled down. Sergent-chef Gaine baled out, but at too low an altitude and was killed. Sub Lt Davibroack was still in the cockpit when his machine buried itself in the ground. The two bodies were brought back to the station mortuary and officers and NCOs of 340 Squadron showed their grief at the loss of their best pilots by mounting a continuous guard for twenty-four hours.

It was business as usual for the unit the next day in bright sunshine. A further three sorties were flown with exercise 'Goliath'. Columns of troops and vehicles were again beaten up. The 'enemy' headquarters also received the attention of the Spitfires on more than one occasion.

On 29 October, the Reverend Pere Goddard held mass in a hangar in memory of Adj. Pottel killed earlier in the month. The minister included in his prayers all members of the French Air Force who had lost their lives in the service of their country. In the afternoon the squadron continued their participation in exercise 'Goliath' when Mustangs were intercepted near Falkirk in less than ideal weather conditions. This was followed by 340 Squadron 'attacking' Hurricanes near Stirling. Two Hurricanes collided and crashed in the ensuing action. The next day the funerals of Gaine and Davibroak took place in Dirleton Cemetery. There was a large cortege made up of squadron personnel and staff from RAF Drem and a firing party was provided by the RAF Regiment. In the afternoon, Reverend Goddard presided over a happier event when the daughter of Lt Kennard was christened in the pilots' room at B-Flight with a reception afterwards in the officers' mess. Yet another accident occurred on the last day of October when Sgt Rosa made a wheels-up landing after his engine cut out at 300 feet—fortunately, he was unhurt.

Training was terminated, given the impending move to RAF Perranporth on 9 November. Proceedings were livened up two days before when a 96 Squadron Mosquito overshot and crashed into a dispersal hut. Two of 340's men in the building at the time received only minor injuries. The next day, the majority of 340 Squadron pilots travelled to their new base by road and a special train carried the servicing echelon.

During the autumn, 340 Squadron and its sister, 341 Squadron, flew convoy patrols over the Southwest Approaches. Early in 1944 they were joined at RAF Perranporth by a third French squadron, forming 145 Wing. After the Allied invasion of Europe, 340 Squadron spent much of the summer in Normandy. In November, its Spitfires returned to Britain and were based at RAF Biggin Hill before returning to Drem for the third and last time on 17 December 1944. Its arrival posed problems as the servicing echelon was top-heavy, containing around fifty-five more NCOs than there would be in the British equivalent. The eleven adjutants were housed in the NCO billets with two bunks to a room. The NCO pilots had to sleep thirteen to a Nissen hut.

A vertical aerial photograph from 7,500 feet of HMS *Nighthawk* (Drem) on 8 October 1945. The notations depicting the runway layout are on the original print. (*Fleet Air Arm Museum*)

On 19 December, 340 Squadron commenced readiness duty at Drem. Two Spitfires (Mk IXb) were ready to scramble immediately with a further two at thirty minutes notice. On taking off in formation for a sector reconnaissance, FS Montaut's engine failed and he crashed from around 100 feet. Montaut was taken to the Astley Ainslie Hospital in Edinburgh, suffering from multiple minor injuries. Most of the remainder of the squadron arrived on 22 December, but two Spitfires and an Auster remained stuck at RAF Biggin Hill. On 26 December there was a formation practice and later the readiness section was scrambled against a hostile aircraft approaching the Aberdeen area. The Spitfires were vectored north but returned forty-five minutes later after an uneventful patrol. It was learned later that a Bf 109 flown by a defecting pilot had crash-landed at RAF Dyce shortly after the section had been scrambled. The squadron log book asks: 'can we claim one destroyed through fear?' As the German military machine began to crumble there were a number of similar defections, including a Ju 52 transport that ditched in the sea off Aberdeen.

At the beginning of the New Year, a missing Fleet Air Arm Firefly was the subject of an unsuccessful search and rescue mission. Cross-country flying and low-level formation training were carried out. Dive bombing was practised on a new purpose-built range at Musselburgh, and air-to-ground firing at the Gullane range. It was impossible to practise squadron landings, owing to recent rain and snow that had softened the grass strip. No. 340 Squadron was put on a non-operational basis on 11 January, the first time in the conflict that RAF Drem had no fighter aircraft on alert. The same day, Sgt Davila in Spitfire PT781 had been given the green Aldis lamp signal in poor visibility. On suddenly seeing an aircraft taxiing in his path, he managed to get his Spitfire sufficiently airborne to 'jump' over it, damaging his propeller blades and holing the radiator. Davila was unaware of this at the time and the loss of coolant caused overheating on the subsequent flight. On 13 January 1945, three Dakota transports arrived from Antwerp with six new pilots and forty airmen, including seven armourers from 340 Squadron who were no longer required by the 145 Wing of the 2nd Tactical Air Force. By 15 January, the squadron had its full complement of twenty-seven pilots. Over the next few days there was snow and rain which limited flying, but when there was a hard frost this usually made the grass runways firm enough be usable.

An instruction was received on 20 January 1945 that 340 Squadron was to move to RAF Turnhouse, where 289 and 290 Squadrons were due to move out. Ships carrying 290's ground equipment had been sunk by German E-boats, which delayed the move. Drem was snowbound for the last week of January. The thaw began on the 29th, and on the last day of January, 340 Squadron left Drem for the last time. In February this Free French unit departed to Europe where it spent the closing days of the Second World War.

The Polish Squadrons

The Polish Air Force, flying near obsolete aircraft against vastly superior numbers, fought with great distinction against the German invasion of September 1939. Towards the end of that year, Britain accepted over 2,000 Polish airmen into the Royal Air Force Volunteer Reserve. In the meantime, the Polish Air Force had reformed in France with about ninety operational aircraft and 7,000 personnel on strength.

Many Poles fled to Britain to swell the ranks of their countrymen already in the RAF. The Polish-British Military Agreement, signed in early August 1940, permitted the formation of the Polish Air Force under RAF operational control. There were numerous other nationalities from occupied Europe in the RAF, but the Poles were the most numerous. Many Polish pilots were taught to fly the Spitfire at 58 OTU, RAF Grangemouth while others were trained to become night fighter pilots at 60 OTU East Fortune. From September 1942, the large number of Polish trainees necessitated the formation of a wholly Polish section.

Numbers of Polish soldiers were also in Scotland. After February 1942, the 1st Polish Armoured Division was largely based in East Lothian and during March 1942 the 10th Mounted Rifles, an armoured regiment, arrived in Haddington where it remained for over a year. Aircraft based at Drem were often involved in exercises with this regiment.

By the end of 1943 there were a total of fourteen Polish squadrons (including ten fighter squadrons) and a complete infrastructure in existence. No. 307 Squadron, the only Polish night fighter squadron, was re-equipped with Mosquitoes at the end of 1942. During May 1943 it began flying missions from RAF Predannack, Cornwall, to intercept Ju 88s attacking shipping in the Southwest Approaches. The squadron needed a break, so on 9 November the first Mosquito flew north to Drem, with the remainder arriving over the following two days. They became one of a small number of RAF Mosquito Squadrons to be based at this airfield.

Initially, most of the time was spent in training. On the night of 13 November three Mosquitoes were unsuccessfully scrambled to intercept enemy aircraft flying southwards off the Scottish coast. A few days later, three Mosquitoes (Mk VI) were dispatched to RAF Sumburgh in the Shetland Islands to operate under Lerwick Fighter Control. Jerzy Dansz, one of the pilots who delivered a Mosquito to Sumburgh, described the airfield:

Polish airmen of 309 Squadron at RAF Drem in 1944. (*Wilhelm Ratuszyski*)

The flight from Drem took 1 hour. I found the airport not very big, fashioned in between rocks requiring the approach directly from the sea but perfectly adequate for a Mosquito. Living conditions are very basic, even worse than in Drem where we slept in wooden cabins, heated by iron stoves. In Sumburgh our boys felt as if they were living on an aircraft carrier. But they were not bored, there was plenty of work to do.[1]

There was still plenty of Luftwaffe activity over the Shetland Islands by units based in nearby occupied Norway, in contrast to Drem, where enemy aircraft had been notable for their absence for a couple of years. Excitement was not long in coming for the Polish newcomers. While flying an Atlantic reconnaissance patrol on 22 November, FS Jaworski's Mosquito intercepted a He 177A heavy bomber, 120 miles north-east of the Shetland Isles. The crew continued shooting at the Heinkel until they ran out of ammunition. It was last seen diving towards the sea with large amounts of smoke coming from its engines and was later confirmed as crashed. This was the first He 177 shot down by the Poles. A few days later, Mosquito DZ741 shot down a torpedo carrying Junkers Ju 88, a long way north of the Shetland Islands. On 9 December Mosquito HJ928, piloted by Jan Pacholczyk, shot down a Ju 88D-1 (8H+AH). The detachment at RAF Sumburgh had a major setback on 20 December when Mosquito NF11 (DD618) on a non-operational flight, with pilot Flt Lt Pfeiffer and radio operator Plt Off. K. Kesicki on board, suffered an engine failure. The pilot attempted to land on one engine, but stalled and crashed into the sea shortly after mid-day. Both its crew members were killed.

On 13 January 1944, four Mosquitoes took off from RAF Sumburgh to carry out a successful raid—Operation Rhubarb—on German bases in Norway. While flying towards a fjord near Stavanger, where they were intending to attack Blohm und Voss Bv 138C flying boats, one of the pilots spotted a Junkers W34, a small transport plane, and shot it down. On the approach to the fjord, two of the Mosquito crews engaged in shooting the flying boats on the water. WO Wisthal reported one destroyed and another as probably destroyed. Flt Lt R. Zwolinski claimed one as probably destroyed. Flying north, they shook off several FW 190 fighters. The other pair of Mosquitoes caused damage to the railway system and a fishing boat. All returned back to their base safely.

Back at Drem there was an inconclusive scramble on the night of 16 December. Otherwise, little had happened except for a fire in a hangared Mosquito Mk II (HG911), thought to have been caused by an inspection lamp arcing. January 1944 was also a quiet month, with much time devoted to familiarising personnel with the new Airborne Interception (AI) radar, Mark VIII. Its revolving disc aerial was located in the Mosquito's nose taking the place of the four machine guns previously housed there, thereby reducing the aircraft's offensive armament to four cannon under the cockpit floor. The squadron's Mosquitoes (NF Mk II) were to be replaced by Mosquitoes NF Mk XII and NF Mk XIII, equipped with the AI Mk VIII radar. On 19 January No. 1 Conversion Flight equipped with the Mosquito VII, the first version to have the AI Mk VIII radar, arrived from RAF Church Fenton to train the Polish airmen on this equipment.

On 21 January, 307 Squadron accepted seven long-range Mosquitoes (NF Mk XIII), plus an NF Mk XII a few days later. On 13 January, a Mosquito II was lost in a fatal crash. WO L. Szemplinski and Plt Off. Frank Tillman had taken off from Drem to fly up to Peterhead for a co-operation exercise with the Royal Navy. The Sector Controller informed the pilot that the weather at the destination was very poor and had cancelled the flight to Peterhead, instructing him to carry out flying in the vicinity of Drem where the weather was good. Unfortunately, the Mosquito had already flown into the unfavourable weather. A short time later it flew into Greenleys Hill, which was close to the coast and obscured by low cloud. The aircraft was totally destroyed and its crew killed. They were laid to rest in Sleepy Hill Cemetery, Montrose.

During much of February 1944 the squadron was grounded because of windy weather and snow at the end of the month. When conditions permitted, the Mosquito crews trained intensively. The re-equipping of the Squadron with new versions of the Mosquito continued. On the night of 11–12 February, a Mosquito NF Mk II and one of the new NF Mk XIIs participated in 'Bullseye' exercises. The next day Sgt R. Kielczewski bounced his Mosquito HK139 on take-off, collapsing one of the undercarriage legs. Fortunately both crew escaped unhurt. There was an alarm on the night of 18–19 February, with two Mosquitoes NF Mk XII being scrambled, but no contact was made. This was the last month that 307 Squadron was based at Drem. On 2 March 1944, the unit was relocated to RAF Coleby Grange. The main task now for the Mosquitoes was to patrol the Humber Estuary where the enemy had become very active.

Drem did not have to wait long for the Poles to return. A-Flight of 309 Squadron touched down there with their Hurricanes (Mk IV) on 23 April 1944. B-Flight, the other part of the unit, was posted to RAF Hutton Cranswick, Yorkshire. This squadron had a long association with Scotland, having been formed at RAF Renfrew near Glasgow in October 1940. Its initial equipment was the Westland Lysander— maximum speed just over 200 mph—designed for carrying out reconnaissance for army units. Rather surprisingly, when the squadron became operational towards the end of 1940, its task was to defend the Clyde Estuary with the Lysanders. The following spring, 309 Squadron kept a flight of aircraft at RAF Scone, where it did its best to intercept German planes passing over Perth. Although scrambled several times, the Polish Lysanders had little chance of catching the much faster German bombers. In May 1941, 309 Squadron moved to RAF Dunino, in Fife, on the opposite side of the Firth of Forth from Drem. Here the squadron was given a task more appropriate to their aircraft. They carried out low-level reconnaissance and picked up messages as well as performed artillery spotting for the Polish troops responsible for protecting Fife, which was regarded as vulnerable to an invasion by German seaborne troops.

Hence, it was appropriate that in the closing years of the Second World War, 309 Squadron would be again responsible for safeguarding the coast around the Firth of Forth. Squadron members were not enthusiastic about reacquainting themselves with Scotland. They were hoping that they would be in the forefront of the invasion of Europe to wreak revenge on the Germans for occupying their homeland. In January 1944, due to the planned invasion of the continent, the squadron's role was changed from fighter reconnaissance to fighter bomber. The Poles exchanged their Mustangs for worn-out Hurricanes (Mk IV) to bomb targets on the enemy coast. The aircraft's range proved to be insufficient and, in April, the squadron again exchanged their aircraft, this time for the equally fatigued Hurricane Mk IIC. Meanwhile Sqn Ldr Golko, a bomber pilot with no experience on fighters, became the unit's new CO. In April, 309 Squadron, with their 'new old' planes, was sent to Drem to defend the area against German raiders flying from Norway. By this time, sightings of enemy aircraft in south-east Scotland were almost non-existent and Drem was in its twilight years as a major fighter airfield. The Poles operated the only fighter squadron there for much of 1944.

By 25 April, 309 Squadron had commenced operations by having two Hurricanes at immediate readiness during daylight hours. With summer and the long-light evenings approaching, pilots and their ground crews were required to put in long hours. On the first day of duty, the aircraft were released from readiness at 10.30 p.m. after scrambling in the afternoon. There was a further alarm on 30 April, which again proved fruitless. The remainder of A-Flight carried out training flights, including air-to-sea firing.

The first of May saw two Hurricanes scrambled over North Berwick, but they were recalled. On 4 May, the aircraft were 40 miles out to sea before their potential victim was identified as 'friendly'. There was further excitement the following day when two Hurricanes were ordered to take off to search for an Allied aircraft which required guiding to its home airfield. Before making contact, the planes were recalled as the stray aircraft was out of range. The task of guiding it back to base was taken over by another Sector.

There was a further scramble on the afternoons of 6 May and again on 9 May, when there was a report of possible enemy activity off Buddon Ness at the mouth of the Firth of Tay. The report was found to be without foundation. All was then quiet for the rest of the month. A number of coastal patrol flights between the mouth of the Firth of Forth and St Abb's Head were flown by a single aircraft after sunset. Additional patrols were flown, sometimes by two Hurricanes, to cover the area around the Firth of Tay towards the end of the month. Cine gun practice, air-to-air firing, interception sorties and cloud flying were included in the training routines. There were also 'Driver' exercises involving the Royal Navy and 309's Hurricanes. These exercises aimed to develop radio communication skills and co-ordination between Allied ships and their fighter cover. They involved three Hurricanes, one of which was the 'attacking' aircraft referred to as the 'Driver'. The other two were the protective fighters, which were given the height and range of the 'enemy' aircraft from the air defence controllers on the ships.

These exercises, which were held frequently—sometimes daily—throughout the summer months, initially met with mixed results. On 7 May 1944, the Hurricanes were in contact with the naval vessels for about one hour before returning to base at 1850:

> At first communication was bad but improved later in the exercise. Directions were good with the exception of one or two minor slips in procedure.[2]

'Driver' made a total of twenty-two attacks on the enemy. Bad communications and incorrect fighter procedures on the part of the Navy dogged the exercises.

On 25 May, 309 Squadron provided air cover for shipping heading north from the Firth of Forth. A total of twenty-six sorties were flown between 8.10 a.m. and 7 p.m. with two Hurricanes airborne at any one time. Not surprisingly, no enemy aircraft put in an appearance. Two Hurricane pilots did get an opportunity to fire their guns at targets on the last day of the month. A barrage balloon had broken adrift in an area 2 miles west of the Bell Rock. The first Hurricane pilot was ordered to shoot it down, which he successfully accomplished. Later in the afternoon a second Hurricane destroyed another stray barrage balloon to the north of the Bell Rock Lighthouse.

By 1 June, 309 Squadron had two Hurricanes on immediate readiness every night from 4 a.m. until almost midnight. They were rarely called on to scramble as even false alarms now rare. Some standing patrols flown in the late evening also proved uneventful. The good summer weather enabled the three Hurricanes (Mk IIC) that had recently been modified to carry out aerial photography. The F24 cameras on the aircraft produced both vertical and oblique aerial pictures as well as stereo pairs. Over the next few months the Hurricanes' services were in great demand, including photographing the Perth area for Polish Staff College and shooting a mosaic of photographs of the area round Moffat for the Staff Camouflage Officer of the Scottish

Army Command. On 19 July, a demonstration of air support was put on by four Hurricanes (Mk IIC) for pupils of the Polish Staff College.

A reconnaissance plane took photographs of the headquarters, then a squadron of Mustangs were to dive-bomb the premises. As there were no Mustangs available, 309's Hurricanes played this role. They also stood in for the Typhoons which were to be the next attackers, then for a fighter squadron making cannon attacks on targets of opportunity. The demonstration was regarded as very successful with the spectators able to hear all communications between the ground controller and the aircraft through loudspeakers.

Otherwise July was a quiet month at Drem. No. 309's Hurricanes remained at alert for an elusive enemy. One section was maintained at immediate readiness from around 4.30 a.m. to 12 a.m. At 11.10 p.m. on 17 July an unidentified aircraft was reported in the vicinity of Cupar, Fife, but on investigation nothing was seen. Standing patrols continued to be flown, commencing at around 11 p.m. with one Hurricane covering the Dunbar-Fifeness and the Fifeness-Arbroath area. During this month, 309's B-Flight moved closer to their colleagues at Drem—from RAF Hutton Cranswick to RAF Acklington. The detachment to RAF Acklington ceased around a month later when B-Flight moved to RAF Peterhead.

During August the Drem-based Hurricanes carried out several exercises with army units. The first took place on 3 August and involved the Artillery Field Regiment of the Czechoslovakian Independent Brigade. The Hurricanes' task was ranging and neutralisation involving a battery of 25-pounder field guns located on the Lammermuir Hills, approximately 7 miles south of the village of Garvald, East Lothian. A radio link was installed in a white scout car, enabling the pilots to communicate with the ground forces. Colonel Marek, the Artillery Regiment CO, was in attendance and was well pleased with the outcome: 'An excellent shoot demonstrating the splendid co-operation between the army and the RAF'.

A similar exercise was held the following day, but the weather conditions were not so amenable with ground haze developing in the afternoon. One pilot could not see where the HE shells were landing so he requested the gunners use shells that released smoke instead. A similar exercise was held on Otterburn Ranges on 1 September with D Battery, 3 Royal Artillery Reserve Regiment. Six sorties were arranged with each pilot given two targets, the first for registration and the second for neutralisation. Firing at ranges of 6,000 to 9,000 yards, the pilots directed their shots well.

Further diversion from the routine of standing patrols and training flights occurred on 12 August 1944, when two of 307's Hurricanes (Mk II) were ordered to guide a friendly aircraft to base. The pilots flew above the cloud at 14,000 feet where the visibility was excellent. The friendly aircraft, a Liberator, was then seen flying below them at 12,000 feet. The fighter pilots descended and signalled the Liberator to follow them, but despite all their gestures the Liberator crew refused to deviate from their course. The pilots reported this to the sector controller who instructed the Hurricanes to return to base and to leave the Liberator to continue on its way.

At the beginning of September, information was received from Air Defence of Great Britain (ADGB) that 309 Squadron would receive 'new' Mustangs (Mk I) to replace their Mk IIs. In the summer of 1944, the unit had initially been informed that it would receive more modern equipment in the form of the Spitfire Mk IX LF, only to be told it was to be the elderly Spitfire Mk II. Bad weather at the beginning of September made the airfield unusable. When conditions improved, the first Mustang I arrived from 41 OTU. Despite poor weather the squadron carried out numerous training flights, including cross-country, low flying, cine gun, aerobatics, high altitude, dive bombing, air-to-air firing, and battle formations. On 21 and 22 September King George VI and Queen Elizabeth visited Edinburgh. They slept in the royal train on the branch line to Aberlady, East Lothian. With the dire state of the runways at Drem brought on by the rain, air cover was provided by 309's B-Flight based at RAF Turnhouse, near Edinburgh, flown down from RAF Peterhead especially for the royal protection duty.

Until October, 309's stay at Drem had been remarkably free of crashes. On the 1st, Flt Lt Baranski in a Hurricane IIC (LF650) landed short and struck the sharp outside edge of the concrete perimeter track. The starboard tyre burst, collapsing the undercarriage leg and damaging the propeller and wing tip. On the 19th, a Mustang Mk I (AP177) landed with its undercarriage up after a test flight. The pilot was unhurt. On the 27th, on another test flight, the engine of a Mustang Mk I (AP170) cut out at 100 feet just after take-off. It then fired, only to cut out again. This continued as the aircraft lost altitude and made a belly landing in a field at Ballencrieff Mains Farm, approximately 2 miles from the airfield. The pilot, Flt Lt Miniszewski, was unhurt but the aircraft suffered damage to its engine, propeller and radiator.

It was not all bad news that month for 309 Squadron. It received the Mustang Mk III to replace the recently delivered Mk I, whereas the earlier versions of this aircraft had been restricted to fighter reconnaissance because of the low power ratings of their Allison engines at altitude, the Mustang Mk III had an American-built Rolls Royce Merlin. It was among the best of the RAF's fighters, remarkable for its great operational range when carrying drop tanks. As a consequence, 309's role changed from that of a fighter reconnaissance unit to a purely fighter one. The flying personnel also changed when the ten most experienced reconnaissance pilots were transferred to other units. Along with the new aircraft, there was a new squadron commander—Sqn Ldr Glowacki, an 'ace' and a hero from the Battle of Britain. He requested that the detachment of B-Flight at Peterhead be withdrawn, as he thought 309 Squadron could be trained more efficiently if it was a single unit. On 21 October, its five Mustangs (Mk I) touched down at Drem. This was the first time all the aircraft were based there.

Even while the squadron was training, it still provided fighter cover for south-east Scotland with aircraft at readiness until midnight. Scrambles in the autumn months but they were few and far between. At the end of the month, Drem's Achilles heel was again revealed when the runways became unserviceable because of poor weather. According to the CO of the station:

> The aerodrome has been unserviceable on a number of occasions this month due to heavy rain. This is causing some concern owing to the fact that the surface is not drying out as quickly as it should. Action is being taken by Air Ministry Works Department.[3]

A line-up of North American Mustang III operated by 309 Squadron and manned by Polish airmen in 1944. (*Wilhelm Ratuszyski*)

North American Mustang IIIs of 309 Squadron preparing to take off in 1944. The Garleton Hills are visible in the background. (*Wilhelm Ratuszyski*)

Characteristically for 309 Squadron, the checkerboards denoting a Polish Squadron were painted close behind the spinner's band, as seen on these Mustang III. (*Wilhelm Ratuszynski*)

North American Mustang IIIs of 309 Squadron taxi to take off. (*Wilhelm Ratusznski*)

The rain lasted into the next month and on 6 November it was decided to move some of the Mustangs to RAF Turnhouse to maintain fighter cover. This airfield had the luxury of concrete runways in contrast to the grass at Drem. The aircraft returned to their base three days later when the airfield was again serviceable.

On 11 November a signal was received from 13 Group Headquarters ordering 309 Squadron to move to Peterhead to carry out intensive training for bomber support. At the beginning of the month six Mustangs (Mk I) had been posted there for a couple of days to carry out convoy patrol duties. The squadron left for its new base two days after the order was received. Fourteen Mustangs (Mk III) took off at 2.55 p.m. north along the Scottish coast. The station commander of Drem expressed his appreciation for the care that the Polish personnel had taken of the buildings. A small detachment of four Mustangs (Mk III) remained to provide fighter cover. There was an accident on 27 November when Flt Lt Zajchowski's undercarriage collapsed after touching down at the end of a training flight. Royalty visited Clydebank at the end of the month with fighter cover provided by two sections of 309's aircraft deployed from RAF Peterhead to RAF Turnhouse. The detachment at Drem was rather surprisingly not involved in this detail.

Little occurred at Drem until all of the Squadron's aircraft were ordered south to RAF Andrews Airfield, Essex, to operate under 133 Wing. On 19 December, the Poles ceased to maintain their state of readiness at Drem and handed over responsibility for fighter cover to 340 Squadron Free French Air Force. The changeover was originally intended for 12 December, but was delayed as the French were weather bound at RAF Biggin Hill.

Due to adverse weather conditions in southern England, the detachment of four Mustangs were unable to leave for RAF Andrews Field until the end of December. No sooner had they arrived at their new base and been reunited with the rest of 309 Squadron than they were escorting large formations of Lancasters and Halifaxes on bombing raids over Germany. The Nazis were certain to be defeated, but the Polish pilots' dreams of freedom for their homeland would have to wait until the collapse of the USSR, half a century hence.

Allied Bombers

Although RAF Drem was a Fighter Command airfield, it did occasionally play host to bombers. When hostilities commenced in 1939, the RAF operated mainly slow, twin-engined Blenheims, Hampdens, Wellingtons, and Whitleys, all designed for primitive airfields and able to use the grass runway Drem. As the war progressed, Bomber Command graduated to operating predominately four-engined aircraft including the legendary Avro Lancaster as well as the Handley Page Halifax and Short Stirling. New airfields were constructed with hardened runways to accommodate these large machines and existing runways were upgraded.

In 1940, it was decided that all future airfields would have paved runways and that grass runways were suitable only for small training establishments. Official records do not make mention of any RAF four-engine bombers ever landing on Drem's grass runway, although an eye witness reported one instance of some Lancasters arriving by night and leaving after lunch. In November 1944, Coastal Command visited the station with a view to using it, but came to the conclusion that the airfield would not be suitable for use by heavy aircraft.

Early in the war, RAF planners decided to concentrate the bomber force in East Anglia, Lincolnshire, and Yorkshire, with training units being based mainly in the Midlands. In 1941 there were only two Bomber Command bases in Scotland—20 OTU at RAF Lossiemouth with Wellingtons and nearby 19 OTU at RAF Kinloss with Whitleys.

Throughout the war, ground crews for the fighter squadrons that deployed to Drem were ferried there in Handley Page Harrows of 271 Squadron. In 1937, the Harrow was one of the first monoplane bombers delivered to the RAF, but by 1939 all had been relegated to training or converted to transports. The latter version, sometimes nicknamed *Sparrow*, flew in and out of Drem for much of the war without difficulty.

Among the first RAF bombers to use Drem during the Second Wolrd War were Hampdens, unfortunately in tragic circumstances. On 21 December 1939, twenty-four Hampden Bombers of 49 and 83 Squadrons based at RAF Scampton and of 44 Squadron based at RAF Waddington, Lincolnshire, set out to locate and destroy the German pocket battleship *Deutschland*. They were acting on reports that it had been seen off the coast of Norway. The bombers failed to locate their objective and headed back across the North Sea towards Britain. Low on fuel, they headed for the nearest airfields in Scotland. In the process, the Hampdens of 49 Squadron became separated from the main force. As they made landfall at Blyth, Northumberland, they were intercepted by 43 Squadron's Hurricanes and escorted to RAF Acklington, the home base of the fighters. Hampden Mk I (L4072) ran out of fuel while attempting to land and struck the Church of Christ, close to the edge of the airfield. The aircraft crashed and burst into flames, claiming the lives of two of its crew. Another 49 Squadron Hampden ran out of fuel and crash-landed in a field north of Belford, Northumberland.

Fate treated the remaining fourteen aircraft little better. The commander believed he was heading for Peterhead and the sanctuary of the airfields at Lossiemouth and Kinloss. In fact, due to a navigational error, the aircraft were much further south and approaching the mouth of the Firth of Forth. As the formation was flying very low over the sea it went undetected by the radar chain until the last minute, but alarm bells began ringing when the Hampdens made landfall a short distance south of Dunbar. A revenge attack had been expected on Drem for the losses it had inflicted on the German bomber force that attacked Rosyth Naval Base two months earlier. No. 72's Hurricanes and 602's Spitfires were scrambled by Turnhouse Operations Room shortly after 3 p.m. to intercept what was thought to be a surprise attack.

In a dark and foggy December sky, the Spitfires bore down on the twin-engine bombers and riddled them with machine-gun fire. Hampden L4090, which was already flying on one engine when it was attacked, crashed into the sea at North Berwick. The local school children dashed down to the seashore to see what was happening. One of those present recollected:

> With lots of Spitfire fighter aircraft zooming about just above roof top level, word quickly went round that they had just shot down a bomber into the sea a few hundred yards off the old disused Victoria Pier. In addition to numerous naval patrol craft that were quickly on the scene a local fishing boat, named *Caithness Lass*, put out to help pick up any survivors. As a few of these saturated aircrew clambered ashore at the old Victoria Jetty and trundled up past the open air swimming pool, we were looking to see the Germans, as we thought, and to everyone's surprise and dismay saw only our own RAF uniforms. The story came out soon after that several Hampden bombers returning from an operation over the Norwegian coast failed to give the correct identification signal for the day and our defence Spitfires promptly brought it down just south of Craigleith Island.[1]

The aircraft reportedly sank within one minute. Of the crew of four, three survived including Sgt Tony Reid, who before the war had been an airline pilot flying the British Airways Lockheed 14. LAC Gibbin, the gunner, was killed during the attack. Once the leader of 602 Squadron recognised the bombers as being friendly the attack was aborted, but not before a second Hampden (L4089) had been downed in the Firth of Forth. Although it sank within fifteen seconds and its dinghy did not inflate, all four crew survived. The remaining Hampdens, with their fuel tanks almost dry, were forced to land at Drem.

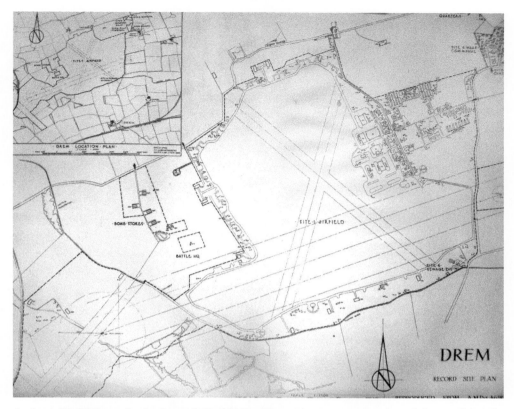

A plan of RAF Drem in the Second World War. The main runway runs from left to right at the southern end of the airfield. Interestingly, a complex of runways is depicted at the south-west corner of the plan, which almost constitutes a second airfield. However, they appear to have never been constructed. (*Aldon Ferguson*)

The following day, a Court of Enquiry was held at Drem. It exposed the confusion that existed when the formation of bombers flew over East Lothian. The Royal Observer Corps, for example, identified the aircraft as Hampdens, as did the Hurricane pilots of 72 Squadron:

> ... whilst the aircraft recognition of the 602 Squadron Spitfire pilots seems to be based on the premise that if it had two engines it was German, as the statements of two of the attacking pilots demonstrated.

The investigation rather surprisingly placed the blame for the tragedy on the bomber pilots: 'The onus of establishing identity rests with themselves'. Naturally, the Hampden crews were less than happy with this finding. On their departure from Drem they expressed their feelings for their hosts by bombarding the airfield with rolls of lavatory paper which they had removed from the airfield's toilets.

In the early months of the war there were numerous examples of Allied aircraft being fired on in error. One possible explanation is that many German aircraft had been developed in secrecy in the years preceding the war. The Allies had few photos of them and only sketchy details on a number of the lesser known types. No. 602 Squadron was itself involved in another incident of friendly fire not long after the incident with the Hampdens. One of its Spitfires on convoy escort was vectored onto a 'hostile' aircraft shadowing the convoy and fired a short burst at it. Fortunately, the pilot soon recognised it as an RAF Avro Anson. It was supporting new-style roundels, which in part was responsible for the fighter pilot's misidentification. No one in the squadron knew anything about the new markings. Compounding this was the fact that it was later discovered that the Spitfire pilot was colour blind.

Sgt Tony Reid, who survived the Hampden that crashed into the Firth of Forth, had the bad luck to be involved in another case of 'friendly fire', only a few months later. On 3 March 1940 he was flying a Hudson with an old friend who had also been a pilot with British Airways. They were on a routine flight, taking photographs of RAF airfields in south-east England so that the effectiveness of the camouflage could be assessed. While their Hudson was flying in perfect weather over Gravesend, the aircraft was attacked and shot down in flames by three Hurricanes. Tony Reid was the only member of the crew who managed to bale out, but had to spend four months in hospital undergoing skin grafts for burns before he was able return to flying.

On 12 February 1941, eleven Whitley bombers landed at Drem after a bombing raid on Germany. On this occasion they did not receive a hostile reception. There were five from 51 Squadron, one from 78 Squadron, RAF Disforth, Yorkshire, and five from 58 Squadron, RAF Linton-on-Ouse. Most of them departed over the next few days, although one Whitley of 58 Squadron did not leave until 18 February.

Until 1944, 19 OTU at RAF Kinloss operated a large number of Whitleys for training purposes. They often took part in fighter affiliation exercises with the Drem-based squadrons and visited the airfield from time to time. One Whitley (T4157) was damaged when it overshot in bad visibility on 27 December 1942. Another dropped in on 5 August 1943, after an engine had cut out at 10,000 feet; fortunately, it restarted when the aircraft dropped to 2,500 feet, but the pilot decided to make an emergency landing at Drem, where the Whitley stayed overnight. Wellingtons also occasionally touched down at Drem. On 28 August 1943, seven were diverted there from an exercise, probably because of poor weather. All had landed by 7 a.m. and it rained heavily all day.

By spring 1943, the Allies had driven the Germans out of North Africa with the help of the First Tactical Air Force. Experience had shown that the most successful and adaptable close support aircraft was the fighter bomber. Plans being laid for the invasion of Europe included the establishment of a Second Tactical Air Force, initially within Fighter Command, and in the summer of 1943 all the remaining light-medium day bombers with Bomber Command were transferred to it. No. 226 Squadron became part of the Second Tactical Air Force in November of that year and spent a couple of weeks at Drem in July 1943, refining their skills.

On 19 July, 226's newly delivered Mitchells (Mk II) took off in a formation of seven—a box of six with one behind—from their base at RAF Swanton Morley in Norfolk for the one-hour-thirty-five-minute flight to Drem. Some of the ground crew were transported in Harrows. No time was wasted, an exercise being flow the same afternoon. At 3.30 p.m., six aircraft rendezvoused with no less than ten Spitfires of

340 Squadron over the airfield at 10,000 feet. The Mitchells were in the air for around two hours, but one aircraft developed a runaway prop and had to land on one engine. Flying the following day was hampered by low cloud but some flying was done in the afternoon when six Mitchells took off at 6 p.m. for another exercise.

On 21 July, six aircraft, escorted by 340 Squadron, took off in the evening to carry out a practice attack on Dundee. Spitfires from the OTU at RAF Balado Bridge, near Kinross, were also detailed to participate, but in the end did not appear. The Mitchells flew out to sea in excellent weather for 30 miles before turning north-west, crossing the coast near Arbroath at 9,000 feet. Attempts were made by Hurricanes from RAF Tealing to intercept them. Two of these 'enemy fighters' that attacked the formation were bounced by the escorting Spitfires. After the 'bombing run' on the city, the formation headed towards the Bell Rock Lighthouse. The two Hurricanes then attacked again, but were repelled by all six escorting Spitfires. The following morning 'heads were again popped round the tent flaps to see a morning fog on the hills—so that's what Scotch mist looks like'.[2] As on the previous day the fog soon cleared and flying was possible. Six aircraft carried out a simulated attack on the naval base at Rosyth. They commenced their exercise by rendezvousing over Holy Island: 'this squadron didn't stay there long!' A second attack was made on the same target later in the day.

On the 23rd, there was little flying in the morning due to poor weather. Eventually six Mitchells took off and were escorted by three of 340's Spitfires to make a simulated bombing attack on Prestwick airfield. Over the target area they were attacked by fighters from RAF Ayr. After the exercise, the Mitchells and 340 Squadron Spitfires landed there. On the return leg of the journey, the bombers made a practice attack on Waverley Station, Edinburgh. This time the escort was provided by 64's Spitfires (Mk V) from RAF Ayr and 340 Squadron were the attackers: 'Scotland is not looking particularly the worse for wear but the Squadron has a few days to go yet'.[3]

On the 24th, Aberdeen was the target. A second simulated bombing raid escorted by nine of 340's Spitfires was flown in the afternoon, when Glasgow Docks received the bombers' attention. The mission was not a success as the 'enemy' fighters did not turn up and the visibility was poor. A third sortie was flown against Rosyth Naval Base. This time there were frequent fighter attacks on the Mitchells, 'too numerous in the view of the crews who were swearing freely when they landed'.[4] The following day the mist was slow to clear, curtailing some of the training programme. Six Mitchells took off in the evening when conditions had improved but were still not ideal. Fighter affiliation was carried out over an area to the south of Perth. Six of 340's Spitfires performed the attacks which were mainly head on. Two days later an attack was carried out on the Army Headquarters at Aberdeen.

On their last day of their detachment to Drem, 226 Squadron received a visit from AM HRH The Duke of Gloucester. He showed great interest in their activities and clambered all over a Mitchell. After the royal visit, the aircrew climbed into all sorts of inconceivable positions aboard a Mitchell to pose for the squadron photograph: 'The ground crew were a bit impatient during the posing, as the NAAFI van was standing close by'. In the evening, seven aircraft took off for the last exercise of the detachment. Four were to attack Rosyth at high level and a further three to perform a low-level raid on Sector Control at Edinburgh, where the Duke of Gloucester would be observing the exercise. Unfortunately, the programme could not be completed due to adverse weather: 'Cloud was very low over the hills—and the hills around here look nice but would not feel so good!' Instead 340 Squadron put no less than twelve of their Spitfires in the air and carried out escort and attacks on the Mitchells at very low level in the vicinity of Drem airfield.

No. 226's Mitchells departed for their home base at 9 a.m. on 29 July. Seven aircraft were to depart, but one went unserviceable and was left behind with a ground party working on it. Commandant Fornier of 340 Squadron escorted the formation as far as Newcastle in his Spitfire. Among the Mitchell aircrew was Arthur Jones DFC who recalled the following about his visit to Scotland:

> There was often low cloud around 800 feet or so during the Squadron's detachment to Drem. We flew across other airfields in the area at a height of 500 feet. This annoyed their controllers who fired off red Very cartridge warnings ... We carried out a mock attack on Edinburgh flying over the sea at a height of 10,000 feet. The anti-aircraft crews said they would have shot all the 226 Squadron aircraft down. When asked by the aircrew at what height did they think the Mitchells were flying at they said 15,000 feet. They were 5,000 feet out and would have been unlikely to have shot any of them down.

The day after returning to RAF Swanton Morley, Arthur Jones's Mitchell was in action over the Dutch Coast, circling a downed US airman in a dinghy. Suddenly eight Me 210s arrived on the scene and shot up the Mitchell, which crashed into the sea 60 miles off Texel, Netherlands. Arthur Jones fortunately managed to escape from the downed aircraft and spent five days in a dinghy before being rescued by the Royal Navy. He commented that his 'stay at Drem and the associated exercises with the fighter aircraft had been of little good'. On a more positive note, Arthur Jones survived the war and lived into the twenty-first century.

In the latter part of the war, the US Army Air Force had large numbers of four-engine Flying Fortress and Liberator bombers based in Britain, mostly concentrated in East Anglia and the neighbouring counties. There were no operational American airfields in Scotland and activity by their aircraft in this part of Britain was somewhat limited.

However, Americans had served with the RAF squadrons at Drem since the beginning of the war. On 4 April 1944, Captain Wootten of the American IX Fighter Command was at Drem to discuss the accommodation of one USAAF unit there. This seems to have progressed beyond the discussion stage, as on 22 April, the 75th Station Complement Squadron arrived. These units consisted of around a 100 personnel including engineers, airfield controllers and specialists in airfield defence, who prepared sites for the operation of US aircraft. The 75th stayed at Drem until the beginning of June, when it moved to RAF Scorton. There is no evidence that any aircraft were based at Drem in connection with this unit, but Kenneth McDowall, a plane spotter, who lived at the edge of the airfield recollected that 'the best beat-up of the war was made by four USAAF Lockheed Lightnings'. This seems to be evidence that US fighters did sometimes come there. Boeing B-17 Flying Fortresses also occasionally visited Drem on training flights. One took some WRNS officers for a flight 'and not just a quick circuit either!'

B-17G (42-317150) from 306 Bombardment Group based at RAF Thurleigh, Bedfordshire, touched down at Drem on 3 February 1944, while on a cross-country exercise. It stayed overnight and the crew prepared to depart after dinner on the following day. They managed to start three engines, but the fourth had a faulty starter. The pilot taxied the aircraft towards the runway, but it became bogged in the soft earth. The Duty Engineer came to the American's assistance and organised a crane and tractor to pull them free. He also offered to repair the engine, but the Americans refused, saying they had taken off on three engines before, as it was not the first time they had experienced this trouble. The pilot then began taxiing, but after 10 yards the Flying Fortress again sank into the mud. The duty engineer, perhaps with a premonition of disaster, said the tractor was not available as it was tea time and advised the pilot to stay until the following morning, by which time he would have the faulty engine repaired. The pilot replied that he would like to take off as soon as possible, so they could be home by dusk. Eventually the plane was again pulled free by the tractor and reached runway 32, which was partly uphill and uneven. A strong breeze was blowing, but the pilot informed Flying Control that he was satisfied with the conditions. It appeared that the B-17 commenced its take-off some 300 yards short of the end of the runway and out of line, further shortening of the length of run available. The flying control officer realized that the take-off was dangerous, although by then it was too late to intervene.

The aircraft had become airborne when the port aileron struck the top of an aircraft shelter pen. The aileron broke off, but the aircraft staggered on for a further 150 yards before crashing in a field, where it burst into flames. The fire engine arrived almost immediately, but the conflagration was so great that nothing could be done. Rescue efforts were further hampered by exploding ammunition. The crash claimed the lives of the four US crew—Lt A. Mosley, 2-Lt W. Ellertson, 2-Lt M. Roskovich, and 2-Lt E. O'Malley. Two British servicemen—Naval rating W. L. Rowe (784 Squadron) and RAF Airman Hodgkins, attached to the radar station at RAF Dirleton—who were hitching a ride to England with the Americans, also died. On 5 March, four American officers arrived from RAF Thurleigh to identify the bodies of the American airmen and interview witnesses to the crash. Their report put the entire blame on the pilot: '100% pilot error in attempting to take off on three engines with fourth windmilling and not using full length of field for the run'.

Although over 100 aircrew are thought to have lost their lives in crashes in East Lothian during the Second World War, such a large loss of life in a single incident was rare. There were a small number of exceptions, in addition to the Flying Fortress disaster. On 20 April 1945, just days from the end of the conflict in Europe, a Wellington Mk X (LP760), from 19 OTU based at Kinloss, disintegrated in flight and crashed at Bankheads Farm, near Humbie. All six of its crew perished.

A month earlier, on 19 February 1945, Lancaster III (NE179) of No. 1669 Heavy Conversion Unit crashed within sight of Drem airfield, just south of Fenton Tower, Kingston. The pilot under instruction took off on a cross country training flight with six crew. The route entailed flying out to sea 85 miles east of Edinburgh, then to 25 miles north of Glasgow, then returning to its base in England via Southport. The flight engineer, also a pilot, was flying the aircraft approaching Edinburgh at 20,000 feet. In order to check the camera settings for a vertical picture of Edinburgh, the flight engineer had to go down into the nose of the aircraft. When approaching North Berwick he handed over the controls of the aircraft to the captain, who replaced him in the pilot's seat.

The automatic pilot was not connected and he did not have time to plug in the intercommunication or to do up the parachute harness. The plane began to dive, so he slowly trimmed back the controls. After descending about 2,000 feet it went into a much steeper dive. The Lancaster was now diving vertically, but the pilot managed to regain control at about 5,000 feet by applying elevator trim and closing the throttle. On recovery the aircraft climbed vertically and stalled. The same cycle of events occurred several times until the Lancaster crashed.

According to witnesses, the aircraft was performing violent aerobatics and appeared to be out of control. Fg Off. H. Carr, an Australian and FS Wifani, a New Zealander, parachuted to safety from around 500 feet. The other crew members were still in the aircraft when it crashed. Plt Off. A. Denaro (the pilot), Sgt Hodges (pilot engineer), and Plt Off. D. Gould were gravely injured and Sgt H. Beaumont (navigator) was seriously injured; Sgt Waters was killed. The crew were collected by an ambulance from Drem as the one sent from RAF East Fortune, the nearest airfield to the crash, became bogged down. Two of the injured crew later died of their injuries. Crash investigators stated that 'the elevators were unmodified and the nature of the failure was typical of that of a Lancaster in a high speed dive without Mod. 1131 incorporated'.

In spring 1945, Drem was handed over to the Fleet Air Arm, which would have seen an end to regular visits by RAF bombers, although they would have still frequently flown over the area on exercises like that of the ill-fated Lancaster.

12

Search and Rescue

Today, search and rescue operations are synonymous with the helicopter. The first helicopters were not delivered to the British armed forces until 1945, so during the Second World War downed pilots had to rely on being spotted from the air and then rescued by high-speed launches or amphibious aircraft.

In 1939, the RAF had a number of high-speed, air-sea rescue launches stationed around the coast. Other than this, little thought had been given to the rescue of pilots. Apart from the humanitarian aspect, this did not recognise that pilots were the RAF's most important asset. They took a long time to train and could not quickly be replaced. Many of the early air battles of the war took place above the English Channel. By the time the high-speed rescue launch arrived on the scene, the pilot—who may have survived the initial crash—had drowned or been overcome by exposure. Had help arrived sooner he may well have survived. Frustrated by the needless death of their colleagues, various suggestions were put forward by pilots to their superiors in Fighter Command to make the rescue service more effective.

Aircraft crew could spot a pilot floating in the water more easily than someone on a high-speed launch so, in early 1941, a small number of search and rescue flights were established flying Westland Lysanders. Prior to this, pilots often flew their fighters over the sea to try and locate a downed colleague. The fast Spitfires and Hurricanes were ill-suited to the task, but fighters from Drem persisted in going in search of missing aircraft until the closing years of the war. One of the most notable examples of such a mission was the search for a missing BOAC Lockheed-14 Super Electra airliner G-ACNG, flown by a pilot that had once transported the prime minister. On 23 April 1940, a Blenheim of 29 Squadron (29 Squadron's log book refers to it incorrectly as a de Havilland DH86) unsuccessfully searched the area around Loch Lomond where the plane had reportedly come down. The airliner was found some time later burnt out on a mountainside, all five occupants dead.

Another example of a rescue in the days before there were specialised aircraft for this role occurred on 20 December 1941. A Spitfire of 340 Free French Air Force Squadron, piloted by Maurice Daligot, had crashed into the Firth of Forth. No less than ten Spitfires from the same squadron took off to search. Additional fighters from 611 Squadron, also based at Drem, assisted in the operation. Soon after the accident a rescue launch pulled two pilots from the water near the reported position of the Frenchman. It was not until ninety minutes later that these men were found to be the 'wrong ones'. They were the crew of a Swordfish and were not even known to be missing. The following day, air-sea rescue boats were still looking for the pilot, accompanied by several aircraft: 'Every square yard of water in the target area explored time after time and not a trace of pilot or plane, dinghy or parachute'.

On 1 October 1941, 278 Squadron—the first specialised air-sea rescue squadron—was formed. It initially operated Lysanders and had detachments at several airfields in Scotland including Ayr, Peterhead, and, from April 1942, Drem (there is no mention of the latter posting in the squadron log book). By the end of 1941 there were six air-sea rescue squadrons. Four were equipped with Lysanders and Walruses; the latter, being amphibians, could land in the sea and pick up the downed airmen. Two other squadrons flew Ansons, which were able to operate at night. The next air-sea rescue unit at Drem was a flight from 281 Squadron based at RAF Ouston, near Newcastle, which arrived on 29 June 1942. Initially non-operational because of a shortage of senior NCOs—the final complement was two officers, five sergeants, one corporal, and twelve airmen—the unit's first flights from Drem were not until 15 July.

The squadron operated three Defiants, handed down from fighter squadrons, modified to carry an M-Type dinghy in a special pack on the under-wing bomb racks. Drem was one of the first RAF airfields to have the benefit of these modified Defiants, first operational in March 1942. During the first part of 1943, 289 Squadron received Avro Ansons as well as Walrus amphibian aircraft. The first Anson appears to have arrived for the detachment at Drem by June and a Walrus was in use the following month.

The first practice mission (homing on a smoke flare) was held at Drem on 13 July 1943. The following day, an air-sea rescue exercise was carried out with a seaplane tender from Tayport. The first operational mission was flown from Drem on 24 July 1942 when Plt Off. Cushman and FS Hall, air gunner, searched for a reported parachute descent—it turned out to be a punctured barrage balloon. On 28 July, Plt Off. Cotton in Defiant T4000 dropped a yellow-painted barrel into the sea 40 miles east of Montrose to serve as a target for an exercise. On his return to Drem, Cotton was instructed to look for a downed pilot reported off Crail, but he was ordered to call off the search when the pilot was picked up by a nearby boat. By this time Cotton was short of fuel and had to land at the Naval Air Station at Crail. He had just taken off again when sector control informed him that there was an aircraft in distress off St Abb's Head. He joined a second aircraft flown by Plt Off. King at the search area and saw three Spitfires orbiting over a convoy. It was found that the IFF (Identification, Friend or Foe) signal of one Spitfire was erroneously sending an SOS. At the end of a demanding day both Defiants finally returned to Drem.

6 August 1942: 281 Squadron Defiant scrambled at 1.17 p.m. (three minutes from 'readiness' to take-off). Search for a Hurricane called off. Aircraft had crash-landed on land.

11 August 1942: Plt Off. King's Defiant took off at 4.25 a.m. Search for the dinghy of a downed Hampden called off at 5.40 a.m. when the dinghy was picked up by a high-speed launch.

19 August 1942: Search throughout the day for a crashed Whitley north-east of Holy Island, Northumberland. Plt Off. Cotton eventually sighted the aircraft, lying 100 yards off Holy Island and reported the bomber could be salvaged.

24 August 1942: Plt Off. Cotton's search in the afternoon for the pilot of a downed Hurricane was abandoned when no trace of the plane could be found.

5 October 1942: A six-hour search by three Defiants of the sea off Cockburnspath, Berwickshire for a Bristol Blenheim. Only the pilot's parachute was found.

17 October 1942: A two-hour search by Plt Off. Cushman (Defiant) for a Whitley bomber. No trace found despite a second search.

November 1942: Two Defiants searched for a Fairey Battle believed to be in the sea off Berwick-upon-Tweed. No trace was found.

14 February 1943: A four-hour search by three Defiants for two Drem-based 197 Squadron Typhoons which had crashed in the Lammermuir Hills. Afterwards Plt Off. Cotton searched for the pilot of an aircraft downed in the Firth of Forth near May Island. The pilot was rescued by boat. The following day, the wreckage of the Typhoons was discovered on the hills.

22 February 1943: An unsuccessful two-hour search by two Defiants—N1613 and T3912—for a Beaufighter in the sea 20 miles east of the Bass Rock. The crew were picked eventually up by boat.

3 May 1943: Sgt Burgess's Defiant was diverted from air-gunnery practice (the aircraft retained machine guns in the rear turret) to search for a Bristol Beaufighter reported down in the sea. A large patch of oil and a dinghy were sighted. A high-speed launch later retrieved the pilot's body.

5 May 1943: A four-hour uneventful search by two Defiants north-east of Dunbar. Oil spotted, but thought not to have been caused by a downed aircraft.

27 June 1943: FS Colbourne airborne at 3.05 p.m. to search for a ditched Fairey Swordfish 6 miles east of Leven, in Fife. One of several small boats picked up the pilot's body.

2 July 1943: A single aircraft search near Grangemouth located a downed Lancaster on the south bank of the River Forth. After returning due to radio failure, the search aircraft returned to guide a navy boat to the wreckage.

19 July 1943: 281 Squadron aircraft searched for two Walrus aircraft reported downed 4 miles east of RAF Leuchars, Fife. Pieces of wreckage were seen and picked up by a high-speed launch.

28 July 1943: The pilot of a Fairey Swordfish was spotted clinging to the tail wheel of his crashed machine. Whilst endeavouring to drop a rescue dinghy, Sgt Burgess misjudged his height and flew into the sea. Fortunately, he and his crew man, AC Vincent, were rescued unhurt by a fishing boat. Sgt Burgess then directed the boat to the pilot in the sea who was successfully rescued. Burgess and Vincent later spent the night in sick quarters at Crail.

30 July 1943: FS Fisher and crew took off at 5.30 a.m. to look for a Mosquito in the sea off Montrose. Some wreckage was located which was investigated by a high speed launch but there was no sign of any survivors.

31 July 1943: FS Burgess in an Anson searched the sea between St Abb's Head and North Berwick for the crew of a Beaufighter who had baled out. After forty-five minutes a dinghy with one occupant was sighted and picked up by a high-speed launch. No other survivors were found.

5 August 1943: An Anson was sent in heavy mist and low cloud to investigate a Flying Fortress down in the sea a mile off Berwick-upon-Tweed. The weather at the time was very bad with. After a difficult and unsuccessful search, the Anson returned. Later Plt Off. King did a sweep around the coast but saw no survivors.

16 August 1943: An Anson and another aircraft of 281 Squadron searched unsuccessfully for a downed Mosquito. The information given to the Ansons was later found to be inaccurate.

18 August 1943: Walrus W3083 was on a flight to test its radio when 'one belligerent seagull encountered off the Bass Rock flew into the starboard main plane, freeing two smoke floats, breaking a spar in the wing'.

19 August 1943: FS Colbourne and crew in an Anson searched for three hours forty minutes for a Wellington suspected down in the sea off Fifeness. A second aircraft joined in but only patched of oil were spotted.

5 September 1943: At 7.45 a.m. Sgt Cullimore and three crew members in an Anson attempted in heavy rain and a gale to intercept a lost Wellington. An hour later, when the Anson had managed to get within 3 miles, the radar plot of the distressed aircraft faded. Sgt Cullimore descended through cloud at 250 feet to search the sea 20 miles east of Stonehaven, but the search was called off due to the extremely bad weather. The Anson landed back at Drem at 11.10 a.m. with Sgt Cullimore and his crew 'having put up a very good show indeed'. Two more Ansons took off to search

at 1.05 p.m. and 3.45 p.m. The second aircraft, flown by FS Fisher, located a dinghy with three occupants. An M-type dinghy was dropped which the survivors managed to reach from their own craft.

8 September 1943: Both the Walrus aircraft based at Drem were reported to be unserviceable.

30 September 1943: An Anson flown by Fg Off. J. Dow (RCAF) with three crew members on a navigation exercise, crashed into Mellock Hill 3 miles north-east of Glendevon. WO Roberts (RCAF) was seriously injured and two other crew were slightly hurt. The Anson was a write off.

8 October 1943: An Anson was scrambled at 12.50 p.m. to 7 miles from May Island where a Beaufighter had dived into the sea. Only wreckage and oil was located. The search was resumed when an observer was pulled from the sea by a boat. The Walrus was airborne for two-and-a-half hours, but found no trace of the pilot. Later in the day the observer died from his injuries.

10 October 1943: Exercise 'Thomson' was held in conjunction with the Army and the Home Guard in bad weather. Two home guard observers in FS Fisher's aircraft were very sick.

12 October 1943: FS Cullimore with three other crew members in Anson 'Alpine 14' searched for a Beaufighter that had crashed east of Eyemouth. A Lysander also circled the area where pieces of wreckage were sighted. The rescue launch failed to appear and FS Cullimore flew down to Berwick-upon-Tweed and found it still in the harbour. He instructed it via radio to join the search but nothing was found.

19 October 1943: Anson 'Alpine 6' and the Walrus, both with three man crews, searched for a Drem-based 340 Squadron Spitfire that had crashed into the sea 3 miles north-east of the Bass Rock. Arriving on scene within ten minutes, they found a Spitfire orbiting the position marked only a patch of oil. The rescue aircraft returned to Drem.

Towards the end of October, the AOC Group visited Drem. Plt Off. Dow was interviewed and received a reprimand and a three-month loss of seniority for his involvement in the crash of the Anson on 30 September 1943. No. 281 Squadron received a 'new' Anson from 280 Squadron. On examination it was found to be old and in bad condition.

November 1943 began with a spell of bad weather. Aircraft were dispatched to RAF Ayr to reinforce the detachment there, which was involved in an operation at Port Ellen. The crew of both the Walrus and the high-speed launch got into trouble and had themselves to be pulled from the sea by crew of a destroyer. The final mission flown by 281 Squadron's Drem detachment occurred on 21 November 1943. Fg Off. King was diverted north during a test flight to a reported crash near the Fleet Air Arm station at Easthaven near Angus. A second aircraft was scrambled but both were recalled as the crashed aircraft had come down on land. No. 281 Squadron's association with Drem came to an end on 22 November 1943 when it was absorbed into 282 Squadron, which had been formed at RAF Castletown with a mixture of Ansons and Walruses at the beginning of 1943. A farewell party for 281 Squadron was held at the Dirleton Hotel on the 29th. The detachment at Drem was now under the control of 282 Squadron as was that at RAF Ayr.

24 November 1943: FS Colbourne searched for a Beaufighter reported missing off Berwick-upon-Tweed at 3 a.m. in an area that extended 35 miles out to sea. Rain reduced visibility down to 100 yards in places, causing the search to be abandoned.

28 November 1943: An Anson searched at first light for a Swordfish that had come down near Fifeness. After returning due to bad weather, the renewed search—joined by a Walrus—found a dinghy and some small pieces of wreckage.

2 December 1943: At 10 a.m., FS Walters searched the sea off Montrose for a downed Oxford. Twenty minutes later, Fg Off. King's Walrus joined in. The aircraft returned after two and three hours respectively. The crashed Oxford was located on land after a thorough search had been made in bad weather.

18 December 1943: Fg Off. Daw and his crew took off at 8.30 a.m., followed by a second aircraft a short time later, to search for a 'civil airliner'—a Lockheed 18 Lodestar recently transferred from BOAC to the Norwegian Air Force—in the sea some 16 miles north of the Bell Rock Lighthouse. Around 250 square miles were searched. Six RAF Hampdens also took part. Nothing was found.

19 December 1943: A search was made for a landing barge, which was adrift. It was discovered at the Isle of May being towed by a fishing vessel.

22 December 1943: While on a practice flight, FS Walters and crew were directed to search for a 485 Squadron Spitfire in the sea near St Abb's Head. By the time they reached the position, the dead pilot had been picked up by a destroyer: 'Our aircraft arrived in position in 13 minutes from the time of the phone call from Ops. A very good show but unfortunately an unhappy ending'.

1 January 1944: Four operational sorties were flown for over twelve hours in search of Beaufighter II V8135, which had crashed into the sea off the Farne Islands while on a night exercise. Nothing was found.

5 January 1944: Fg Off. King and crew were scrambled at 4.16 p.m. to look for the crew of Beaufighter JL425 from RAF East Fortune, which had crashed in the sea about 3 miles south of May Island when flying in formation at 1,000 feet.

No survivors were found although a partially inflated dinghy was seen floating in the sea.

10 January 1944: The Ansons and Walrus were diverted from a training flight to a crash site 12 miles north of Drem. Fg Off. King landed his Walrus on the sea and searched around the scene of the crash. Apart from some wreckage and a dinghy, nothing was found.

15 January 1944: WO Burgess's Anson was diverted from an air-sea rescue exercise to search for a Barracuda downed 3 miles south of Fifeness. The Walrus was sent to assist and taxied on the sea around the site. Its crew were then informed that the three crew of the Barracuda had been picked up earlier by a boat.

18 January 1944: Plt Off. Dow's aircraft was instructed to search for a Hawker Hurricane in the Stirling area. Bad visibility in the area made the search impossible.

20 January 1944: At the request of flying control officer, FS Colbourne and crew plotted the position of grounded balloons around Gullane.

29 January 1944: FS Colbourne and crew were scrambled at 9 a.m. to search 96 miles north-east of Drem where the radar plot of a Halifax had faded. They were airborne for over four hours, but saw nothing. A further two unsuccessful sorties were flown by 282 Squadron until the search was abandoned at 5.20 p.m. An Anson was flown from the detachment at RAF Ayr to assist as Drem had only one aircraft available.

30 January 1944: FS Colbourne and crew were scrambled at 1.15 p.m. to an area some 100 miles east of Drem where a Warwick was orbiting a dinghy. The Warwick was a version of the Wellington bomber used by Coastal Command for search and rescue. They arrived to find three Warwicks overflying the scene. Despite the numerous rescue aircraft, the dinghy was lost from sight. A further aircraft was dispatched from Drem to relieve FS Colbourne, but it had to return because of a faulty compass. The dinghy was again located but the daylight was fast fading.

31 January 1944: FS Colbourne and his crew continued the search. The plan was to cover an area of the North Sea 110 miles from base, some 50 miles long by 25 miles wide. Just over half the area was covered with no result. A Whitley discovered the dinghy some 30 miles north of the search area. A high-speed launch was directed to it and found several survivors on board. No. 282 Squadron was congratulated by 13 Group for its efforts, particularly in view of the poor serviceability of the flight's aircraft. Keeping the aircraft serviceable was a constant battle for 282 Squadron's detachment and other rescue units based at Drem. Often there was only two or three aircraft available. In an emergency, flights based at RAF Ayr and RAF Castletown would send additional aircraft and vice versa.

At the end of January 1944, 282 Squadron's association with Drem came to an end. On 1 February the unit reformed to operate Warwicks at Davidstow Moor under the control of Coastal Command. No. 278 Squadron took over the air-sea rescue flight at Drem. Its headquarters was at RAF Coltishall in Norfolk, but it already controlled a number of aircraft in Northern Scotland, including RAF Sumburgh, RAF Peterhead and RAF Castletown.

6 February 1944: The first rescue mission flown by 278's detachment involved five sorties in search of a Wellington, last seen over Drem flying north. The mouths of the Firth of Forth and Firth of Tay were searched but nothing was seen until 5.30 p.m. when an empty dinghy was reported by a Beaufighter 7 miles off St Abb's Head. It was not possible to locate this in the short time left before nightfall. The following morning another search was made for the dinghy.

10 February 1944: An Anson took off in the afternoon to search for a Fleet Air Arm Barracuda that had come down in the sea, 1½ miles from Crail. The crew were rescued by a fishing boat.

17 February 1944: One Anson went to Ayr to assist in a search for an aircraft that had crashed into the sea off Arran.

Only six sorties took place between 20 and 29 February due to a shortage of aircraft and bad weather. Earlier in the month one Anson had been loaned to RAF Castletown. There was a delay in its return as it was found to be in need of a complete overhaul.

2 March 1944: An Anson took off at midday to drop food to the crew of the aerial lighthouse* near St Abb's Head, which had been cut off by heavy snow. Later, there was a search for a Barracuda reported in the sea close to Elie. A destroyer and two fishing boats also searched the area, but found only a petrol tank and a deflated dinghy. (*The aerial lighthouse should not be confused with the shipping lighthouse at this location. It was one of a series of light beacons visible only to aircraft approaching the east coast. These navigation lights were part of the 'Occult' project).

4 March 1944: Two aircraft searched for a Mosquito reported in the sea near the Bell Rock. Nothing was found.

13 March 1944: Two Ansons took off at 9.45 a.m. and 12.20 p.m. to search for a Spitfire pilot reported to have baled out east of Lanark. The search was carried out in a very strong wind but visibility was good. The pilot was later found dead in the aircraft which had been located at Carstairs the previous evening. The Spitfire XIV RB172 was from 91 Squadron, also based at Drem.

20 March 1944: FS Cullimore's Anson searched the Firth of Forth area for over three hours from 7 a.m. for Beaufighter JL652, reported missing from RAF East Fortune

and last heard of over the airfield. Nothing was found and Coastal Command took over. A second Anson then searched for a Beaufighter R2452 from RAF Charterhall that had disappeared off St Abb's Head while flying at night. A further two aircraft joined this search, but again nothing was found.

28 March 1944: At 2.50 p.m., FS Cullimore and crew in an Anson and Flt Lt Emus and crew in a Walrus searched for an aircraft reported to have gone into the sea north-east of Fifeness. Cloud from 500 feet down to sea level made searching difficult, but oil and wreckage were eventually sighted 1 mile off Fifeness. Flt Lt Emus landed and, aided by the high-speed launch directed by FS Cullimore, picked up some of the wreckage which was strewn along a 1,200 foot line. There was no sign of the pilot who presumably died instantly. The wreckage was later identified as a Hurricane. This was the last recorded operation by an air-sea rescue squadron based at Drem.

No. 278 Squadron continued to train during the first part of April 1944 despite being restricted by poor weather. On 15 April 1944, Coastal Command took over responsibility for all the search and rescue flights under the control of Fighter Command, including 278 Squadron. This meant that many airfields in Scotland lost their aircraft employed in this role. The detachment at Drem was informed to move to RAF Portreath, in Cornwall. Aircrews remained at readiness until 12.01 a.m. on the 21 April. Later the same day, three Ansons and two Walrus departed and the last of 278's aircraft left shortly after 11 a.m. on 22 April 1944. Thus ended Drem's role as a base for air-sea rescue units.

No. 309 Polish Squadron, flying Hawker Hurricanes out of Drem for much of 1944, was sometimes called upon to fly searches. For example, on 21 July 1944 two of their aircraft were requested to search to a suspected crash site between St Andrews and Bell Rock Lighthouse. Nothing was found during the fifty-minute search. Just over a month later Hurricanes took off from Drem at 6.30 a.m. to look for a Mosquito that was reported down in the sea approximately 6 miles east of RAF Leuchars. After a few orbits over the area at low level, an oil patch, a few pieces of plywood, and a dinghy or parachute were seen. A short time later, a Coastal Command Warwick was guided to the debris by the Hurricanes. It dropped markers and the Hurricanes then returned to Drem.

On 1 February 1945, Anson NK945 was on a flight from RAF Kinross to RAF Castle Bromwich, in Warwickshire, when it flew into a snowstorm. The pilot turned back but struck the crest of Turf Law, in the Lammermuir Hills, 4 miles north-west of Oxton. The aircraft broke up and rolled into a steep valley. The wreckage was hidden by snow and not found until seven days later by a shepherd. Two of its crew, Flt Lt R. Ferguson and POA Davidson, were killed instantly. The third, Flt Lt Václav Jícha (a Czech), survived the impact, but died from exposure as he crawled through the snow looking for help. He was a distinguished fighter pilot, who took part in the Battle of Britain and had shot down seven enemy aircraft before his death. Sub-Lt Farquharson arrived here in another Anson on the following day to assist in the recovery of the bodies. Flt Lt R. Ferguson was buried in Dirleton Cemetery and Flt Lt Václav Jícha in St Mary's Roman Catholic Cemetery, in Haddington.

13

Airfield Defences

The threat of invasion had long concerned those responsible for the defence of the realm, but never was the threat of enemy troops rampaging through the land greater than in the early years of the Second World War. A great deal of effort was put into constructing invasion defences along hundreds of miles of coast. The beaches of the Firth of Forth were rapidly covered with numerous kinds of obstacles to deter a German seaborne landing and soon concrete blocks covered all the beaches of East Lothian. Pillboxes and machine-gun posts were hastily built to protect road junctions and other potential targets.

There were several such defences in the vicinity of Drem airfield. Neighbouring RAF Macmerry was protected by a large number of pillboxes. Drone Hill radar station was similarly protected—these concrete structures now constitute some of the few surviving remains of this important complex. There was not only a fear that German troops may mount a seaborne invasion, but that units may arrive in large gliders. To counter this, wooden poles were erected on potential landing sites–at the density of one per acre on Castlemains farm, a short distance from Drem airfield. Later they were overshadowed by the six 90-foot radio communications masts situated at three sites there.

On Drem airfield, the fighters were dispersed around the boundary to reduce the chances of being hit by enemy bombs. Blast protection was provided by fighter pens usually constructed of sandbags. Unusually, this airfield had at least one small log stockade to protect aircraft. In spring 1940, City of Glasgow Squadron dispersed their Spitfires along the eastern boundary from the petrol farm southwards, despite the fact that 'it will entail a long walk for some'. Other measures considered for reducing the likely casualties of a bombing raid included having maintenance personnel sleep off the airfield and pilots living at dispersal points, only coming to the mess for meals and washing. At other airfields, tarmac runways were painted to camouflage them. There was no need for this with the grass runways at Drem. Second World War aerial photographs show the airfield to be very well disguised, the runways blending smoothly into the surrounding landscape. The airfield maintains a checkerboard field pattern as if a variety of crops were still being grown on it.

The fighter squadrons scattered their aircraft around Drem, and they sometimes flew them to other airfields. Macmerry Airfield, a short distance west, had been used as a landing ground in the 1930s by the Edinburgh Flying Club. It was first considered for the dispersal of fighters in March 1940, but at that time the site was heavily populated with construction workers. At the beginning of June, the state of the site had improved. Runways had been marked out, but the surface had not yet been prepared nor the grass cleared away. When 602 (City of Glasgow) Squadron landed a number of their aircraft here as an experiment, they were almost shaken to pieces by the bumps in the ground. Despite this, Spitfires regularly migrated here to spend the night.

Initially, one of the attractions of operating from here was that the pilots could sleep in the clubhouse, but by July this was no longer available and instead they had to spend the night under canvas next to their aircraft. No. 263 Squadron's Hurricanes were the next to use Macmerry—for a few days in November, 1940. The following year, on 16 January, 607's Hurricanes deployed here from RAF Usworth. The Duke of Kent visited them a few days later. One of their aircraft crashed near Haddington on 9 February, killing Plt Off. Burwell-Phillips DFM. At the beginning of March the whole squadron moved the short distance east to Drem. From this time on, the threat of an enemy attack on airfields in south-east Scotland began to recede and there was less need to conceal aircraft away from their main base.

A brick pillbox, built to defend the hangars at Drem and photographed in 2015. (*Malcolm Fife*)

The feared blitz on Drem never materialised, but it occasionally received the attention of a lone raider. An enemy aircraft approached the airfield from the south at 1 a.m. on 30 August 1940 and dropped ten bombs approximately ¾ mile from the eastern boundary. All fell in open country, causing little damage other than a wounded bullock. Four high-explosive bombs were dropped in fields on the south side of Fentonbarns Farm in a straight line 50 yards apart on 1 November 1940. One fell close to the main Dirleton-Drem road. On 16 April 1941 five high-explosive bombs were dropped to the north of the airfield, falling close to Inereil Lodge, Archerfield, Dirleton. Again, little damage was done. A further two bombs fell on Archerfield Estate the following month and on the same day, 6 May 1941, the enemy came somewhat closer to hitting Drem airfield, when a further three bombs landed near the west side. In the evening of 12 August 1942, four high-explosive bombs were dropped within the airfield's boundary, though only slight damage was caused. On 25 March 1943, three phosphorous incendiary bombs were discovered to have fallen in a field on Kilduff Mains Farm, near Drem. These were the last known German bombs to have fallen on East Lothian during the Second World War.

Throughout the conflict, the personnel underwent regular drills to deal with the possible threat of poisoned gas released by enemy aircraft. Two of the amenities buildings would function as gas decontamination centres if required; one hut was a shower block and another would serve as a drying room. Close by was the decontamination and first-aid block. After a gas attack, personnel entered the building by walking through a bleach tray. Those that were contaminated and injured could be hosed down while still in the first-aid area; of course, the use of gas was a two-way threat, Britain had also manufactured large stocks of mustard gas, which RAF aircraft would spray on German troops if they landed on British beaches. This lethal chemical was stockpiled in underground storage tanks on the north-west corner of RAF MacMerry for potential use by 614 Squadron's Lysander IIs. The A-1 main road now runs over this site.

Many more bombs would have probably fallen on Drem airfield were it not for the creation of several decoy sites. A dummy airfield (known as a 'Q' site) was created at Whitekirk, a few miles to the east in the summer of 1940. As by this stage of the war most raids took place at night, this 'airfield' was no more than a series of lights that resembled runway approach lights. At 12.30 a.m. on 14 July 1940 (only a short time after the 'airfield' came into operation), an unidentified aircraft dropped three light bombs, two of which caused substantial craters, while the third only partially exploded. Another bomb fell in a cornfield and two others landed in wet clay on open land, causing no damage. At 1.30 a.m. on 27 July another four bombs were dropped, creating two substantial craters a short distance from the obstruction lights and further bombs fell on 4 August and 2 October 1940. The site was too successful for its own good, as there were complaints from people living close by that their lives were being put in danger by the close proximity to the mock landing lights. The decoy airfield was then moved to a more remote location at Blackloch, close to Halls Farm on the edge of the Lammermuir Hills. It first received the attention of the Germans when ten high-explosive bombs fell in its vicinity on 25 August 1940. The following morning another eight bombs fell on the site. The latter fell at an angle of around 45 degrees to the flare path. Two bombs fell in a potato field and a further five landed in a corn field, causing only slight damage to the crops. The remaining one fell on a grass field and caused no damage.

In spring 1940, Col. John Turner, who was responsible for these decoy sites, urged RAF Command to adopt the practice that aircraft on operational airfields should be completely hidden from view and dummies dispersed over the airfield in the same manner as the real ones. At first this idea received little enthusiasm from the senior RAF officers. Eventually, some had second thoughts. During July 1940 Drem had the distinction of being the first airfield to have dummy aircraft installed. They took the form of eight 'Hurricanes' while a similar number of real fighters were hidden in woods bordering the airfield.

At this time Richard Atcherley had just taken over command of the airfield. When he was not experimenting with ways of improving the landing lights (which eventually lead to the creation of the Drem Lighting System), he was devising many and diverse methods to make Drem less vulnerable to attack. His twin brother David was in command of RAF Castletown at the other end of Scotland and they were often referred to as the crazy twins. This lead to great competition between the two of them as to who could make their base most secure. Richard Atcherley had the highly polished staff car, he inherited from his predecessor George Keary, covered in camouflaged paint. All the personnel were then mobilised to carve out hides for the aircraft in the woods on the edge of the airfield. The work did not progress as fast as he wished, so he persuaded the headmaster of Fettes College in Edinburgh to dispatch double-decker bus loads of his pupils to assist. Their efforts were rewarded by flights in some of Drem's aircraft. Richard Atcherley also decided that Drem would construct its own air raid shelters. For this scheme he had the airmen remove 60 yards of track from a disused railway line. The rails were the bend into a 'U' shape. Corrugated iron was then applied to form the walls and roofs of the shelter. While this was taking place, a train appeared on what was believed to be the deserted railway line. Railway officials informed the local constabulary who searched in vain for missing sections of track.

In one of his more eccentric moves, Richard Atcherley had the army personnel responsible for manning the Bofors anti-aircraft guns relieved of their duties and replaced with local game keepers, and a few poachers, on the assumption that their marksmanship would be better than that of the military. Unsurprisingly, this arrangement incurred the wrath of the Army and was discontinued. However, the scheme to conceal Drem's fighter aircraft in the woods was continued at least for another two years. No. 64 Squadron's log book records in May 1941 that 'landings and take-offs were made in the landing ground in the backwoods'. It appears there was virtually an airfield within an airfield by this stage. On 22 April 1942, the clearance of Spinney Woods began. No. 611 Squadron was instructed to provide ten men each day for this work and on the first day, eight trees and three roots were cleared in three hours. Richard Atcherley's career did not progress much beyond this, despite all his innovations. Apparently, his unorthodox behaviour did not sit well with some of the higher echelons of the RAF.

Initially the airfield was guarded by Army units based in East Lothian. Later in the war, the RAF Regiment was created to defend its airfields and installations. The garrison strength at Drem on 26 March 1942 was one company of 70 Borders Regiment, consisting of three officers and 210 other ranks. They were armed with six spigot mortars and eight .303 Vickers machine guns on loan from the RAF. In addition there was 2845 Squadron, RAF Regiment, with two rifle flights and one anti-aircraft flight with four twin-Lewis machine guns and two quad-Vickers .303 machine guns. A lorry-mounted Hispano gun and a number of Armadillo armoured fighting vehicles with .303 Lewis light machine guns provided a mobile defence. The RAF Regiment also had six .303 Vickers machine guns and six Smith guns on strength.

In the event of an emergency, reinforcements would be drawn from the RAF station personnel, who would be armed. These consisted 150 men in the first line, ninety in the second line, and 250 in the third line. Those in the first line could be made available without seriously disturbing the operational role of the airfield, while the second line would involve withdrawing certain clerks, and those in the third line would only be used for defence duties in a last ditch stand when flying was unable to continue. The reserves had access to four Armadillo armoured fighting vehicles, eight Vickers .303 machine guns, and seventeen Lewis .303 light machine guns. Their main weapon was, however, the standard .303 rifle of which 400 were available.

Most of the heavy anti-aircraft batteries in south-east Scotland were concentrated around Edinburgh and Rosyth naval dockyard. Various lighter units provided defence for Drem against low-level intruders. No. 72 Light Anti-Aircraft regiment detachment was replaced on 29 December 1941 by the 20th Light Anti-Aircraft Regiment. In the summer of 1942 the 10th Polish Light Anti-Aircraft battery took over, but departed on 22 September 1942, leaving the airfield without any form of anti-aircraft defence for a while.

Target practice for the gunners was often provided by locally based aircraft. In addition, the main role of 289 Squadron based at RAF Turnhouse was to supply aircraft for mock gunnery practice by artillery units in south-east Scotland. From time to time they performed the role of 'enemy aircraft' for gun batteries in East Lothian and the radar station at Drone Hill. This squadron operated a variety of aircraft handed down from front-line units, including Lysander III, Hudson III, Hurricanes, Oxfords, and Defiants and often flew the short distance from RAF Turnhouse to Drem on training flights. In the latter part of 1944 a detachment was permanently based at Drem, staffed with around four flying crew and seventeen maintenance personnel.

Finally, pilots at Drem were sometimes sent on escape and evasion exercises. As well as testing their skills at avoiding capture, this training also served to probe the defences of the airfield. One such exercise took place on 10 March 1943. No flying could take place that day owing to bad weather. Ten pilots of 65 Squadron were dumped from a blacked-out van, some 10 miles away from Drem, with the intention of returning and entering the Intelligence Office undetected. They wore civilian dress, mostly with battle dress trousers, and carried with them sixpence in coppers. Sqn Ldr J. Storrar and Flt Lt J. Grey got back within two hours with the assistance of an Army car, which

The roof of Drem's Battle Headquarters as it has survived into the twenty-first century. It is situated well away from the main part of the airfield, which can be seen in the distance. (*Malcolm Fife*)

they stole in Haddington. A further two pilots returned undetected, having walked all the way back across the countryside. Of the three other pairs of pilots, one got onto the perimeter track at Drem, but was caught near the Flight dispersals. The other two were captured by members of the RAF Regiment before they reached the airfield, but Sergeant P. Taylor later managed to escape and reach the Intelligence Office.

Life at Drem

In 1940, the bagpipe-playing Reverend Sutherland suggested to CO Richard Atcherley that the personnel might benefit from more spiritual instruction and that it would be a good idea to bless the aircraft. One of 602's Spitfires and one of 605's Hurricanes were polished and rolled out onto the parade ground to be duly blessed by the padre. Most of the Drem personnel and many local bigwigs were witness to this unique ceremony, but all were eclipsed by the presence of legendary Scots entertainer, Sir Harry Lauder. Atcherley persuaded him to put on an impromptu performance in one of the hangars later the same evening.

The blessing of the two aircraft did not have the desired effect, as both were involved in accidents within the next three days. The 602 Squadron Spitfire ran into a boundary hedge during a night landing. Tragically, Hurricane L2115 crashed near Dunbar on the 24 June, killing pilot Barry Goodwin. Although there were no more blessing of aircraft at Drem, church parades were a significant feature of life. They were not always the most popular of activities. An entry in the station log book for 17 October 1943:

> … after finding that the voluntary system of church parade had not been a success in the past, the method of detailing 25% [of the personnel] every fortnight was re-instated and the first church parade was held today on the station parade ground.[1]

Despite being an operational airfield, Drem was able to host air cadet camps, mainly from well-known Edinburgh schools. There was always one or two aircraft on strength other than fighters which were suitable to give the students a flight.

During July 1940, schoolboys from Fettes School, Edinburgh, had been helping to clear woodland to extend the aircraft dispersals. As a reward for their hard work, they were offered a flight. All the serviceable aircraft from the station flight were called on—two Tiger Moths, two Harvards, a Fairey Battle, plus a borrowed Bristol Blenheim. Four schoolboys were packed into the Blenheim, flown by Richard Atcherley, who had a reputation of being a daredevil. The boys were subsequently treated to an inverted flight over the airfield at minimum altitude: 'Even after that experience the boys said they enjoyed the flight, so obviously they teach them how to be diplomatic at Fettes

Pilots of 602 Squadron playing a game of chess for the benefit of the press. The preferred game while on readiness alert was Ludo… (*602 Squadron Museum/SCRAN*)

College'. Despite tempting fate on numerous occasions, Richard Atcherley survived the war and lived to an old age.

Another station commander, Peter Townsend, was involved in a hair-raising flying incident in 1941. On a local flight with a Polish officer, he flew through telephone wires. On landing, the Pole threw his arms around Townsend, saying it was the most thrilling experience of his life. Not long after the Regional Post Office Chief phoned, complaining that 'one of your blasted pilots has flown through my telephone wires'. Townsend replied that, when he discovered who was responsible, he would have the pilot disciplined. Later he was appointed the Royal Equerry and become well-known because of his friendship with Princess Margaret.

Although some of the squadron log books express dismay at being posted to Drem, most revised their opinion after having spent time there. Unlike other Scottish airfields, it was close to several busy towns and Edinburgh—always popular with military personnel—was only 20 miles away. However, Sqn Ldr René Mouchotte was not won over:

> Edinburgh can be regarded as the handsomest city in Britain. Great squares, wide avenues, fine monuments—but what gloom. How chilly it is! The character of the people is apparent merely from their way of walking in the streets. One might fancy it is against the

law to laugh. In public places people stand motionless, talking in low voices. The shops close at four o'clock. The 'black out' and the winter make the place even more dismal. I understand it is the same in peace time.[2]

'Beer patrols' to local pubs were the major activity for those with free time. Early in the war, entertainments were low on the list of priorities, but as the danger of attack on Britain receded, the station log book gives as much attention to entertainments as it does to operational activities. Drem even had its own cinema on base, which also doubled out as a theatre.

Although there was always a number of pilots on duty, ready to scramble at short notice, Christmas was the time for numerous parties and dances. No. 340 Free French squadron log book records festivities for 26 December 1941 in great depth:

Last night we drowned all our troubles in a cask of red wine sent up from Free French Headquarters, there was enough to drown even more troubles than we've had—220 litres [58 gallons] of it. Some we mulled and some we drank cold and some in spite of ourselves, we had to leave for another day. Quite a lot went to the good woman who runs the YMCA, who'd never tasted mulled claret before and after her first mug of it never wanted to taste anything else. She was still at it this morning when we went in to pay the bill and enjoying it better than ever. We had the party after midnight mass which was said in the next room. There was a cold buffet—stodgy but sufficient—and a long table loaded with presents for the men which had poured in for the week before, we drew lots for them and there was something for everyone. There was also a Christmas tree, painfully cut with our own hands and one blunt pocket knife in the Spinny towards dusk and there were the Tahitians who played their guitars and sang their songs and everyone was happy. There never was a noisier party nor one with less breakages and yet there wasn't a glass left, next morning. We'd been drinking out of glasses with a red *Croix de Lorraine* on them, and souvenir-hunters took a fancy to them.[3]

By 1943, the Christmas celebrations would last for much of December. On 17 December, the Officers Mess Christmas Dance took place with many guests and officers from RAF Turnhouse and RAF East Fortune. Officers of 307 Polish Squadron supplied the decorations—life-size drawings of dancers in national costume cut out and fixed to the walls—and, the next day, a party was given for the children. On 24 December, a Christmas dinner was held in the Airmen's Club for sergeants, followed by a dance. On Christmas morning, both RAF and WAAF sergeants were entertained to drinks in the Officers Mess, then officers and sergeants served Christmas dinner to airmen and airwomen. Paper hats were provided for all. On Boxing Day, a dance was held in the WAAF NAAFI for the benefit of those airwomen who had been on duty on Christmas Day. A further dance was held on New Year's Eve in the NAAFI and continued for one hour into 1944.

The following year, there were again elaborate Christmas Day festivities. Father Christmas arrived in the station's Auster and handed out gifts at the children's party, and again the officers and senior NCOs served Christmas dinner to the airmen and airwomen.

The station band performed and the day concluded with an all-ranks dance in the NAAFI. On Boxing Day, the officers played the other ranks in a fancy dress football match.

Throughout the war, ENSA (*Entertainments National Service Association*) gave numerous shows at Drem. In early 1944, they included 'French Without Tears', 'Too Young to Marry', and 'Nine to Six'. Later in 1944, Turnhouse Dramatic Society gave a performance of 'Laburnum Grove' in the cinema attended by a small audience, 'which may have been due to the coldness of the hall'. There appears to have been some audience participation at the shows, as it is recorded that some were drowned out by the rival chanting of 'Scotland the Brave' by 602 (City of Glasgow) and 'There'll always be an England' by 609 West Riding, Yorkshire.

The Albatross Club, a new airmen's and airwomen's club for all ranks not above corporal, was opened on 25 October 1943. It was in the NAAFI building adjoining the cookhouse and consisted of a lounge, reading and quiet room, games room, and billiard room, and there was even a grand piano.

There were numerous other distractions in the form of weekly and monthly dances. In February 1943, 65 Squadron's log book records:

> At the Sergeants Dance held this evening, the Medical Officer and the Engineer Officer enlivened the proceedings with exhibitions of dancing which were energetic if unorthodox, whilst our Lothario of B-Flight demonstrated once more his powers of attraction. The absence of sundry of our lords and masters believed to be due to the exhausting effect of intruder operations into Edinburgh on the previous evening.[4]

There were also impromptu parties and social events at Drem throughout the war. In the summer of 1941, the station commander, Wg Cdr Eeles, gave a party for officers at his home serving sausages, chips, ice-cream and beer, but 'no casualties'.

On 15 April 1944, 29 Squadron held a party in the Officers Mess to celebrate the twenty-fifth anniversary of the unit's active existence:

> The occasion was marked in appropriate style. The unfortunate ban on travelling in the Firth of Forth area (in connection with the impending invasion of France) threatened to dampen festivities at one time by preventing an importation of sufficient glamour, but strong reconnaissance parties successfully raided local haunts, returning with full 'bags'. When the patrols reached base, they found the Squadron at a high state of readiness and the more attractive targets were rapidly singled out by visual means.[5]

The Fighter Command Band gave a well-attended performance in Drem's NAAFI on 5 August 1943 in conjunction with a tour of stations in Scotland. Drem formed its own band in 1944, which gave regular performances on the airfield and it often went under the billing 'The Dremlins Band Wagon'. For the more intellectually inclined, there were discussion groups; among the topics they discussed were 'euthanasia', 'I want to be an actor', and 'is an accent a drawback in social and business life'.

In the summer of 1943, the weekend activities included football, cricket, golf, and tennis. On 22 July the annual sports day was held in good weather with a large turnout. In the winter rugby, hockey, and netball were also played against the Home Guard, RAF East Fortune, and teams from other stations. Local landowners would sometimes invite pilots to shoot on their estates in the Lammermuirs. No. 64 Squadron log book relates:

> CO and half a dozen pilots did a spot of shooting although the bag was negligible, the afternoon was really enjoyable. Believe a few rabbits gave themselves up.[6]

A more low-brow form of relaxation was a rat hunt undertaken by members of 29 Squadron 'with the assistance of 'Peter', 'Binder' and sundry other dogs of the neighbourhood. Final score: one destroyed (confirmed). Our casualties, a bite on 'Peter's' nose'. One of the more bizarre activities for an operational airfield was one hour's compulsory gardening for station headquarters staff and equipment personnel. On 30 June 1943, the station commander, the adjutant, assistant adjutant, and some two dozen personnel led the way by hoeing and weeding several rows of lettuces in front of their offices. A year later it was recorded that the gardens were a great success, providing peas and other vegetables for the messes. In June 1944 it was decided to go ahead with bee-keeping as well.

Throughout the war, Drem had a small number of its own aircraft for transporting urgent supplies or personnel known as the station flight. At the beginning of the war there were two Miles Magisters, P2469 and N3806, which were used for flying practice, including cross-country flying in addition to communications duties. Other types known to have been possibly used included Blenheims, Defiants, Fairey Battles, and de Havilland Rapides. A Gloster Gladiator may have also been based here; one was recorded as still being on charge by RAF Turnhouse as late as 1945. Drone Hill radar station also attracted a number of visitors to Drem. Miles Magisters flew in vital spare parts and more exotic flying machines—autogyros—were used for radar calibration and trials. One, a Cierva C.30 V1186 of the Signals Wing crashed near Drone Hill in March 1941.

During May 1943, a detachment of 141 Squadron's Beaufighters flew north from their base at RAF Wittering to Drem for training on the Serrate device. The ground crew were transported in a Harrow aircraft. Among them was Don Aris who recollected the following about his brief posting at Drem:

> At Drem, with only a few ground crew on the detachment, we were kept very busy. Apart from the Serrate training, there was a lot of air firing practice which as an LAC armourer, kept me very busy. There was an urgency to get the crews ready for the Serrate operations. For the first time in years it was, for me, a brief period of servicing aircraft that were not operating–same job, same aircraft but your heart was not in it as they were not ops. My diary records that the food at the airmen's mess was awful and we used to go often to eat at the parachute café which my memory says was opposite the main gates. Whilst there I had two 36 hour passes and went to Edinburgh for the first time and saw what a beautiful city it is. We often used the camp cinema and among the films we saw were Gold Rush, What a Man, Black Sheep of Whitehall, Too Many Blondes, Goldwyn

Follies, Me and My Girl, San Francisco and a Yank at Eton–what names for an ancient film buff. I remember the strange, to us, uniforms of the Free French ground and aircrews of 340 Squadron Spitfires Vb's and there was a detachment of Beaufighter II F's of 488 Squadron. I also remember seeing Fleet Air Arm chaps, unusual to us to see naval airmen servicing aircraft. My memory of Drem some 60 years on is of the pleasant surroundings with North Berwick Law to the east. It was no better or worse than the many airfields I served on except for the food! On 13 June 1943, we left Drem at 11 a.m. by air and arrived at Wittering at 1.00 p.m. We were on immediate duty at the flights with the rest of the squadron preparing for the start of the first Serrate bomber support opps that night of 13/14th June, 1943.[7]

William Wharam, who lived with his family in North Berwick, served on the ZZ tender at Drem in the closing stages of the war. One day, when he was walking along a nearby beach, a low-flying Beaufighter suddenly appeared and opened fire on some targets moored in the sea. Bullets struck the beach and some passed between Wharam and his wife and children. As the Beaufighter departed, the pilot wiggled his wings to acknowledge that he had seen them on the beach.

The Parachute Café was a popular rendezvous for personnel based at RAF Drem. It has long since been demolished. (*K. Chalmers-Watson, RCAHMS/SCRAN*)

15

VIP Visitors

At the outbreak of the Second World War, it was thought that London would be the first target in the sights of German bombers. Hence it came as a surprise to many when the enemy concentrated its first aerial attacks on Scotland, particularly in the vicinity of the Firth of Forth. Drem—which prior to the declaration of war was just an obscure training airfield—was suddenly thrust into the limelight. With little else happening in other parts of Britain during the early months of hostilities, the press devoted numerous column inches to the exploits of the first Spitfire pilots to see action in the Second World War, although for security reasons, it would often not be mentioned by name.

Drem hosted several press delegations. On 10 March 1940, a party of around twenty journalists were given a conducted tour of the facilities. They were shown the Link trainers, the station armoury, the parachute section, and a hangar used by 602's Spitfires, followed by a screening of cine camera-gun films and a demonstration of a Spitfire firing on the stop butts. The highlight of the visit was a scramble by 602's Spitfires to 'attack' two Blenheim aircraft. Air Vice Marshal Sandy Johnstone commented in his memories that is was 'a ruddy dangerous performance'.

Drem also received attention from foreign journalists. M. Claude Blanchard from *Paris Soir* was shown round the airfield on 24 April 1940 and two years later Professor Gonsalez Montesinos from the Mexican newspaper *Novedades* was shown round the airfield.

The visit most highly regarded in the history of the airfield was that of King George VI on 26 February 1940. Arriving not by air but by train, the King awarded 602's Sqn Ldr Farquhar Fighter Command's first DFC of the war, for playing a leading role in the downing of the first German bombers over Britain. Although the King frequently visited Edinburgh in subsequent years, he never returned to Drem. In September 1944 the station log book bemoans this fact after the royal train spent the night close by in a siding at Aberlady. By then Drem had shifted from the limelight.

The Duke of Kent, fourth son of King George V, lunched in the Officers Mess and carried out an informal inspection of the station on 14 September 1940. A member of the RAF Welfare Branch, he would tour RAF stations unannounced and often unrecognised, driving his own car. He paid a return visit on 20 January 1941. In

King George VI inspecting a line up of airmen in front of the hangars at RAF Drem.
(*Museum of Flight, National Museums of Scotland/SCRAN*)

Two press photographers pose for their photograph while covering the Royal visit by King George VI to Drem on 26 February 1940. In the background can be seen Spitfires of 609 Squadron. (*Museum of Flight, National Museums of Scotland/SCRAN*)

August of that year he was killed in a plane crash in the north of Scotland. Later in the war, the Duke of Gloucester, who held the rank of Air Marshal, paid a visit of inspection.

A small number of senior politicians also visited Drem; on 3 September 1940, Sir Ronald Campbell, the British minister to Washington, and Sir Archibald Sinclair, the Secretary of State for Air, arrived in a de Havilland Express DH 86 N6246 of 24 Squadron. This unit specialised in ferrying high-ranking military officers and government officials around the country. Their aircraft were sometimes put to more mundane use, such as the Dragon Rapide G-ADEV, which conveyed freight to Drem in early January 1940.

Throughout the war, numerous high-ranking officers would descend on Drem on morale boosting visits. In early 1940, when the airfield was the focus of attention, Sir Edward Ellington and Sir John Salmon, both Marshals of the RAF, came to Drem. In the summer, another Marshal of the RAF, Lord Trenchard, the first Commander of the RAF and creator of the Royal Auxiliary Air Force, visited. Sandy Johnstone, at that time a pilot with 602 Squadron, recorded the following entry for 10 June 1940 in his diary:

> On returning I found Boom Trenchard at the dispersals. The Grand Old Man was in terrific form and in no time at all had us all firmly believing that the German Air Force was made up of nothing but a bunch of cissies. I always feel it is a privilege to talk to him, for he somehow symbolises all that is best in the Royal Air Force. There he was wearing an old pattern uniform with turn-up trousers, no scrambled egg on his service cap, still carrying his white walking stick and holding his audience with every word he uttered.[1]

Unlike many of the other high-ranking officers, who only put in a fleeting appearance, Lord Trenchard continued his relationship with Drem and other fighter airfields in Scotland, making inspections and giving lectures on his theories of air warfare.

Visits were not confined to high-ranking officials and members of the press. Personnel at Drem would often find themselves giving tours of the station to numerous other military personnel, often deployed nearby. For example in August 1943, around 350 members of the Royal Observer Corps spent four hours looking around the airfield and enjoying a comprehensive programme which included screening of security films. Thirty-eight senior Polish Army officers paid a visit on 26 September 1944, to discuss army air co-operation and were treated to demonstrations by Spitfires, Typhoons, and Mosquitos. Two months later, a Polish Air Force unit came to take photographs of record of 309 Squadron, manned by their countrymen and at that time based at Drem.

16

Innovation

Drem's contribution to the development of the RAF night fighter force was not restricted to the training of specialist aircrews. Several important innovations were developed at the airfield.

There were few night-flying navigation aids at the outbreak of the Second World War. Locating the airfield was hard enough, landing in the dark was outright hazardous, particularly with enemy aircraft in the vicinity. Runway lighting often consisted of nothing more than paraffin lamps or flares that would be extinguished if there was a danger of the airfield being bombed, leaving any Allied aircraft to remain in the air or to divert elsewhere. It might be as long as thirty minutes before the flares were relit. Various innovations were tested throughout Britain in an effort to overcome this problem. In late 1939, while stationed at Drem, Hiram Smith had experimented with a slide projector to facilitate the correct angle of approach at night–red indicated too low, green too high, white was correct. Regrettably, his idea was never taken up.

A wind of change blew through Drem when Wg Cdr Richard Atcherley took over as station commander in June 1940. Unlike his predecessor, Atcherley was full of ideas and willing to experiment with any innovation that would improve the operational capability of his airfield. He had a strong background in night flying. In the 1920s he flew an airmail route between Cairo and Baghdad, for which he invented an ingenious system of path-finding marker bombs. A decade later, he was a test pilot at Farnborough evaluating new engines, including the Merlin, which went on to power the Spitfire. Once his day's work was over at Farnborough he carried out unofficial experiments in night flying using his own Avro Avian. He devised a series of reflector prisms to serve as a flare path, fitting a headlamp to the Avian to light them up as he came into land. Another of his nocturnal activities was to carry out reconnaissance flights over roads in southern England while Army exercises were being held to see if he could spot troop movements. Fearing a serious accident, Atcherley's commanding officer eventually put an end to his night flying. In 1934, Atcherley befriended Sir Guy Hambling, one of the largest shareholders in Imperial Airways, who had a private airfield on his estate at Rookery Park, Suffolk. Reflector studs were erected there so Atcherley could fly in from Farnborough after dark to experiment with his night-landing equipment.

Richard Atcherley, early on in his career in the RAF. He became station commander of RAF Drem in June 1940 and was responsible for inventing the 'Drem Lighting System'. (*RAF Museum*)

At Drem, Atcherley, now aged thirty-five, was in charge of his own airfield and used the opportunity to develop his ideas. With materials in short supply, he put in a request for wire to construct a telephone line to a hill some 5 miles away, where a group of airmen was living in tents; this was just a ruse to obtain materials for his runway lighting system. The mounts for the lights were constructed of wood and concrete in the workshops at Drem. In its final form the system consisted of three parts, the runway lighting, the approach lighting, and the outer circle lighting. At each corner of the runway were 10-foot poles, each displaying a narrow beam of light, which was not visible from above, but showed white lights to the centre of the landing strip and red lights away from it. Some 25 yards to the left of the centre line of the runway were three flare lights and an angle-of-glide indicator. A row of markers was installed at ground level along the edge of the runway at 100-yard intervals. Two amber glass screens were then placed 400 yards from the runway to act as a distance marker. Funnel lights guiding the aircraft to the approach were placed on 15-foot poles at the end of the runway, these were unscreened white lights with six on each unit. The whole airfield was then surrounded by an outer ring of twenty-three white lights, equally spaced in a circle of 2,000-yard radius from its centre. A mobile floodlight with its own power source was positioned on the left-hand side of the active runway close to the glide path indicator. All the other airfield lighting was powered

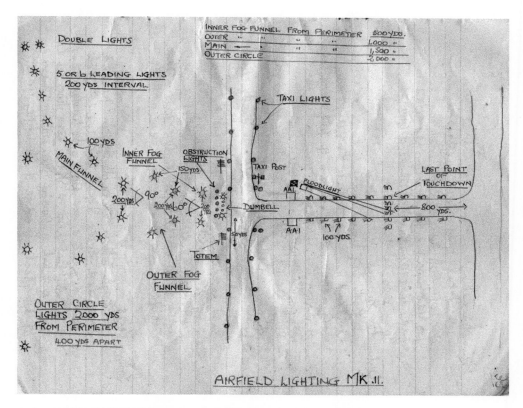

A sketch of the Airfield Lighting System (Mk II) based on the Drem Lighting System. (*RAF Museum*)

by the mains supply and could be switched on and off at will. If there was a power failure the mobile floodlight could operate on its own power.

A pilot approaching the airfield would fly around the outer circle of lights and then commence his approach above the funnel lights. At an altitude of about 500 feet, two white vertical beams of light from the poles at the rear end of the runway became visible as did two vertical beams of red light on other poles on the approach. As the pilot came into land, the glide path indicator would appear green if the aircraft's approach angle was correct. This lighting system could be switched on and off at the flick of a switch should the need arise, so that even during an air raid the airfield lighting could remain on. Most of the light was supplied by ordinary light bulbs, their beams screened by metal shields so they were only visible at an altitude of 500 feet or lower. Thus aircraft could continue to land and take off during an attack. An enemy aircraft flying overhead would see no runway lights or the large outer circle of lights enclosing the airfield. Although the original lighting system was designed with Spitfire pilots in mind (who usually made a curving approach when landing) the innovation was soon adopted at many other airfields.

It became known as the 'Drem Lighting System', much to the disquiet of many of Richard Atcherley's colleagues, who thought it should have been named after him.

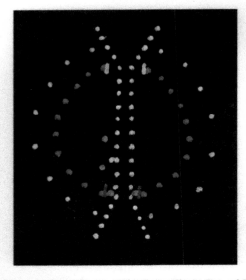

This diagram shows the Drem Lighting System. The Outer Circle, Funnel Lights and Runway Flare Path are all white lights. The inner circle with blue lights is the taxiway. At each end of the runway are Totems, either showing white lights (far-end of runway) or red lights (near-end of runway). These indicate landing direction. At the near-end of the runway is the Glide Path Indicator, which shows Amber/Green/Red, depending on whether an approaching aircraft is Too High/Correct Glide Slope/Too Low. A white double-flare and two amber lights on the left hand side of the active runway were distance indicators.

A diagram of the Drem Lighting System for night landings. (*Former Drem Museum*)

In December 1940, Atcherley's posting at Drem came to an end, when he assumed command of 54 Operational Training Unit responsible training night fighter pilots, but he continued to refine his invention:

> Whilst at Church Fenton I did a lot of work on the original Drem System which had been rather messed up when the Ministry of Supply took over production. I installed an improved layout which became the prototype for all other service airfields.[1]

By the end of 1941 this lighting system was in the process of being installed at eighty bomber and twenty fighter stations.

Drem Airfield's contribution to innovation in air warfare extended far beyond improved runway lighting systems. In December 1942 the Radio Development Flight was formed at Drem, with a small number of Boulton Paul Defiants and Bristol Beaufighters. The innocuous name of the Flight disguised its true purpose. Air Ministry scientists had developed equipment that allowed RAF night fighters to lock onto the radar transmissions of their opponents. It went by the name 'Serrate' and was a homing device that also gave a visual indication of the enemy's location on a cathode ray tube. Aircraft such as the Beaufighter were fitted with both Air Interception radar AI Mk IV and the Serrate. Both systems fed into the same cathode ray tube. By the flick of a switch the operator could tell from the Serrate that an enemy plane had detected his aircraft with its radar and roughly where it was. Then, by changing back to the AI radar, the operator could get a precise bearing on the German aircraft and hunt it down.

The purpose of the Radio Development Flight was to supply practice targets for aircrew of operational squadrons to train in the use the Serrate equipment. Drem was chosen as it was thought that the German radio and radar intelligence services would have less chance of discovering details of the new invention than if it was based in airfields in the south of the country. The Beaufighters and Defiants carried transmitters intended to replicate the radar signals of the enemy night fighters, but it was later found that there was a fault with this set-up. The radar display in the fighters tracking these mock enemy aircraft bore little resemblance to that transmitted by the airborne radar carried in German aircraft.

The first crews to make use of this facility were six pairs of pilots and navigators from 141 Squadron, who arrived in their Beaufighters on 12 May 1943. They were commanded by Wg Cdr Bob Braham, who by the age of twenty-three had already shot down twelve enemy aircraft, eleven of them at night and was dubbed by the press 'The Night Destroyer'. On 14 June 1943, on completion of the training, 141 Squadron commenced Serrate operations from a number of bases on the coast of southern England. To the end of September their Beaufighters, while supporting RAF bombers on night raids, achieved great success, destroying seventeen enemy aircraft and damaging a further six. On the 5 July the Radio Development Flight was renamed No. 1692 Flight and its Beaufighters and Defiants were later augmented with some Mosquitoes. In the autumn of 1943 a number of other units took part in the Serrate training programme including 239 Squadron, equipped with the Beaufighter Mk IF.

Training at Drem came to an end when No. 1692 Flight departed south to its new base at RAF Little Snoring, in Norfolk.

Another technological development to which Drem contributed was 'Moonshine'. This was a radar counter-measure device that radiated strong return pulses to the radar that had detected the aircraft in which it was fitted. It created the impression of a much more sizeable force than really existed. Moonshine was used to confuse the standard German early warning radar, the 'Freya'. A small number of aircraft equipped with this technology could make it appear that a formation of over 100 RAF bombers were approaching Europe. The Germans would scramble their fighters to intercept this spoof raid, wasting valuable fuel and resources. The actual bomber formation would often appear much later when the enemy defences had been worn down by numerous false alarms. The development of Moonshine first began in late 1941. The following year trials took place at RAF Tangmere using a Defiant, which proved the concept worked. A secret memo dated 19 May 1942 sheds the light on the development of the project:

TRE are manufacturing at Swanage certain radio countermeasures apparatus to be known as 'Moonshine' for installation in and operation from aircraft. It has been decided that the aircraft in which Moonshine is to be installed will be Defiants and Headquarters, Fighter Command, have undertaken to establish one Squadron of twelve aircraft and six reserves of which six aircraft and three reserves will be fitted with Moonshine. This squadron will be located at Heston. In order that the technical and operational implications of Moonshine may be ascertained preliminary trials are being arranged. To avoid interception and interpretation by the enemy of experimental transmissions these trials will be carried out at Drem. A Ground Controlled Interception [station] modified to the enemy frequency is being installed at Drem for the purpose of these trials. Intention is to carry out Moonshine trials and complete installation of Moonshine in 6 and 3 reserve Defiant aircraft in readiness for operational application. Headquarters, Fighter Command, have loaned a mobile GCI for the trials at Drem. This has been modified by TRE and is being moved to Drem under arrangements made by 80 Wing. It is anticipated that this convoy will arrive at Drem on 22.5.42.

Trials—Two Defiant aircraft have been prototyped to receive the Moonshine installation. TRE have undertaken to fit the first two Moonshine equipments in this aircraft. It is anticipated that these will be completed by 24.5.42. Headquarters, 11 Group is requested to arrange for two pilots and two observers RDF to report to Heston on 24.5.42 to take over the aircraft and fly them to Drem. Headquarters, Fighter Command, is requested to arrange for the attachment to Drem for the period of the trials of sufficient ground personnel for the maintenance of the Defiant aircraft and one experienced CHL operator to observe results at the Ground Controlled Interception [station].[2]

Further trails and training were carried out at Drem when another nine Defiants arrived from RAF Northolt on 20 July 1942. Moonshine was put into operational use on 6 August 1942. In the autumn, 515 Squadron's Defiants (Mk II), conducted successful operations with this equipment while based at RAF Heston. On occasions over 300 enemy fighters were airborne trying to intercept 'ghost' formations of Allied bombers.

This was not the end of Drem's association with this electronic countermeasures project. In November, a small number of Bostons, fitted with Moonshine equipment on an experimental basis, flew north from TFU Defford to Drem. They were joined by two similarly equipped Defiants. Two of the locally based fighter squadrons were requested to simulate an operation, which involved using Cockburnspath Chain Home Station on the Berwickshire Coast to simulate an enemy radar station. A different version of the Moonshine concept was used to deceive the Germans into believing that the Allied D-Day landings in Normandy in June 1944 were actually occurring in another part of France.

The Fleet Air Arm and HMS *Nighthawk*

Throughout the latter years of the Second World War, RAF Drem played host to several Fleet Air Arm squadrons. Eventually, the Royal Navy displaced the RAF from this airfield completely.

When war broke out, the only Royal Naval Air Station in Scotland was at Donibristle in Fife. There was then a rapid expansion with new facilities being built around Scapa Flow, in the Orkneys, and at other locations scattered throughout the country. Generally, the Fleet Air Arm operated independently from the RAF, each having their own airfields.

Rather unusually, there was a Fleet Air Arm training unit—784 Squadron (night fighter training)—based permanently at Drem from autumn 1942 onwards. Formed on 1 June 1942 at Lee-on-Solent, near Portsmouth, it was equipped with two Chesapeakes, six Fairey Fulmars and several Ansons to serve as radar trainers. The aircraft moved north to Drem on 18 October 1942, probably to coincide with the opening of the Dirleton GCI radar station and to take advantage of the local airfield's reputation in training RAF night fighter pilots.

The Fleet Air Arm preserved few of their records at the end of the Second World War, so only sketchy details survive of their activities at Drem. More Fairey Fulmars were received by 784 Squadron after training had begun. From autumn 1943 some of the trained crews were actually attached to RAF night fighter squadrons, the most successful being Lt (A) D. Price RNVR and Sub-Lt (A) R. E. Armitage RNVR, who were each awarded DFCs for their exploits with 29 Squadron.

As with all the other squadrons involved in training at Drem, there were numerous minor accidents. Fulmar DR717 suffered an engine failure on 26 May 1943, and the following month Fulmar BP789 experienced the same problem. In the same year, several aircraft experienced problems with their undercarriage. Instead of landing back at Drem, they generally flew to the Fleet Air Arm station at Donibristle on the other side of the Firth of Forth, which specialised in the repair and overhaul of naval aircraft and thus was well placed to rectify any damage inflicted on the aircraft during their emergency landings. Fulmar DR744 made a forced landing there with its left undercarriage leg retracted on 25 October 1943. The following day, another Fulmar (DR660) had problems with its landing gear and also put down at Donibristle. Early the following month, yet another Fulmar (BP836) scraped along the runway with its undercarriage completely retracted. Not all the Fulmars that descended on Donibristle had problems with their landing gear, BP820 had to make an emergency landing as its connecting rods had fractured.

There were also a number of more serious accidents. Sub-Lt D. Boniface RNZN was making his first night landing at Drem on 18 January 1944 when he flew into a group of trees near Good Row, Whitekirk, killing himself. It is believed Boniface had mistaken RAF East Fortune for Drem Airfield.

On the first day of 1945 a Firefly (Z2053) crashed 3 miles off the Fife coast near Crail while on a non-operational flight. The pilot, Lt H. W. French RNVR, and Lt R. H. Teuton RNVR of 784 Squadron radioed that they were baling out. The aircraft was seen to hit the sea, but, despite an extensive search, no trace of the crew was found.

In the latter part of 1944, the Fulmars began to be replaced with Fairey Fireflys. The Vought-Sikorsky Chesapeakes, which acted as targets for the fighters equipped with AI airborne radar, in turn gave way to the North American Harvard. During the same year, 784 Squadron formed three operational flights to operate from the British-built escort carriers HMS *Campania*, *Nairana*, and *Vindex*. Their aircraft were involved in the work-up of the recently launched carrier HMS *Campania* in the Firth of Clyde during April and May 1944. On 3 June 1944 this vessel was allocated to the Western Approaches Command with 813 Squadron embarked.

Autumn 1942. Fleet Air Arm 784 Night Fighter Squadron Instructor's Course. Note the majority are Volunteers Reserve (VR), indicated by the wavy rank insignia on the uniform cuff. (*Fleet Air Arm Museum*)

This unit flew Swordfish, Wildcats, and Fulmar night fighters. No. 784 Squadron provided some of their aircraft to operate under their control in August. A similar arrangement was operated for the carrier HMS *Vindex* with them supplying night fighters to supplement the Sea Hurricanes and Swordfish of 825 Squadron. The third escort carrier HMS *Nairana* sailed from the Clyde to cover convoys to Freetown and Madagascar with a detachment of 784 Squadron on aboard in early 1944. Many of the deployments lasted a few weeks and others were limited to a few days before the aircraft returned to Drem.

While 784 Squadron was a permanent fixture at Drem in the latter part of the war, a number of other Fleet Air Arm units also deployed there, including 884 Squadron on 10 April 1943. Prior to this it had afforded fighter protection to the North African invasion. It then returned to fighter defence at RAF Turnhouse, operating under the control of 13 Group, RAF Fighter Command. At this time 884 Squadron was equipped with Seafire Mk IIc, a naval version of the Spitfire. The squadron departed at the beginning of May 1943, spending most of the next two months back at RAF Turnhouse. Fleet Air Arm Seafires returned to Drem on the 11 June 1944. A composite unit of 801 and 880 Squadrons with eight Seafires moved in for a few days from Skeabrae while their carrier HMS *Furious* was undergoing repair. While at Drem they operated under the control of RAF Fighter Command providing local air defence. Four of their Seafires took off on fleet patrol on 14 June 1944 as fighter cover for the battleship HMS *Warspite* entering Rosyth Dockyard on tow.

No. 770 Squadron, a Fleet Requirements Unit providing aircraft to act as practice targets for Royal Navy ships, moved in from RNAS Dunino, Fife, on 16 July 1944. It was to be based at Drem alongside 784 Squadron and one RAF fighter squadron on a permanent basis. Nos 770 and 784 were commanded by Lt-Cdr Beard and had their headquarters in Rose Cottage. No. 770 squadron had thirteen officers and 127 other ranks, while 784 Squadron personnel included twenty-three officers and 212 other ranks. Around the same time, the flying control caravan for the airfield was finally completed and '[gave] a great deal of satisfaction, especially in wet weather'.

Three days after its arrival at Drem, 770 Squadron carried out trials with winged targets resembling miniature gliders, the first time these devices had been flown from a grass airfield. One successfully landed back on the runway with only slight damage to its nose and wing skid. Among the more conventional equipment operated by 770 Squadron were Seafires, Blenheim IV, Hurricane II, and Martinet target tugs. During 1945, around three Mosquitoes were delivered to 770 Squadron. They spent much of their time at RAF Charterhall, in Berwickshire. One of these machines, a Mosquito B.25 (KB617), was badly damaged when its right undercarriage leg collapsed on landing on 29 June 1945. Jim Malcolm, who was serving with 770 Squadron at that time, recalled that the aircraft was on a delivery flight to the unit:

> I believe one of the transport crew members was a woman who walked down the damaged wing sweeping her helmet off letting her hair flow free and should have received an Oscar for her entrance.[1]

Fairey Fireflies (NF) of 1792 Squadron. (*Fleet Air Arm Museum*)

A Fairey Fulmar of 784 Squadron, Fleet Air Arm. (*Fleet Air Arm Museum*)

In late 1944, with victory in Europe on the horizon, the RAF began to contract, although the defeat of Japan was still a distant prospect. Accommodation for a naval fighter school with seventy-eight aircraft was needed in Central Scotland. The Admiralty suggested the following airfields be considered—RAF East Fortune, RAF Charterhall, or RAF Milfield. The RAF was unhappy to relinquish any of them and instead offered RAF Dyce (now Aberdeen airport). This was unsuitable for the Admiralty's requirements so RAF Drem was offered. It was accepted, although it was considered 'unsuitable for the safe operation of modern aircraft'. On 19 February 1945, the Air Ministry offered to loan RAF Drem and RAF MacMerry to the Admiralty on condition that the Admiralty agreed to continue to house one RAF training squadron at Drem (other accommodation for it was expected to be found by May) and for it to be used in an emergency by one night fighter squadron. Drem became a Naval Air Station on 21 April 1944.

The Admiralty requirement for RAF Drem and RAF MacMerry was to house an expanded Naval Night Fighter School and the Fleet Requirements Unit for the ships operating from Rosyth. At an internal Admiralty meeting on 22 February 1945, the Director of Naval Air Operations spoke:

> [He] explained that the whole of our night fighter training depended on the availability of Drem. If we have to move elsewhere, the programme must be put back at least 2 and probably 4 months.

It was proposed that Drem be a 'tender' (as in 'a vessel attendant on other vessels') to Donibristle and then become an independent command on 1 June 1945 at which date MacMerry airfield would commission as a tender for Drem. It was originally intended to name Drem HMS *Skua*, but this was changed to HMS *Nighthawk*, as it was thought more appropriate for a night fighter station.

The first inkling the RAF personnel had at Drem that their airfield would shortly pass to control of the Royal Navy was in February 1945 when a number of naval personnel came to inspect the airfield. Around the same time, new drains were laid which improved the serviceability of the runways. By 30 March 1945 there were no RAF squadrons based at Drem, but some thirty-seven officers and 326 other ranks remained. There were already a similar number of Fleet Air Arm personnel attached to 784 and 770 Squadrons and the Naval Air Section. A meeting was held on 6 April to discuss the transfer of control. Among those present were Wg Cdr Harris RAF (Drem's CO) and Lt-Cdr Kite and Lt-Cdr Abbey from the naval air station at Donibristle. It was suggested that the terms of transfer should be 'lock, stock and barrel' with a few minor adjustments made locally. The fate of the civilians employed by the RAF was brought up at the meeting, as was the contracts for coal, coke, gases, petrol, oils, and lubricants already made by the RAF. The radar training unit SCR 584, which operated a small number of Spitfires, would remain at Drem.

Advance Royal Navy parties arrived on the 14 April 1945. The RAF personnel still stationed at Drem were then transferred to the control of 17 Group, Coastal Command, and were gradually moved to RAF Dyce. The last ever entry in RAF

Drem's station diary stated that they 'finally decided on 12th [April] to hand over Drem to Navy by 21st! Shambles complete and utter'. The RAF absence from here was short-lived. No. 603 (City of Edinburgh) Squadron had returned to their home base of RAF Turnhouse on 28 April 1945, after spending the latter part of the war in North Africa. Some of the ground crew had been with this unit since the outbreak of the war. While at RAF Turnhouse, news of the surrender of Germany was received. An entry for 603 Squadron's log book on 7 May 1945 is finely understated—'apparently the war is over'. Some less welcome news received the same day was that the squadron had to move to Drem. By the following day their Spitfires (LF Mk XVIe) were ready to scramble. The squadron still had one vital task to perform and 'Great Happenings [were] expected at Drem [on the 8th].

The Germans were expected to send a delegation of their armed forces officials to surrender in Norway. Their arrival was scheduled for the 9 May, but was postponed due to heavy rain. The next day, a patrol intercepted a Flying Fortress off St Abb's Head, but there was no sign of the German delegation's aircraft. The waiting continued until 11 May. In the afternoon, patrols were flown in sections of four aircraft at 2,000 feet in an effort to rendezvous with the Germans. Twenty sorties were flown without any sightings, but the last two sections of four led by Flt Lt Batchelor and Flt Lt Sergeant encountered three white Ju 52 transports flying at 1,000 feet.

In the fading light, they were escorted to Drem by the Spitfires, landing at 8 p.m. According to the local press there were eighteen officers on board the aircraft, including a lieutenant colonel from the Wehrmacht and another from the Luftwaffe. They appeared sullen and frightened and stood with bowed heads.

German officers arrive from Norway in a Junkers Ju 52 to surrender on 11 May 1945. (*IWM*)

German officers about to board a Leyland bus. The Drem control tower—thought to be a locally modified Night Fighter Watch Office—can be seen in the background. (*IWM*)

A delegation of German officers arrive at Drem by a Junkers Ju 52 transport. It is painted completely white in compliance with the terms of surrender. (*Aldon Ferguson*)

Shortly after their arrival, they were transported by car to a mansion house near Edinburgh for interrogation. The naval officers were taken on board a Royal Navy warship anchored close to the Forth Rail Bridge for questioning. On 13 May, two of the Junkers returned to Norway with some of the German officers.

After this, 603's stay was anti-climactic. On 17 May, two aircraft were scrambled for an air-sea rescue search, but after patrolling for some time they returned as it was too dark to continue. Numerous training flights filled in the time. Some of the more experienced pilots relieved their boredom by looping their Spitfires around the narrow spans that joined the large triangular sections of the Forth Rail Bridge. Towards the end of May, 603 Squadron moved its dispersal to the south side of the airfield. Like all Royal Navy shore bases, HMS *Nighthawk* was run like a ship. On an aircraft carrier, aircraft were picketed down if not in use and the same rule applied here. RAF pilots thought the naval practise merely amusing at first, but after a while the novelty wore off. They would be ordered to scramble only to find that their Spitfires had been tied down; this lead them to poke fun at the Royal Navy regulations. The sailors were only allowed out of the camp at specific times, as they would be on a ship, where they would be transferred ashore on liberty boats. One night, some of the 603's pilots made a mock-up of a small boat on wheels and pulled it past the sailors waiting to leave camp.

For the remainder of May, 603 Squadron continued with their training programme, punctuated by spells of torrential rain on 20 May.

> Opportunity was taken by those who remained in camp to enjoy the luxury of a morning in bed and during the day table tennis and snooker and bridge were played as the weather was less than kind.[2]

The following day the weather had improved and 'practice flying was carried out all day, formation, cine gun and aerobatics being the main items on the programme'. The squadron also had an Auster aircraft on strength, which they used from transport and other tasks. The weather deteriorated again on the last day of the month and the opportunity was taken to clean all the aircraft, each pilot being responsible for furbishing his own machine. There was one last entry in the squadron logbook for May:

> The month has been strangely quiet after the active months of March and to a certain extent April. Scotland has treated the Squadron indifferently [referring no doubt to the poor weather and rain].[3]

In June, 603 Squadron members had assumed that they would shortly return to RAF Turnhouse, their home base. They were in for a shock:

> Today the squadron heard with real chagrin that the move to Turnhouse had been postponed and that they were to move to Skeabrae in the Orkneys. So the ground crew find themselves posted 'overseas' again. They have been home from the Middle East for

almost 5 months. Several sorties were made to Turnhouse to find out the 'whys' and 'wherefores' of the move and Turnhouse turned out an excellent lunch and its usual first rate hospitality, seeming to regret the posting as much as we did.[4]

The main party of 100 airmen and two officers left on the night train to Thurso on 13 June. The next day it was the turn of their Spitfires (LF Mk XVIe) to depart. When their wheels left the ground, it marked the end of Drem's association with RAF fighter squadrons.

There was at least one unscheduled return by an RAF Spitfire. On 14 January 1946, a number of aircraft from 164 Squadron took off from RAF Turnhouse to exercise with eight Mustangs. The squadron leader's Spitfire (Mk IX) had developed a 'temperament' some months previously and while flying over East Lothian his aircraft 'packed it in' at 9,000 feet. He made a forced landing at Drem, none the worse for the experience.

The originally intended complement of HMS *Nighthawk* was 105 aircraft—one Firefly training squadron, one Hellcat training squadron, one first-line Firefly squadron, and two first-line Hellcat squadrons, excluding reserves to be held at Donibristle or Dunino naval air stations. There were proposed dates of transfer to Drem of additional squadrons:

Hellcat training squadron	1 May 1945
1791 Squadron, first line	16 June 1945
892 Squadron, first line	26 June 1945
891 Squadron, first line	23 July 1945

In June 1945, the requirement was reduced to eighty-two aircraft. One of the first-line Hellcat squadrons was removed, with the result that the Fleet Requirements Unit for Macmerry was reassigned to HMS *Nighthawk*. The detailed breakdown of aircraft:

Activity	Units	Aircraft
Firefly Training	784 Squadron	16 Fireflys
	1 First-line squadron	24 Fireflys
	Classrooms	5 Ansons
Hellcat Training	Training squadron	9 Hellcats, 6 Harvards
	1 First-line squadron	16 Hellcats
	Classrooms	6 Ansons

In addition, twelve aircraft of 770 Squadron, the Rosyth FRU, were to be held at Drem. It is not clear if the proposed numbers of aircraft were actually achieved.

Aircraft movements were boosted by Fairey Barracudas on training flights from the naval air station at Crail and transport aircraft from 782 Squadron at Donibristle. Beechcraft 17 Staggerwings came and went on communications duties.

No. 732 Squadron was reformed at Drem on 15 May 1945 for single-seat night fighter training, and it had nine Grumman Hellcats, six Ansons, and six Harvards. Its existence was short-lived, as it was amalgamated with the other night fighter training squadron at Drem on 7 November 1945. No. 892 Squadron, flying Hellcats (Mk II NF), operated from Drem from 6 July to 2 November 1945. It had only recently been formed in Northern Ireland and while at Drem worked up to operational status. No. 892 was the Royal Navy's first front-line squadron to operate the Hellcat in the night fighter role. At the end of the year it embarked on the carrier HMS *Ocean*.

In the summer of the same year, two other front-line squadrons flying Fairey Fireflys also made use of the night fighter training facilities at Drem. The first to arrive was 1791 Squadron, which had been formed on 15 March 1945 at Lee-on-Solent naval air station; the squadron then embarked on the aircraft carrier HMS *Puncher* before coming to Drem. Their twelve Fireflys (NF.Mk I) were based here for two months from 18 June to 18 August 1945. After the Japanese surrender on 14 August 1945, the squadron was disbanded the following month at the Fleet Air Arm station at Burscough.

No. 1792 Squadron was formed on 15 May 1945 and received twelve night-fighter versions of the Fairey Firefly. It arrived at HMS *Nighthawk*, Drem, on 29 August 1945 to work with the night-fighter school. Its stay ended on 27 November 1945 when they departed for the Fleet Air Arm station at Machrihanish to prepare for their embarkation on the carrier HMS *Ocean*.

With all hostilities at an end, the Fleet Air Arm began to contract rapidly. Training continued at Drem into 1946, but there would be no further deployments of front-line squadrons there. There were numerous accidents to the aircraft based at HMS *Nighthawk*. No. 784 Squadron's MB392 suffered a starboard oleo collapse on touch down on 12 April 1945. The same failure resulting in a belly landing for this aircraft two months later. A Firefly, MB474, of 1791 Squadron overshot the runway and

A Fairey Firefly of the Fleet Air Arm receiving attention outside a hangar. (*Fleet Air Arm Museum*)

crashed into a railway cutting on 1 July 1945. Its pilot, Sub-Lt W. Cumming, escaped unhurt, but just over a month later he was involved in another accident. The left wing of Firefly WB469 hit a tree while approaching the airfield. The surviving records give no clue as to fate of the pilot or his aircraft. Sub-Lt J. Harrison taxied his Firefly MB441 into another aircraft, damaging his propeller and mainplane on 7 May 1945. On 24 October MB436 of 784 Squadron skidded on mud and collided with MB468.

Tragically, there were also a number of fatal accidents. Two occurred on the 7th and 8th of August 1945; Sub-Lt J. Marshall and Midshipman Pilot Steele of 784 Squadron were both killed when their Firefly MB447, on a night-flying GCI exercise, crashed into a hillside near Garvald, East Lothian. Initially it was thought that the aircraft may have come down in the sea and a Vickers Warwick of 279 Air-Sea Rescue Squadron searched the coastline. It was assisted by two Sea Otters that flew down from RAF Banff. After an unsuccessful searched they landed at Drem.

The second crash involved a Hellcat JX966 of 892 Squadron in which Sub-Lt O. Norwood perished. Unlike most wartime accidents which received little or no mention in the press, the (Edinburgh) *Evening Dispatch* ran several paragraphs on this incident:

> A Fleet Air Arm lieutenant lost his life when his plane—a Hellcat—crashed into the top of a hill near Heriot today. The plane coming in from the east struck a dyke and the fragments were scattered over a square mile of moorland. A farmer who saw the pieces of wreckage, climbed the hill early this morning and found the pilot sitting with his head in his hands, dead. He had been badly burned. The crash occurred on the hill farm of Brothershiels, about 2½ miles from the village of Heriot....
>
> The plane coming in from the east skimmed a field of corn with its wing tips and struck a dyke. It removed about 10 yards of the structure, went on and was shattered in pieces on the hill. The engine was found 250 yards from where the plane struck the wall.[5]

The hills were covered in mist in the early morning and this was thought to be a contributing factor to the crash. Ironically, on the same newspaper page that featured this crash was the headline 'HIROSHIMA DISASTROUS RUIN'. The aircrews that lost their lives in these accidents had been training for a mission that would never take place. Japan surrendered a few days later on 14 August 1945.

Drem was finally declared surplus to naval requirements on 31 December 1945. With the departure of 784 Squadron to Dale Naval Air Station on 1 February 1946, flying came to an end. Drem was never reduced to 'care and maintenance' (as originally foreshadowed), but proceeded direct to decommissioning and transferral back to the Air Ministry on 15 March 1946, when the RAF took it back on a caretaking basis as a satellite of RAF Turnhouse. At this time Drem had Nissen hut accommodation for 2,181 personnel of all ranks.

As early as July 1944 it was recommended that 'a considerable area of unused Emergency Landing ground be de-requisitioned'. Nothing appears to have been done by February 1945 and there was talk of letting it for agriculture purposes. A letter dated 11 November 1945 confirms the disposal of the Mungoswells site immediately and the Luffness Mains site as soon as the blister hangars were removed. Six stone cottages on the boundary—two at the northern entrance and four in a terrace near New Mains Farm buildings—were authorised for disposal in August 1947. By that time three of them had been occupied by squatters and by October all six had been.

An Air Ministry minute of 20 October 1952 confirmed that Drem was now surplus to requirements and was to be re-allocated for agricultural use. The Ministry of Food occupied three Bellman hangars for the storage of bagged grain and other buildings were used as an egg-box depot. Other than a brief spell in the 1980s when there was a landing strip for light aircraft, the runways have never been used again.

Drem today would be recognisable to someone that served there in the Second World War. It is still possible to walk around part of the perimeter track. A two-bay aircraft dispersal survives on the south-west corner, still in good condition, complete with its blast shelters (it was one of only two of this type on the airfield). Concrete foundations and a brick border are the only remains of ten rectangular pens on the north-west corner. The site of the command bunker on the western edge can still be seen, although it has been filled in, and the nearby control tower has long since disappeared. On the opposite side of the airfield, some of the large Bellman-type hangars remain and clustered round them are numerous small buildings once used by the engineers. A brick-built pillbox stands to the south of them.

Near the main road several of the accommodation blocks are now shops and businesses such as Fenton Barnes Farm shop. Many of the former hangars and buildings at Drem are used by several companies for a variety of purposes and on land next to them there is a mushroom farm.

One can imagine that those who served at Drem to preserve the freedom of the country against a tyrannical enemy would approve of the use to which their airfield had been put. The grass runways from which the Spitfires and Hurricanes operated have been given over to arable crops. Horses graze in neighbouring fields.

The Chalmers-Watson family, who purchased the site of the original First World War airfield, still run their businesses here. At weekends the buzz of aero engines resonates on the south side of the former airfield—not military aircraft on some mission, but small radio-controlled machines, being flown by aircraft enthusiasts. Perhaps there is a Spitfire among them.

Members of 732 Squadron, Fleet Air Arm, with a Grumman Hellcat in 1945.
(*Fleet Air Arm Museum*)

A view of the site of Drem Airfield in 2015. The perimeter track is in the foreground and in the distance the airfield buildings. The main runway was between the two. (*Malcolm Fife*)

Opposite above: Another view of the site of Drem Airfield in 2015, looking towards the technical area, which included the hangars. (*Malcolm Fife*)

Opposite below: The ground-controlled interception station at Dirleton, now converted into houses. It is a conspicuous landmark for visitors to Yellowcraig Beach. The immediate ground is private property. (*Malcolm Fife*)

Gravestone of Sergeant D. W. Hall RAF, who was killed on 30 August 1941 when his Bolton Paul Defiant crashed near Gifford. (*Malcolm Fife*)

Opposite above: 'Fenton Barns'—a number of the smaller airfield buildings have been utilised to form a retail park. This is the estate and administration building. Another serves as a farm shop. (*Malcolm Fife*)

Opposite below: The gravestones of two New Zealand Airmen, Fg Off. J. Dasent and Sub-Lt D. H. Boniface, in Dirleton Cemetery. The latter died when his Fairey Fulmar crashed near Whitekirk. (*Malcolm Fife*)

A line of RAF gravestones in Dirleton Cemetery, in view of Drem. (*Malcolm Fife*)

Appendix:
Flying Units Present at
Drem Airfield

UNIT	CODE	FROM	DATE IN	DATE OUT	TO	AIRCRAFT
151 Sqn		Liettres (F)	21/2/19	10/9/19	disbanded	Camel
152 Sqn		Liettres (F)	21/2/19	30/6/19	disbanded	Camel
3FT	S/SFTS	formed	17/3/39	27/10/39	disbanded	Hart, Anson, Oxford, Audax, Don, Magister, Tiger Moth
602 Sqn		Grangemouth	13/10/39	14/4/40	Dyce	Spitfire
609 Sqn		Acklington	17/10/39	19/5/40	Northolt	Spitfire
72 Sqn		Leconfield	28/10/39	12/1/40	Leconfield	Spitfire
111 Sqn		Acklington	7/12/39	27/2/40	Wick	Hurricane
29 Sqn		Debden	4/4/40	10/5/40	Debden	Blenheim
603 Sqn		Prestwick	14/4/40	5/5/40	Turnhouse	Spitfire
245 Sq		Leconfield	12/5/40	5/6/40	Turnhouse	Hurricane
602 Sqn		Dyce	28/5/40	13/8/40	Westhampnett	Spitfire
605 Sqn		Hawkinge	28/5/40	7/9/40	Croydon	Hurricane
263 Sqn		reformed	12/6/40	28/6/40	Grangemouth	Hurricane
145 Sqn		Westhampnett	14/8/40	31/8/40	Dyce	Hurricane
263 Sqn		Grangemouth	2/9/40	28/11/40	Exeter	Whirlwind
111 Sqn		Croydon	8/9/40	12/10/40	Dyce	Hurricane
141 Sqn		Turnhouse	15/10/40	24/10/40	Gatwick	Defiant
232 Sqn		Skitten	24/10/40	11/11/40	Skitten	Hurricane
607 Sqn		Turnhouse	8/11/40	12/12/40	Usworth	Hurricane
611 Sqn		Hornchurch	13/11/41	3/6/42	Kenley	Spitfire
258 Sqn		Duxford	3/12/40	14/12/40	Acklington	Hurricane
43 Sqn		Usworth	12/12/40	22/2/41	Crail	Hurricane
603 Sqn		Southend	13/12/40	28/2/41	Turnhouse	Spitfire
7 AACU det		Castle Bromwich	19/12/40	22/3/41	Castle Bromwich	various

Unit	Location	Date	Date	Location	Aircraft
43 Sqn	Crail	1/3/41	4/10/41	Acklington	Hurricane
607 Sqn	Macmerry	2/3/41	16/4/41	Skitten	Hurricane
600 Sqn	Catterick	14/3/41	27/4/41	Colerne	Beaufighter
260 Sqn	Skitten	16/4/41	19/5/41	Middle East	Hurricane
64 Sqn	Turnhouse	20/5/41	6/8/41	Turnhouse	Spitfire
123 Sqn	Turnhouse	5/8/41	21/9/41	Castletown	Spitfire
410 Sqn	Ayr	6/8/41	16/6/42	Ayr	Defiant,
64 Sqn	Turnhouse	4/10/41	17/11/41	Hornchurch	Spitfire
141 Sqn det	Ayr	11/10/41	23/1/42	Ayr	Beaufighter
340 Sqn	Turnhouse	20/12/41	29/12/41	Ayr	Spitfire
242 Sqn	Ouston	1/6/42	11/8/42	North Weald	Spitfire
453 Sqn	reformed	18/6/42	26/9/42	Hornchurch	Spitfire
222 Sqn	Winfield	18/8/42	16/8/42	Hornchurch	Spitfire
222 Sqn	Biggin Hill	20/8/42	22/10/42	Biggin Hill	Spitfire
65 Sqn	Lympne	11/10/42	29/12/42	Ayr	Spitfire
784 Sqn	Lee-on-Solent	18/10/42	15/1/46	Arbroath	Spitfire
				Dale	Chesapeake, Fulmar, Proctor, Anson, Reliant, Firefly, Hellcat
197 Sqn	Turnhouse	25/11/42	28/3/43	Tangmere	Typhoon
124 Sqn	Martelsham Heath	29/12/42	21/1/43	Martelsham Heath	Spitfire
Radio Dev Flt	formed	?/12/42	5/7/43	re-designated 1692 Flight	Beaufighter, Defiant.
65 Sqn	Machrihanish	10/1/43	29/3/43	Perranporth	Spitfire
130 Sqn	Perranporth	30/3/43	30/4/43	Ballyhalbert	Spitfire
884 Sqn	HMS Argus	10/4/43	5/5/43	Grimsetter	Seafire
186 Sqn	reformed	27/4/43	3/8/43	Ayr	Hurricane
340 Sqn	Turnhouse	30/4/43	9/11/43	Perranporth	Spitfire
141 Sqn det	Wittering	12/5/43	11/6/43	Wittering	Beaufighter

1692 (RD) Flt	4	Radio Dev Flt	5/7/43	10/12/43	Little Snoring	Beaufighter, Mosquito, Defiant, Wellington, Hurricane, Oxford, Anson
488 Sqn		Ayr	3/8/43	3/9/43	Bradwell Bay	Mosquito
96 Sqn		Church Fenton	3/9/43	8/11/43	West Malling	Mosquito
281 Sqn		Woolsington	6/10/43	22/11/43	into 282 Sqn	Walrus, Anson
485 Sqn		Hornchurch	8/11/43	28/2/44	Hornchurch	Spitfire
307 Sqn		Predannack	9/11/43	2/3/44	Coleby Grange	Beaufighter, Mosquito
278 Sqn det		Coltishall	1/2/44	22/4/44	Bradwell Bay	Walrus, Anson
148 Airfield HQ		formed	23/2/44	6/5/44	West Malling	Auster
486 Sqn		Beaulieu	28/2/44	6/3/44	Castle Camps	Typhoon
29 Sqn		Ford	29/2/44	1/5/44	West Malling	Mosquito
91 Sqn		Castle Camps	8/3/44	23/4/44	West Malling	Spitfire
309 Sqn		Snailwell	23/4/44	13/11/44	Peterhead	Hurricane, Mustang
801 Sqn det4		HMS Furious	11/6/44	17/6/44	Skaebrae	Seafire
880 Sqn det8		HMS Furious	11/6/44	17/6/44	Skaebrae	Seafire
881 Sqn det8		HMS Pursuer	11/6/44	16/6/44	Skaebrae	Wildcat
770 Sqn	Det. 8	Dunino	26/7/44	1/10/45	disbanded	Martinet, Blenheim, Hurricane, Beaufighter, Spitfire, Mosquito, Seafire, Reliant
880 Sqn	det8		HMS Furious	1/8/44	7/8/44	Skaebrae
340 Sqn		Biggin Hill	17/12/44	31/1/45	Turnhouse	Spitfire
SCR.584 Trg Unit	3L	formed	25/1/45	26/5/45	Manston	Spitfire, Oxford, Anson
603 Sqn		Turnhouse	7/5/45	14/6/45	Skaebrae	Spitfire
732 Sqn		reformed	15/5/45	7/1/45	disbanded	Hellcat, Firefly, Harvard, Anson
1791 Sqn		Inskip	18/6/45	18/8/45	Burscough	Firefly
892 Sqn		HMS Premier	6/7/45	2/11/45	Machrihanish	Hellcat
1792 Sqn		Inskip	29/8/45	27/11/45	Machrihanish	Firefly
Station Flight		formed	?	?	disbanded	Reliant, Traveller, etc.
3 GS		Macmerry	?/4/46	1/9/47	disbanded	Cadet

Endnotes

Chapter One

1. Quarterly Survey of R.A.F. Stations, Nov 1918, (The National Archives).
2. 'History of 41st Aero Squadron, The Reminisces of Sgt W. Mack', *Cross and Cockade Journal*, Vol. 12, No.1. Spring, 1971, pp. 54–61, pp. 72–74.
3. *Ibid.*
4. *Ibid.*

Chapter Two

1. *Haddingtonshire Courier*, 18 July 1924.
2. Smith, David, *Britain's Military Airfields*, 1939–45, (Wellingborough: Patrick Stephens Ltd, 1989) p. 21.

Chapter Three

1. *The War Illustrated*, (The Amalgamated Press Ltd, 18 Nov. 1939), p. 315.
2. Glasgow Museum, Glasgow's Spitfire, Glasgow City Council, 2003, p. 30.
3. *Ibid.* p. 22.
4. *Ibid.* pp. 31-32.
5. *Ibid. The War Illustrated*, p. 350.
6. Buckton, Henry, *Birth of the Few*, (Shrewsbury: Airlife Publishing, 1998).
7. McRoberts, Douglas, *Lions Rampant—The Story of 602 Spitfire Squadron*, (London: William Kimber, 1985), p. 65.
8. Johnstone, AVM Sandy, *Enemy in the Sky*, (California: Presido Press, 1979), p. 41.
9. 602 Squadron Operational Records, The National Archives, 11 July 1940.
10. *Ibid. Enemy in the Sky*, p. 83.
11. McDowall, R., 'Schoolboy Memories of Drem', *Aeroplane Monthly*, Vol. 23, No. 2, Issue 262, Feb. 1995, pp. 60–63.

12. Ziegler, Frank, *The Story of 609 Squadron*, (London: MacDonald, 1971), p. 76.
13. 611 Squadron Operations Record Book, The National Archives, Nov. 1941.
14. *Ibid.* 22 Dec. 1941.
15. *Ibid.* 30 Dec. 1941.
16. *Ibid.* Jan. 1942.
17. *Ibid.* 14 April 1942.
18. *Ibid.* 2 June 1942.
19. *Ibid.*

Chapter Four

1. Mason, Peter, *Nicolson VC-Authorised Biography of James Brindley Nicolson*, (Ashford: Geerings of Ashford, 1991), p. 10.
2. Docherty, Tom, *Swift to Battle No.72 Fighting Squadron, V.1 1937–1942*, (Pen and Sword Books Ltd., 2009), p. 60.
3. 64 Squadron Operations Record Book, The National Archives, 15 May 1941
4. *Ibid.* 26 May 1941.
5. *Ibid.* 9 June 1941.
6. *Ibid.*
7. *Ibid.* 18 June 1941.
8. *Ibid.* 15 June 1941.
9. *Ibid.* 27 June 1941.
10. *Ibid.* 1 July 1941.
11. *Ibid.* 19 July 1941.
12. *Ibid.* 9 August 1941.
13. *Ibid.* 8 Nov. 1941.
14. 81 Squadron Operations Record Book, The National Archives, 2 April 1942.
15. 242 Squadron Operations Record Book, The National Archives, June 1942.
16. 453 Squadron Operations Record Book, The National Archives, 11 August 1942.
17. *Ibid.* 6 Sept. 1942.
18. Mouchotte, R., *The Mouchotte Diaries*, (Bristol: Cerberus Publishing Ltd, 2004), p. 157.
19. *Ibid.* p. 160.
20. *Ibid.* p. 161.
21. 124 Squadron Operations Record Book, The National Archives, Jan. 1943.
22. 65 Squadron Operations Record Book, The National Archives, 22 Feb. 1943
23. *Ibid.*
24. 130 Squadron Operations Record Book, The National Archives, 31 March 1943.
25. *Ibid.* 23 April 1943.

Chapter Five

1. 111 Squadron Operations Record Book, The National Archives, 21 Dec. 1939.
2. 605 Squadron Operations Record Book, The National Archives, 6 June 1940.

3. *Ibid.* 15 June 1940.
4. *Ibid.* 15 August 1940.
5. *Ibid.* 605 Squadron Operations Book, The National Archives, 16 August 1940.
6. 111 Squadron Operations Record Book, The National Archives, Sept. 1940.
7. 43 Squadron Operations Record Book, The National Archives, Feb. 1941.
8. *Ibid.* 30 April 1941
9. *Ibid.* April 1941.
10. *Ibid.* June 1941.
11. *Ibid.* 4 Oct. 1941.
12. 260 Squadron Operations Record Book, The National Archives, May 1941.

Chapter Six

1. 263 Squadron Operations Record Book, The National Archives, Nov 1940.
2. 137 Squadron Operations Record Book, The National Archives, August 1940.
3. Kyle, James, *Typhoon Tale*, (Maidston: George Mann, 2001), p. 95.
4. 197 Squadron Operations Record Book, The National Archives, 19 March 1943.
5. No. 148 Airfield Headquarters Operations Book, The National Archives, March 1944.
6. *Ibid.*

Chapter Seven

1. 600 Squadron Operations Record Book, The National Archives, March 1941.
2. *Ibid.* April 1941.
3. *Ibid.*
4. *Ibid.* April 1941.
5. 96 Squadron Operations Record Book, The National Archives, 22 Sept. 1943.
6. 29 Squadron Operations Record Book, The National Archives, April 1944.

Chapter Eight

1. 410 Squadron Operations Record Book, The National Archives, 20 Oct. 1941.
2. *Ibid.* Dec. 1941.
3. *Ibid.* 8 Feb. 1942.
4. *Ibid.* 15 Feb. 1942.
5. *Ibid.* 1942.
6. *Ibid.* May 1942.

Chapter Nine

1. 340 Squadron Operations Record Book, The National Archives, 7 Nov. 1941.
2. *Ibid.* 12 Nov. 1941.

3. Mouchotte, René, *The Mouchotte Diaries*, (Britsol: Cerberus Publishing Ltd, 2004), p. 116.
4. *Ibid.* 340 Squadron Operations Book, The National Archives, 17 Nov. 1941.
5. *Ibid.* 13 Dec. 1944.
6. *Ibid.* Mouchette, René, p. 118.
7. *Ibid.* 340 Squadron Operations Book, The National Archives, 17 Dec. 1941.
8. *Ibid.* 26 Dec. 1941.
9. *Ibid.* 1 Jan. 1942.
10. *Ibid.* August 1942.
11. *Ibid.* 11 August 1943.

Chapter Ten

1. Gretzywgier, Robert, *307 Dywizon Mysliwski Nocny*, (Warsaw: 2005). (history of 307 night fighter squadron)
2. 309 Squadron Operations Record Book, The National Archives, 7 May 1944.
3. R.A.F. Drem Station Diary, The National Archives, October, 1944.

Chapter Eleven

1. Website, History of Leith, www.leithhistory.co.uk. Recollections of a 1939 evacuee.
2. 226 Squadron Operations Book, The National Archives. 22 July 1943.
3. *Ibid.* 23 July 1943.
4. *Ibid.* 24 July 1943.

Chapter Fourteen

1. Drem Station Diary, The National Archives, 17 Oct. 1943.
2. Mouchotte, René, *The Mouchotte Diaries*, (Bristol: Cerberus Publications Ltd, 2004), p. 117.
3. 340 Squadron Operations Record Book, The National Archives, 26 Dec. 1941.
4. 65 Squadrons Operations Record Book, The National Archives, 7 Feb. 1943.
5. 29 Squadron Operations Record Book, The National Archives, 15 April 1944.
6. 64 Squadron Operations Record Book, The National Archives, The National Archives.
7. Don Aris personal recollections of Drem supplied to author.

Chapter Fifteen

1. Johnstone, AVM Sandy, *Enemy in the Sky*, (California: Presidio Press, 1976), p. 63.

Chapter Sixteen

1. Pudney, J., *A Pride of Unicorns: The Biography of the Atcherley Brothers*, (London: Oldbourne Book Co., 1960), p. 171.
2. 'Moonshine' experiments at Drem, 80 Wing Operation Order No. 2, 19 May 1942, The National Archives, Avia 7/1544.

Chapter Seventeen

1. Personal recollections of Jim Malcolm supplied to author.
2. 603 Squadron Opertations Record Book, The National Archives, 20 May 1945.
3. *Ibid.*
4. *Ibid.* 11 June 1945.
5. *The Evening Dispatch*, front page, 8 August 1945.

Bibliography

Where possible, the text of this book has been based on the RAF Station log book and squadron records preserved in the Public Records Office at Kew. Most of the quotes are drawn from these sources. Unfortunately, few documents survive for the time the Royal Flying Corps were based at Drem or West Fenton Airfield as it was known in the First World War (changed to Gullane Airfield at the end of the war). The Fleet Air Arm records are also very sparse for the time they operated from this airfield in the Second World War.

Books

Beedle, J., *43 Squadron—The History of the Fighting Cocks 1916–66*, (London: Beaumont Aviation Literature, 1966)

Bragg, M., *RDFI—The Location of Aircraft by Radio Methods 1935–1945*, (Paisley: Hawkhead Publishing, 2002)

Brew, A., *The Defiant File*, (Tunbridge Wells: Air Britain (Historians) Ltd, 1996)

Brooke, Field Marshal Lord A., ed. Danchev, A., and Todman, D., *War Diaries 1939–1945*, (Phoenix Press, The Orion Publishing Group Ltd, 2003)

Buckton, H., *Birth of the Few—16th October 1939—RAF Spitfires Win Their First Battle with the Luftwaffe*, (Shrewsbury: Airlife Publishing Ltd, 1998)

Dobinson, C., *Fields of Deception—Britain's Bombing Decoys of World War II*, (London: Methuen Publishing Ltd, 2000)

Ferguson, P. A., and Hamlin, J., *Beware! Beware! The History of 611 (West Lancashire) Squadron, Royal Auxiliary Air Force*, (Reading: Airfield Publications, 2004)

Foreman, J., *RAF Fighter Command. Victory Claims of World War II, Part One 1939-1940*, (Walton-on-Thames: Red Kite, 2003)

Francis, P., *British Military Airfield Architecture—From Airships to the Jet Age*, (Sparkford: Patrick Stephens Ltd, 1996)

Franks, N., *Another Kind of Courage—Stories of the UK-based Walrus Air-Sea Rescue Squadrons*, (Sparkford: Patrick Stephens Ltd, 1994)

Glasgow City Council, *Glasgow's Spitfire, Cultural and Leisure Services* (Museums, 2003)

Hajducki, A., *The North Berwick and Gullane Branch Lines*, (Oxford: The Oakwood Press, 1992)

Hammerton, Sir J., *The War Illustrated Volume 1, Issues 1–20, 16th September, 1939—19th January, 1940*, (London: The Amalgamated Press)

Hughes, J., *Power to the Hunter—A History of Royal Air Force Kinross*, (1994)

Jackson, A. S., *Imperial Airways and the First British Airlines 1919–1940*, (Terence Dalton Ltd, 1995)

Jefford MBE BA, Wg Cdr RAF (Ret.) C. G., *RAF Squadrons, 2nd Edition*, (Shrewsbury: Airlife Publishing Ltd, 2001)

Jeffrey, A., *This Present Emergency—Edinburgh, The River Forth and South-East Scotland and the Second World War*, (London, Edinburgh: Mainstream Publishing, 1992)

Johnstone CB DFC, AVM S., *Diary of an Aviator—An Autobiography*, (Shrewsbury: Airlife Publishing Ltd, 1993)

Johnstone CB DFC, AVM S., *Enemy in the Sky—My 1940 Diary*, (San Rafael, California and London, England: Presidio Press, 1979)

Kyle DFM, J., *Typhoon Tale*, (Maidstone: George Mann, 2001)

Mason Hist. ARAeS, RAF (Ret.) F. R., *Battle over Britain*, (London: Frances K, McWhirter Twins Ltd, 1969)

Mason, F. K., *The Hawker Hurricane—An Illustrated History*, (Manchester: Crecy Publishing Ltd, 2001)

McRoberts, D., *Lions Rampant—The Story of 602 Spitfire Squadron*, (London: William Kimber, 1985)

Mouchotte, R., *The Mouchotte Diaries*, (Bristol: Cerberus Ltd, 2004)

Moyle, H., *The Hampden File*, (Tunbridge Wells: Air Britain (Historians) Ltd, 1989)

Munson, K., *Aircraft of World War II*, (Shepperton: Ian Allan Ltd, 1972)

Norman, B., *Broken Eagles 2—Luftwaffe Losses over Northumberland and Durham, 1939–1945*, (Barnsley: Leo Cooper, 2002)

Price, Dr A., *Britain's Air Defences 1939–1945*, (Oxford: Osprey Publishing, 2004)

Ramsey, W. G., *The Blitz—Then and Now Volumes 1-3*, (London: Battle of Britain Prints International Ltd, 1987, 1988, 1990)

Ross, D., Blanche, B., and Simpson, W., *The Greatest Squadron of Them All—The Definitive History of 603 (City of Edinburgh) Squadron RAUXAF*, Volumes 1 and 2, (London: Grub Street, 2003)

Simpson, J. F. G., *Drem Airfield*, (Gullane and Dirleton History Society, 2003)

Smith, D. J., and Stephens, P., *Action Stations 7. Military Airfields of Scotland, the North-East and Northumberland*. (Cambridge: 1983)

Sturtivant, R., and Balance, T., *The Squadrons of the Fleet Air Arm*, (Tunbridge Wells: Air Britain (Historians) Ltd, 1994)

Sturtivant, R., and Burrow, M., *Fleet Air Arm Aircraft 1939–1945*, (Tunbridge Wells: Air Britain (Historians) Ltd, 1995)

Sturtivant, R., Hamlin, J., and Halley, J. J., *Royal Air Force Flying Training and Support Units*, (Tunbridge Wells: Air Britain (Historians) Ltd, 1997)

Thetford, O., *Aircraft of the Royal Air Force since 1918*, (London: Putnam Aeronautical Books, 1995)

Thetford, O., *British Naval Aircraft since 1912*, (Putnam and Company Ltd, 1971)

Tully-Jackson, J., and Brown, I., *East Lothian at War*, (East Lothian District Library, 1996)

Tully-Jackson, J., and Brown, I., *East Lothian at War, Volume 2* (2001)

Walton, D., Northumberland Aviation Diary, *Aviation Incidents from 1790–1999*, (Northumberland: Norav Publications, Seahouses, 1999)

Ziegler, F. H., *The Story of 609 Squadron—Under the White Rose*, (London: MacDonald & Co. (Publishers) Ltd, 1971)

Magazines

'Aeromilitaria, The Drem System', *The Air Britain Military Aviation Historical Quarterley*, No. 3, 1983, pp. 71–74.

Chapman, P., 'A Bit Young—Air Mechanic William Smith, No. 2 Training Depot Station, RFC/RAF 1917–1919', *Cross and Cockade Journal*, p. 117.

'History of 41st Aero Squadron—The reminisces of Sgt W. Mack', *Cross and Cockade Journal*, Vol. 12 No. 1, Spring 1971, pp. 54–61, pp. 72–74.

Abraham, B., 'Fleet Air Arm Bases—Drem', *Airfield Review*, October 2002 and July 2003.

McDowall, K., 'Schoolboy Memories of Drem', *Aeroplane Monthly*, Volume 23 No. 2, Issue 262, February 1995, pp. 60–63.

'The A-Z of Mitchell's Wonder', *Flypast Special, Spitfire 70*, (Key Publishing Ltd, 2006)

James, D., 'Westland Whirlwind', *Aeroplane*, Vol. 34 No. 5, Issue 397, May 2006, pp. 59–75.

'263 Squadron', *Aviation News*, Vol. 19 No. 14, 23 November–6 December 1990.

Websites

www.bbc.co.uk/history/ww2peopleswar
www.rafdrem.co.uk/history.html